AGITATED STATES

THEATER: Theory/Text/Performance

Enoch Brater, Series Editor

Agitated States: Performance in the American Theater of Cruelty

Anthony Kubiak

Ann Arbor

THE UNIVERSITY OF MICHIGAN PRESS

Copyright © by the University of Michigan 2002
All rights reserved
Published in the United States of America by
The University of Michigan Press
Manufactured in the United States of America
⊗ Printed on acid-free paper

2005   2004   2003   2002   4   3   2   1

A CIP catalog record for this book is available from the British Library.

Library of Congress Cataloging-in-Publication Data

Kubiak, Anthony, 1951–
    Agitated states : performing in the national theaters of
cruelty / Anthony Kubiak.
        p.   cm. — (Theater—theory/text/performance)
    Includes bibliographical references and index.
        ISBN 0-472-09811-X (alk. paper) — ISBN 0-472-06811-3 (pbk. :
alk. paper)
        1. Theater and society.   2. Theater—Political aspects. I.
Title.   II. Series.
    PN2049 .K83   2002
    792—dc21   2001008271

For Susan

Acknowledgments

Although it has been a long stretch between books, it has never been idle time: ten years, in fact, is barely adequate to assess "what went wrong" in some of the theoretical thought of the 1980s and 1990s. This book is a small attempt to realign performance studies, to reinvigorate the reading and performance of dramatic texts, and to question what became the truisms of political and cultural analysis in those decades. No one has been more valuable to me in this long process than Jon Erickson, whose supple mind, incisive analyses, and friendship lie behind every passage of this book. Our discussions and debates over the past decade have influenced my thinking in ways too numerous to cite.

I would like to thank LeAnn Fields, my editor at the University of Michigan Press, for her belief in my work, and for her help and support under sometimes very difficult conditions. She is indisputably one of the most important forces in the growth of performance theory in the past decade. I would also like to thank Lawrence Buell for his early encouragement as I began this project, and for the help and support of others at Harvard during my years there: Werner Sollers, Philip Fisher, Marjorie Garber, and Elaine Scarry were especially kind and helpful to me.

Over the course of years, and especially in recent months, I would like to thank Herbert Blau for his continuing support and encouragement.

Since my coming to the University of South Florida, the support and respect of colleagues and friends has helped see this project to completion. I would like to thank William T. Ross, Sara Deats, Steven J. Rubin, and Philip Sipiora especially, as well as my graduate students, who have had to suffer through many of the ideas presented in this book more times than they deserve.

I would also like to thank all of the people at Inkwood Books, especially Carla Jimenez, Leslie Reiner, and Kamran Mir for their help and support: in the age of Borders and Barnes and Noble, many of us have forgotten the joy and indispensability of the small, committed, community bookstore. And finally, thank you to Susan and Daniel, who, as always, help me find and keep crucial perspective.

Portions of this book have appeared in *Modern Drama* 34, no. 1 (1991): 107–17; *Journal of Dramatic Theory and Criticism* 12, no. 2 (1998): 15–34; *Drama Review* 42, no. 4 (1998): 91–114; and *Performance Research* "On Memory" (December 2000): 30–36.

CONTENTS

*A*CT **4**/Abdication

Prologue

Although deeply and profoundly theatricalized, American culture has never understood its performative nature because, in its tendencies to the materialist, the pragmatic, and the anti-intellectual, it has refused or failed to think through the ontologies of performance. Even today, the preponderant voices in theater and performance theory are of a constructivist, cultural materialist bent, positions that tend to critique theater and performance as document or event or cultural formation from a position seemingly outside the theatrical, or, conversely, through the idea of the performative as a controlling metaphor. The approach of most contemporary performance theory is, as a consequence, ideologically (but not necessarily politically) driven. The major weakness of such ideologically driven positions, as Herbert Blau contends, is their failure to take into adequate consideration the theatricality of their own theoretical apparatus.

The basic problem raised by the various manifestations of the theatrical in America, I suggest, seems less the result of skewed ideology in need of correction, or the naming of particular historical conditions, than a confusion and uncertainty about the more abstract aspects of memory, history, and identity. What is needed, in the case of American cultural history, is a recognition of the depth of the theatrical in our history—and not, in the parlance of much critical theory today, merely performance or the performative—in the formulation of identity, and identity's lack. I am suggesting an embracing, a recognition, a deploying of theater itself as the space within which we can begin to see the profound depths of the theatricality and performativity of American culture: theater as theatricality's cure. Here, then, theater is not the pathology. Rather, the pathology is a refusal to recognize the necessary infection of the social—including the theory that attempts to apprehend it—by the duplicities of the theatrical: that *any* manifestation of the social (including critical theory) is at once theatrical.

But this is not to claim a too rationalist position for the drama. This space of theatrical reflection is not only a space of thought or recognition, but also of emotion (which we now know to be essential to rational thought), and so a space of intensity, brutality, and beauty. Within it we might take the measure of the human, her history and ontopolitics, certainly, but also her fragility, her power, her hopelessness, her damnation, her redemption, concealed as merest possibility. This theater, then, is no mere Brechtian space of distancing, nor is it merely a vehicle for the "return to humanism": the irony is always that within this space of reflection, thought becomes embodied, and in so becoming, becomes strangely secret and hidden. But in a theatricalized culture that has no viable theater—American culture—this hiddenness of thought, like theater itself, is foreclosed, is refused entry into cultural consciousness, and so returns in the hallucinatory remains of enormity—slaughters, genocides, racisms, Civil Wars, and now, children assassinating children en masse.

Introduction/Second Manifesto: The American Theater of Cruelty

From the Standpoint of Content
(American Culture Theater)

On September 11, 2001, the incessant American chatter stopped. We couldn't find the words. Couldn't believe our eyes, yet the enormity of the televised images barely approached the events themselves: inconceivable on the television screen, the impact was far more devastating on site. The enormous crater, filled with debris, and surrounded by cathedral-like skeletons of broken I-beams, was almost instantly baptized *Ground Zero*, the place where nearly three thousand lives were ground to nothingness and dusted over the city like gray snow or crematoria ash. A great and terrible hole opened in our history.

The fact that the scene itself absolutely outstripped the mediated images of the disaster remind us once again of the power of presence, what Philip Auslander calls "liveness": that for all of the gravity of the televised images, the attacks of September 11 suggest terrorism's need for theater and not the mere mediations of film or video. Inasmuch as those events were designed as horrific performances, as actions to be seen and responded to, playing live to an audience of perhaps one million or more in lower Manhattan, the attacks on the World Trade Center derived their perverse impact from a single fact of performance: that the effectiveness of theater has always been directly proportionate to its cost—economic, certainly, but human most importantly.

I am, of course, not suggesting that theater and performance, even those forms that involve direct and real violence (which all perfor-

mance enacts to some degree), are terrorism. Nor am I suggesting terrorism is merely theater. Terrorism, or the experience of it at Ground
Zero or within the plummeting aircraft, is designed to obliterate
thought, consideration, or speculation. Indeed, the pain, the horror, the
terror itself is unnamable. Rather, it is the use of terror as coercive
image that underscores its theatricality. Those in New York and the
Pentagon and in that Pennsylvania field, those at terror's site, must
work through the collision of the real and the seeming on their own
terms. Whether the dissociations of the moment produced the unreal
presence/absence of theatrical experience is—as it always must be—a
matter of individual experience, and in those that survive, exploration,
reflection, and expression. For the rest of us, the mediated images, their
endless repetitions, their ghastly majesty, are the scripts and scores.
And crucial to the effectiveness of those images and scripts is the certainty of the real, appalling violence to which the images point. As we
sat before our television sets, we knew to some degree that what we
were seeing was not real, was a mere shadow of what was happening,
but we also knew the ghosts and shadows of the video images both
masked and indicated a Real violence really occurring elsewhere,
wordless and fathomless.

Since that terrible day, we have all been sorting out our emotions,
debating causes and possible solutions. The central concern has been
deciding where to place the blame, and how to respond, both interna-
tionally and domestically. In our search for those executing terror's
logic, however, one glaring but crucial issue has remained unexamined: the harrowing recognition that the attackers, the Others who
lived (and live) among us like toxic spores, knew us, recognized us,
understood us in a way we do not yet understand ourselves. The attack
was designed especially for us. Its scale, the choice of targets, the sheer
spectacular impact of the images seemed, even in their unthinkability,
constructed with a distinctly American theatricality in mind. The act,
melded with the fundamentalists' eternal abhorrence of theater,
mocked our deeply and historically ingrained desire for the spectacle,
and for transfiguration through the spectacle. The images powerfully
echoed the history of the American disaster and action film, and the
sheer enormity of the act assured its appearance and reappearance in
every home in America, fueling our obsessive need for the repetition
compulsions of the televised image on the evening news.

Finally, though, the terrorist groups underestimated us, underestimated the resiliency of American culture, born of its ability to neutralize

any abomination through television and commerce. The repetition of the images and the inevitable marketing of patriotic fervor suggest the political capital to be had: the buying and selling of flags and slogans and stocks, of course, but also in academia the buying and selling of theoretical positions coming out of those untheorizable events, trying to turn tragedy into theory, turning theory instead into absurdist theater. Taken together, then, the attacks of September 11 seemed a violent indictment of who we are, a people of the spectacle, blind to the theater of it all.

It remains for us, however, to examine the long coalescence of this theater, the theater that has formed us, the theater we refuse to acknowledge: the intense, self-absorbed struggle with who we might be, who we might be becoming. Here, unlike the attacks from without, the theatrical *fort/da* takes other forms. More insidious than gratuitous attacks emanating, Kafka-like, from the burrows and tunnels of Afghanistan is the nagging self-destructiveness at the core of the American mythos. Here the theatricalities are even more unrecognized and unrecognizable.

Adumbrated, then, by the events of September 11, the other crippling violence of American society has, for now, been silenced. Juxtaposed against the foreign aggression, which appeared in the Real like some psychotic hallucination, is an Other, systemic disease: the suppurating wounds inflicted by American violence—child assassins, for example, murdering other children.

Some six months prior to September 11, then, on March 5, 2001, Charles Andrew Williams, of Santee, California, opened fire on his classmates, killing two and wounding thirteen. And while children killing children with guns has been a national pathology for some time now—especially in America's poor, urban neighborhoods, where such shootings have often gone unnoticed and unmourned—the more recent waves seem particularly chilling because they are without seeming cause. In the school shootings, middle- and upper-class young men (largely) vent their rage against a world that has treated them, all in all, remarkably well. In these acts of violence we cannot, in liberal solicitude, point to causes and so "understand" the violence: here there is no poverty, no racism, drug addictions, or gangs. Moreover, these horrors are staged, in some cases rehearsed, in all cases performative, the killer-ego as actor emerging within the mediated eye of cultural America.

Following the causal trail—always a risky business—the most recent prologue for this American jeremiad is perhaps the February 19, 1997, shooting in Bethel, Alaska, in which sixteen-year-old Evan Ramsey walked into the common area of his high school and opened fire, killing a student and the principal after being spurred on by his classmates the night before. Several students stood on a balcony overlooking the common area and waited for the grisly performance. One teacher volunteered in disbelief that it was "like they were going to watch a movie," *as if* they were going to watch a movie: mediation twice-removed.

A year later, on March 24, 1998, Mitchell Johnson and Andrew Golden, thirteen and eleven years of age and costumed in camouflage, planned and scripted an even more horrific act. Concealing themselves in the slash pine and scrub of Craighead County, Arkansas, and using rifles with telescopic sights, they methodically murdered four classmates at Jonesboro's Westside Middle School and wounded ten others, setting the stage with false fire-alarms and stashed weapons, as if the sad slaughter were merely a scene in another action movie.

But horrific as they were, the Bethel and Jonesboro atrocities seemed mere rehearsal for an even bigger event when the killing-performance was "taken on the road" to Littleton, Colorado, almost one year later. On that day—April 20, 1999, the one-year plus one-day anniversary of the Oklahoma City bombing and in obeisance to it— twelve children were murdered by two classmates carrying shotguns and semiautomatic pistols through the halls of Columbine High School. The outrage of the events of April 20 was amplified in other plots in other classrooms and campuses in Port Huron, Michigan, and in Conyers, Georgia—just as it had been the previous year when Kip Kinkel shot and killed his parents and two students in Springfield, Oregon, in the performative afterglow of Jonesboro. By late April the climate of anxiety and fear in schools across the nation was palpable, a result, in part, of a suspicion that news media itself had caused or at least abetted the replication of an especially rabid adolescent mind-set.

Although the seeming copycat nature of the plots in Port Huron and Conyers was terrifying because of their repetitive, performative, even *texted* nature—their seeming theatricality—more harrowing was the threat that, like theater, the performance would settle quickly into repetition compulsions in schools across the nation. The Jonesboro and Littleton tragedies, the events that seemingly triggered mimetic and performative rage in a dozen or more American schools, remain the most disturbing of the recent events because of the rehearsals that preceded them: the enormity was not merely discussed and planned by the killers, it was situated within a virtuality that quite literally bled into the

Real. Both Eric Harris and Dylan Klebold, like Johnson and Golden a year earlier, wore costumes—the infamous black trench coats and, in the days before the bloody show, black clothing, black boots, and sunglasses. They also upped the theatrical ante by producing, directing, and acting in a series of video trailers that functioned as prelude to performance, giving running commentary like film stars pimping their roles on Letterman or Leno, though no one knew it at the time. In some of the videos they quote Shakespeare and note reasons for, and the potential impact of, their particular theater of cruelty: "I can make you believe anything," Harris says at one point to the video camera. And indeed, his theatrical assumptions are echoed—and both echo and eclipse Artaud—by the *Time* journalist writing the story: "[T]his may have been about celebrity as much as cruelty," Timothy Roth writes. He quotes investigating FBI agent Mark Holslaw, who says, "'They wanted to be famous,'" reiterating the tired and predictable "natural born killers" cant. Harris, in fact, in a video moment of characteristically pathetic hubris, states flatly (and incorrectly) that "directors will be fighting over this story." Other tapes are more overtly theatrical, more tightly scripted. In these more self-conscious performances, Harris and Klebold wear their costumes and play out the school murders for other members of the troupe, filming themselves marching among a group of trench-coated vigilantes who open fire on fleeing, and largely faceless, individuals. By way of dress rehearsal, in the days before the killing, they reputedly marched in military formation, in costume, down school hallways in a show of pathological rage and performance art preceding their Grand Guignol, while the act itself, we are told, was, also in the style of the Grand Guignol, "mainly an improvisation."[1]

By way of explanation in the media, we were told they took refuge in fantasy gaming and in Imaginary[2] preoccupations with the Gothic and the occult. Complicating this virtual immersion in the Imaginary was the role those same American media took in insisting on these particular details as somehow the most significant in understanding this schizoid and murderous episode: while Harris and Klebold seemed to be refuting all notions of meaning and value in and through their actions, invoking the very substance of trauma—a horror that absolutely precludes meaning—the media stubbornly tried to find substance in the very "theatricalized" aspects of the events that would seem the most empty of significance. It was at this point, I suggest, both in the minds of Klebold and Harris and in culture at large, that the real and its phantasms met.

Thus in the killings themselves and in their recapitulation as media images, the same point was reiterated: the failure of our culture to separate reality from its illusions, its theater(s). The ambiguous referent here is intentional—culture's theaters and reality's theaters now occupy the same site. Culture (*that* phantasm), in the age of materialisms and critical theory, has become the totality of the seemingly real. Indeed, while editorials in the days following the murders insisted that the "problem" was that a generation of kids could no longer separate the virtual violence of video and computer games and movies from the real violence of torn flesh, unspeakable pain, and the terror of death, nowhere was there discussion of the media's immersion in its own fantasias—the very hallucinatory quality of the news reports in their insistence upon the surreal details of the unthinkable. Thus the condition that some recent theorists dismiss as a sign of virtual cultural schizophrenia—"the psychotic incestuous immersion into the Screen as the material Thing that swallows us, depriving us of the capacity of symbolic distance and reflection"[3]—seems exactly the point both in the seeming dissociation of the killers and in the peculiar repetitive fantasies of the media reporting them.

But this media self-indulgence was only an occultation of the real issue, the issue of the Real. While political leaders were insisting that parents turn off their computers and keep their kids away from virtual violence, the bombs were falling in Belgrade in yet another video arcade–style war of the Real against the Imaginary: indeed, the inability of American political leadership to confront the reality of the war in Kosovo was clearly expressed in its refusal to send ground troops to fight in the unspeakable brutality of a real war. As long as the battle could be fought on video screens from positions of complete dissociation, soldiers and political careers would be safe, the violence would be rendered unreal, the fantasy of saving the Kosovars would remain intact. But this paradoxical wielding of the Imaginary in the Name-of-the-Father[4]—the confusion in the cultural mind between Imaginary and Symbolic orders, a failure to maintain the distinction between them—engenders a "remainder," the "obscene and revengeful figure of the Father-of-Enjoyment, of this figure split between cruel revenge and crazy laughter,"[5] an embodiment of Klebold's infamous laughter and horrific *fort/da* games of "peekaboo" as the killings commenced: enfant terrible, the child's ridicule of the man.[6]

But the proposition that the decadence of the post/modern world—and its fascination with virtuality and the promise of sanitized violence—has borne predictable fruit engenders a counterproposition: spectacular virtual violence (in movies and computer games) is not the cause of American social psychopathology, but is rather the result. Virtual violence is not a cause but a symptom of a prior psychopathology with a short but brutal history. American culture is born of both violence and specularity, not unique in the emergence of cultures, certainly, but unique in its nearly ahistorical brevity and subsequent intensity. Complicating that peculiarly intense history of violent spectacle is the refusal—the repudiation or *Verwerfung*[7]—of both specularity and savagery, and their repression in/as mediation, as if modern mediation were the primary source of the images of cultural and political violence and not the mere means of their dispersal.

Hence in America virtual violence is not the real issue, real violence is. Similarly, the issue is not that young people witness x number of virtual murders before their entrance into first grade, but rather that the repetition compulsions of violent spectacle should appear at all on TV and movie screens. Similarly, the violence of the media is rarely discussed outside particular images of death and mayhem, and yet mediation's most compelling violence might very well be the propagation of an anti-intellectuality that seems the hallmark of American society. Even the most passive images, or perhaps most especially passive images, may produce the kind of inertia against which and within which social/familial violence most easily propagates. All of those self-satisfied images out there become the signs of our dys-satisfaction in here. Television becomes, oddly, a kind of reality principle. Lives are emptied of real content by the reality of the manifestly illusory, an entire culture living within pixilated hallucinations of every conceivable sort while young people, faced with endless illusion, crave the real, a real that is increasingly closed to them—or rather, a real whose critical distance from the Imaginary by way of the Symbolic becomes increasingly foreshortened. Finally, as the real is refused, the last location of the real becomes, perhaps, the very craving for it. Perhaps adolescents like Harris and Klebold become addicted to their virtual worlds because in a world increasingly mediated, at least the addictions are real—in the obsessive-compulsive registers of psychopathology, what I crave most are not drugs, alcohol, or sex, but my addictions themselves. And so in the sign systems of the political, the virtual becomes the very mark, the symptom, the stand-in for reality's lack. Beyond this and through this, the virtual and its addictions have become the real. In the conflation of the two, the concern ceases to be the real violence that chews at our culture's repressed core. We simply seem unable to move from an Imaginary history—a "local" history of image, part, and archive—into the histories of the Symbolic, the "real" history of agonizing individuation and absorption: the history of nationhood.

So while parents and politicians bemoan the ascendancy of the virtual over the real, they forget that American culture, far more than others, is in its very substance virtual, illusory, and has been since its inception. The current crisis is more than political or social, then. It is philosophical and psychic: culture's need to situate and negotiate the Real and the Imaginary (as in, for example, the relationship between the real world and its representations in film and TV) through the articulations of symbolic discourse, through thought, debate, language, and art. I have decided, for this reason, to use an analytic approach that relies a good deal on the terms of Lacanian discourse. Such an analysis, while using many of the ideas of Lacan and contemporary apologists, at the same time is aware of the theatrical as it operates in the aid of the psychic. This awareness of the theatrical deflects, I think, the kind of wholesale capitulation to Lacanian concepts and mind-set that, in the hands of some recent theorists, would exempt Lacan himself from the registers of theatricality. And yet Lacan's very writings—elliptical, throwing us off the scent, approaching seeming more than being—are more indebted to the theatrical than is typically acknowledged. As a result, a sensitivity to the problems of theater and theatricality (as they are developed, for example, in the work of Herbert Blau) is an important aid to understanding the present study. At the same time, while it is not at all necessary to have mastered Lacan to understand the readings that follow, some familiarity with the terms of psychoanalytic thought certainly won't hurt. To this end, I will try to define salient terms and ideas as I proceed, and to question those terms when they prove insufficient. I should also state here that I am certainly aware of the ongoing debates among those using Lacan in cultural and historical contexts, and those employing more Marxist or historicist methodologies. And while I occasionally bring those debates into my analysis when they seem germane, I am not trying to "convert" anyone to Lacan's ideas.

Indeed, the use of psychoanalysis as a diachronic tool of analysis will always raise eyebrows: perhaps the most persistent and persistently misdirected skepticism regarding this sort of analysis is that it is "anachronistic," out of its time, or, more in line with political theory once again, ahistorical. Such skepticism sometimes claims that it is absurd to apply a twentieth-century technique or philosophy to earlier periods because those earlier periods were not themselves conceived within the terms of those same modern techniques or philosophies. Hence we cannot talk about the unconscious in relation to early-nineteenth-century thought or history because this period in history had no modern concept of the unconscious. But what sort of theory—historical, political, or otherwise—is not anachronistic in this sense? Even traditional historiographies apply a historical sensibility to earlier periods that is out of synch with how those periods conceived (or didn't) their own historical epistemes.[8] History as we understand it, Hayden White reminds us, is a mid-nineteenth-century phenomenon.

Beyond the misplaced charge of anachronism, the other main sticking point in the objections to psychoanalysis is a pervasive misunderstanding of the unconscious. The unconscious is in many ways the conceptual anchor of psychoanalytic thought. Produced through the action of repression, the unconscious is, as a result, that which directs us to find substance in otherness, in lack and deficiency. The unconscious is the agency that sends us "beyond" the text—it is the interpretive impulse, in some sense, that finds meaning elsewhere. It is the unconscious that pushes us to ask not what the text/dream/speech says, but what it means.

It was largely the influence of Lacan that moved our understanding of the unconscious away from a more or less Freudian notion of something that is possessed, a thing seemingly *self*-contained (or in the case of the political or cultural unconscious, culturally contained), toward an understanding of the unconscious as process. The unconscious, as conceived by Lacan and postulated by Juan-David Nasio, is radically dynamic and other—not merely changing moment to moment, but, like memory itself, reinvented moment to moment, appearing and disappearing as the gaze turns elsewhere. In an important sense, there is no unconscious until it is invoked, and invoking the unconscious means listening for what lies beneath the word that fails.[9]

In Lacan, I would argue, the unconscious is thus less a set of specific contents than a stance, a way of reading that focuses on what is left unsaid, the remainder, the impulse or fantasy behind manifest fantasy. Analysis thus operates in defiance of psychic censorship, what Lacan called the father's "No!" There is in this schema, then, no recovering the contents of a real past, either as unconscious, or as "actual" history. There is only re-membering the fantasy (and what is America *but* fan-

tasy?), putting together, constituting, reinventing according to what we
see as truth (and the seeing is always the problem). This process, of
course, is also the process of mounting a theater production, whether in
thought or in fact. The "manifest content" (either as historical document
or literary text) may be the same episteme to episteme, but our understanding of its meanings necessarily changes, and oftentimes changes
radically. Some of this changed understanding arises from increased
knowledge—newly discovered documents, newly seen historical relationships, and so on. But there is another way to read these changes in
historical understanding: a rereading of the desires behind them
through the reading and production of the theatrical itself, a rereading
of the fantasy content behind the historical data or literary text. This is
admittedly chancy: there is no empirical "proof" that my readings are
correct. We must look to the effects of these readings: do they open the
texts in question in meaningful ways, resituate them, "estrange" them,
and in so recontextualizing them, give them new life? I believe historical knowledge can be had, but, following R. G. Collingwood and Hayden White, I also believe any reading of history involves rereading the
fantasy that structures the historical narrative. This is one of the tasks of
literary criticism, what Lacan termed "traversing the fantasy."

So in using Lacan to read history as fantasy through the texts of
the fantastical itself—theater—I am in no way refuting history or the
study of historical fact and its interpretations: I am instead suggesting
that the proper object of "historical" psychoanalytic reading is precisely that which cannot be known through the reading of (normal)
history. This sort of analytic reading is legitimized by the necessary
failure of history to speak fully, to tell us more, to tell us all, and to tell
us through a very particular medium, the historically situated play, a
cultural fantasy bound to the repetition compulsions of cultural consciousness—the theater. In fact, Nasio suggests, the Lacanian fantasy,
playing itself out through the (cultural) unconscious, is precisely the
knowledge of repetition.[10] This "knowledge," then, is not knowledge
of some thing, some content. It is merely the knowledge of/that is repetition—a knowledge that is, in other words, *theatrical*. As such, it
appears as a hole around which sign systems revolve, a hole "veiled by
fantasy itself," very like the pierced doubloon fastened to the mast of
the *Pequod*.[11] What is this, again, but theater, a mere seeming that
nonetheless anchors consciousness?

Here, then, it makes little sense to speak of historical causality, the
mechanisms of repression, or true historical content. We are, rather,

seeing the play as an entire symptomology of history's failure. The pathologies presented in the plays I will discuss—aphasia, amnesia, blindness, repetition compulsions, addictions, grief, and bereavement—represent less material history than history's immaterial nightmares. As a nation, as a culture, we carry the marks of those nightmares with us through time. We are the result, the culmination of that history, and our recollection of it is always a recollection of a hidden fantasy marked by the often violent resistance of sheer endurance. The interpretation, in other words, whether of historical document or art object, always occurs as the accumulation of bereavement in the now. The historical reality of *us* is that we carry the burden of our history with us in the present, and it is only in the present that we can understand the past, even though the real traumas of that past are always displaced: elsewhere, behind us, before us, nowhere at all. Here, then, as I suggested above, theater supersedes Lacanian thought, and it is this supersession that I would offer as the theoretical grounding of this study. Theater itself grounds our understanding, our culture/history—and a shifting ground it is. In this context, I suggest, it is not only *we* who do the interpreting, it is also the productions of theater that interpret *us*.

At the same time, using the terms of Lacanian psychoanalysis involves far more than yet another descent into poststructural contingencies.[12] What, finally, has contingency theory[13] accomplished in America but a recapitulation of its seeming unreality? What have theories of the "contingent" and "decentered" self, for example, and insights into the provisional nature of meaning and truth, brought to a culture articulated through a history of disappearances, illusion, and ephemerality? Indeed an important difference between Lacan's philosophy and contingency theory is Lacan's rejection of the notion of the "open," infinite play of signification. For Lacan, there can only be an infinite play of signification and desire within a delimited space because it is the delimitation that *produces* desire's play, the desire to know, the desire for more, for what is beyond, for what I can't have— what Lacan calls desire in the Other. This delimited space is the stage upon which desire emerges, both as theater and as culture. Here is the link between theatricalized America and its (I would contend) failed theaters: what is American history, after all, but just such a continuous staging of desire? America, even now straining at the limits of its "new frontiers" through free-trade agreements and globalized economic growth, America, generating within those ever-expanding limits its own endless play of desire (more markets, more capital) and significance (still the city on a hill, even now believing in its manifest destiny recontextualized as historically inevitable, unlimited, market growth). America, that in staging its desire still deeply believes in the purity of its authentic identity. America onstage rejecting its own theater. And it is, I suggest, on the failed American stage that we can begin to understand the failure of American identity itself.

I arrive, then, at the crux of the present study: the formulation of American culture as theater, and this culture's repudiation of that theatricality as the central fact of American history. I am suggesting here a kind of reading of that American theater, a reading of America as theater. The texts I will be analyzing thus represent more or less a standard anthology of "best" (i.e. most critically acclaimed) American plays and literature. While studies of marginal or lesser-known dramas might provide other powerful insights about American cultural history, my intent is to "read" dominant American culture/history through the plays that have been judged—rightly or wrongly—as "typically American." This list is by no means exhaustive, and hardly objective, and must represent to some extent my own subset of "the most typical" that best illustrates the points I am trying to make.

Although largely chronological, however, this is no theater history, nor is it a cultural studies take on the "theatricality in/of American history." What follows is, instead, an analysis of theater's absent place in our history, a history nonetheless saturated with the seemingly theatrical, the appearance of a phantasmic history, of history as phantasm. This historical memory exists as a kind of subarachnoid scar tissue, the remainders of real trauma and psychopathology that occur only and always elsewhere—the repressed slaveries, genocides, and crimes against humanity that cry out for the large arc of narrative that can never contain them, but also the history of subjective agony and *ecstasis*, a history that resists entry into the linguistic at each turn *through* its history, refusing the movement from trauma to language. This particular history is the site of what Cathy Caruth might call the historical unconscious, what Jacques Lacan called "that chapter of . . . history marked by a blank,"[14] a history of disappearances that reaches back to the pages of the earliest Puritan diaries and continues in the narratives of the evening news. And although recently "rediscovered" (in the reassessments of American melodrama, for example), the theater of American life and culture remains one of the most poorly theorized aspects of our national identity. The results of this neglect, as we have seen, have had more than mere academic effect.

Theatricality was and is the *ungrounded signifier* of American culture, a signifier that is at once everywhere and nowhere. Alongside this
doubling of the theatrical impasse is a failure to recognize theatricality,
and in this, a failure to mount a "real" theater in theatricality's face, so
to speak. There is no viable American theater tradition that stands in
contradistinction to, questions, critiques, the hidden and blatant theatricalities of culture in the manner of Brecht, Beckett, or Pirandello, or
more pointedly in terms of theater's foreclusion, Artaud. We lack a
stage tradition that points to the wavering distance between theater
and the real, a tradition that consciously takes theater as its object.
Instead, we have a theater history that at best provides mere glimpses
of theater's image as/of its own critique. And because, as I would
argue, there is historically no such space in American culture—no
actual space in which the theatricalities that have produced American
culture are themselves reflected upon—we remain blind to theater
when it appears, we do not discern the space of speculation, even as an
absence. Hence the inability to discern the distance between the virtual
and the real, the distance that Lacan gives over to the Symbolic. What I
am suggesting in this study, then, is the profound need for theater (and
not mere performance) within an American culture apparently saturated with it: but a theater disengaged, made strange, opening the distance between stage and gallery, between Real and Imaginary. This
would be a theater of Brechtian gest, to be sure, a theater in which the
performative moment, perpetually dissolving, still appears as the very
instantiation of thought, a theater that thinks—in mind, certainly, but
also in the very nerve-meters of the brain.

In Brecht, then, but in Artaud as well, and in the tension between,
we might begin to detect the contours of one of the most nagging issues
of recent performance theory: the nature of theater's representations,
and the relationship of theatrical text to "performance" and the Real
itself. In a 1998 article in *PMLA*, W. B. Worthen articulates the problem
with subtlety and precision. Discussing the tensions between more traditional engagements with dramatic text and the newer forms of performance theory that try to engage "the performative," Worthen suggests that traditional literary engagements with performativity tend to
focus on the performative function of language as represented in literary texts. Conversely, much performance-oriented criticism of drama,
for all its invocation of the theater, similarly betrays a desire to locate
the meanings of the stage in the contours of the dramatic texts.[15]

In contradistinction, various performance studies have worked out approaches and descriptions of specifically "nondramatic" scenarios that, in their nonscriptedness, seem to challenge the supremacy of the written dramatic score as the epitome or site of cultural meaning and authority. As a result of these challenges, "drama appears to be an increasingly residual mode of performance."[16] In other words, "drama" (which in this case means the dramatic text, or the study of performance through the study of texts as ultimate sources of authority), and its pale sibling, theater, have, in the projects of much performance theory, "given up the ghost" in favor of cultural/performative studies that seem more real, closer to the unconscious playing-out of cultural/gender fears and suppositions. But as Worthen points out, citing, in part, Joseph Roach's idea of theater as surrogation, this belies what actually occurs (or might occur) onstage. The idea that play production is merely reenactment or repetition of an "authorized" playscript is finally quite naive (my term, not Roach's or Worthen's). In Worthen's developing argument, the play-text is no mere "authorized" version of reality or cultural value; it is rather a lens through which experience, thought, and emotion are excruciated, "pulverized" in Artaud's term.

But the text here is still, it seems, subservient to the performative. I would suggest that the text is neither more nor less important than the performative. Once the business of historicist or ideological analysis of play-text is past, once we have dismantled the sexist/racist/homophobic contours of any given text, we should face the paradox that this newly realized content, just like the "authorized" content so berated by theorists, is, in its own way, now the newly authorized meaning of the text. Beyond this, we might recognize that what the dramatic text and its theater ultimately reveals to us is its otherness: the fact that it, like the theatrical production, exists as disappearance, exists elsewhere, finds its meaning where it is not. It is this hiddenness that forms the substance of the theatrical: not the obvious and "hollow" (quoting J. L. Austin) recitation of dialogue, but the concealed act of surrogation that renders theater real.

Reversing the present bias, then: performance, inasmuch as it is theater, is theater primarily *because it occurs elsewhere*. In other words, because theater is at least in part located within the Symbolic order, it can never be where it indicates it is. Moreover, performance and performativity—of gender, race, heterosexuality, queerness—*aspires* to the theatrical when it desires its own otherness, when it is mindful and bodiful, when it is distanced and strange, when it becomes, in Artaudian and Blauian categories, thought. Thus separating performance from text is not only wishful thinking, as Worthen points out, it is bad thinking, or worse, not thinking at all. For it is in theater *as* theory, as dramatic text, that scrutiny of performative aims and occlusions can be undertaken, reconceiving "the text as material for labor, for the work of production":[17] political and economic, certainly, but also the labor of analysis, the labor of "social impossibility."[18] Here, then, theater is not only not moribund, it represents that which gives place to, "interrogates," and frames the performative, gives the performative birth, so to speak, gives it meaning, and also disarticulates that meaning. In the episteme of Returns, we are facing what we might call the "return to theater," the return to the analysis of play-texts closely read and acted. And perhaps it is only there, within the elasticity of textual meaning, that we can begin to understand culture's performativities, *not* through any presumed attention to an authorial code of meaning, but through a willing submission to the rigors of thought and the discipline of theatrical practice. When so engaged, theater becomes the farthest remove from Austin's "hollow utterance"—it is, as in social realism, for example, no mere re-creation of reality, but the creation of the Real. This is theater's paradox and the most common point of misapprehension on the part of those who dismiss theater or relegate it to a paler form of the performative. What makes the work of Karen Finley, Chris Burden, or Rachel Rosenthal so powerful is precisely its theater. What (in my opinion) makes the work of Laurie Anderson or Anna Deavere Smith weak in comparison is precisely the *lack* of theater—or the appearance of theater's double—in their performances: the lack of the sense of meaning or action as occurring elsewhere. One might think the point would be obvious by now after Brecht, Artaud, Grotowski, Schechner, Blau, and others: theater, in production, in its surrogation of the dramatic text, is not make-believe. It is Real, like the recurring, disappearing, terrifying substance of the nightmare itself.

And returning to the very nearly literal Nightmares on Elm Street, the nightmares of the eternal return of American children killing children: these are perhaps distressing not because they are aberrations, not because they signify something deviant, something other than what we are, but because the murderous phantasms of the adolescent mind might be exactly who and what we are. In this scenario, the problem is not that the virtual is confused with the real, but that the virtual—of desire and violence—is realized, is brought into reality. The godlike pronouncements of Klebold—that he will bring about the destruction of the earth, for example—take on a certain horrific truth that at the time was almost too obvious to see: he and Harris did, like Shiva in fury, bring forth the Real "in multitudinous seas incarnidine." In some sense their act was truly an act of dis-illusion.

But which of these arguments is it? In the registers of the psycho-analytic, is the propagation of violence in American culture due to a generalized confusion of categories (real/Imaginary, life/theater, real-ity/virtuality), or the erasure of the Symbolic, the anti-intellectual rejec-tion of the critical distance required for thought? Without theater's standing against theater's double, there is no way of knowing. Putting forth theories, especially theories that further erode the space of the Symbolic, is also not much help. I am suggesting in this book that we need a practiced theatrical eye, and beyond this, a theatrical eye that forces us to see what can only appear in the membranous wounds of mind, the "hauntology" or ghostings[19] of what can only appear as dis-appearance. We need to look beyond materialist performance theory and visibility politics and confront the unbearable scene of the crime, an unconscious taped-off from sight by the very theories that profess discernment, blinded as those theories oftentimes are by the dazzling impact of mere spectacle, mere "performance."

Indeed, today the inability to discern the theatrical often takes the form of a discourse of performativity, that, taking as its point of depar-ture the performative nature of the social, fails to see the historical, rep-etition-bound nature of the theater that gives birth to performance, per-formativity, and the real.[20] The performative, in other words, no matter how seemingly spontaneous, still requires scripts, as Judith Butler's more recent work reminds us, no matter that those scripts be repressed.[21] The irony, of course, is that in the aforementioned post-structural suspicion of the "authorized text," the scripts of past and present are often ignored, or nervously bracketed off (as Worthen's article so aptly points out), even though it is the histories of theatrical practice—including play-scripts—that most powerfully engage with the unconscious scriptings behind stereotype. The most obvious exam-ple of this dialectical struggle between originality and scriptedness would be the work of Stanislavski,[22] or in the present study, the writ-ings of Joseph Jefferson.

This other, essentially repressed, theatricality moves through many levels and kinds of hidden inscription, from the unconscious blocking of Harris and Klebold's grisly and moronic performance sce-nario, for example, into a kind of preconscious staging of the "second level" of scripted, cultural catastrophe. This level is represented best, perhaps, in the contrast between the trials of O. J. Simpson—accused of murder in the domestic/domestic terrorist attack on his wife, Nicole Brown Simpson, and her friend Ronald Goldman—and Timothy McVeigh, accused and convicted of murder in the political/domestic terrorist bombing of the Alfred P. Murrah Building in Oklahoma City, an abomination in which 168 people died. Here, unlike the horror of Littleton, in which the unconsciously scripted violence was, nonetheless, irredeemably real, both the Simpson and McVeigh trials as trials were, though also intrinsically violent, also mere *representations* of the acts of violence that they framed. As such they were clearly and consciously inscripted. But despite the constant references in the media to "the media circus" and to the trial as "theater," the real theater of each, especially in the case of McVeigh, remained largely hidden, even though, through the scenarios of jurisprudence, something like a theatrical narrative emerged in each case.

The trials were near inversions of one another: Simpson, a black film and sports star, prized his celebrity and lived a highly visible life of conspicuous consumption, while also eschewing political or social connections to the African American community in Los Angeles. McVeigh, on the other hand, was a virtually invisible poor white man, a Gulf War veteran and militia sympathizer. Simpson's trial, befitting his quasi-celebrity status, was watched by millions.

Television cameras recorded every nuance of the proceedings, as both Simpson's multimillion dollar legal "dream team" and prosecutors provided nonstop spectacle, from the grisly murder photos blown up many times life-size, to the keenly dramatic moment when Simpson, trying on the shrunken, blood-encrusted gloves found at the murder scene, turned to the jury and cameras and, holding up his hands in a gesture of confrontation and submission, proclaimed with exaggerated, theatrical finality, "They're too small!"

In contrast, cameras were not allowed in the courtroom during McVeigh's trial. His voice was never heard during the proceedings, his one utterance a carefully read quote after the trial was over,[23] an utterance very different from the seemingly unrehearsed ejaculation by Simpson. McVeigh's face remained "masklike," his demeanor impassive. He was forensically aphasic, often nearly autistic, rocking without expression in his chair, staring into space. Simpson's trial, though politically charged in its racial accusations against the Los Angeles Police Department, was never cast in purely ideological terms, while both prosecutor and defense attorney in McVeigh's trial clearly sought to link him to a wider right-wing political movement.

The juries in each case also seemed inverse images of each other. The Simpson jury maintained a decidedly high profile. Some members even achieved minor celebrity status while the trial was still in progress—one female juror went so far as to agree to pose for *Playboy* magazine. McVeigh's jury never achieved such celebrity status. It was, in fact, invisible, hidden behind a black wall during the course of the trial. The differences were perhaps best summed up in the public attitude toward the respective crimes scenes: the Simpson murder scene remained a kind of tawdry secret, visited by tour buses late at night, while the Oklahoma site became a virtual religious shrine, the chain-link fence that cordoned off the devastated building transformed into a reliquary of photos, flowers, and stuffed animals.

The overall effect of these differences was that the McVeigh trial, in all of its aspects, seemed less theatrical, more authentic, than the Simpson trial. But the fact that the suffused and understated approach of both prosecution and defense in the McVeigh trial were calculated within the shadow of the Simpson trial precisely for their theatrical value was lost on most observers. And though the somber theatricalities were plentiful in the McVeigh trial, they were obscured by the fact that the participants in that trial acted well, in contrast to the Simpson participants, who acted poorly. The McVeigh trial was simply better theater. The very opening of the trial, for example, began with the paradoxically sobering but histrionic unveiling of a huge found sculpture that had been slowly rolled into the courtroom on a dolly: the blackened, twisted rear axle of the Ryder truck that held the bomb, completely covered by the compelling and ministerial black veil. This moment was nothing less than prologue and theme for the entire trial—the slow and understated revelation, a virtual forensic striptease—of the distorted mechanisms of terrorist ideology. The unveiling of the twisted wreckage also foreshadowed the performative centerpiece of the McVeigh trial, the testimony of the victims and the victims' families. Not only the photos of twisted bodies and shattered concrete, but also the faces of the witnesses—drawn, contorted, and wrecked—who masked their emotional scar-tissue with crumpled Kleenex, twisted handkerchiefs, and trembling hands. These testimonials were certainly heartrending and appalling, but they were also carefully selected and rehearsed, and followed a very fine line between sheer ghastliness and empathy—a reenactment par excellence of Aristotelian terror and pity preceding catharsis.

But these aspects of the trial largely went unnoticed. The critics were in effect "taken in" by the theatrical at the specific moment that the theatrical seemed to disappear. The Simpson trial was a prosecutorial failure because it detached itself from theater. The Simpson fiasco became *merely* performative and thus emptied of significance. The narrative of jealous, stalking, murderous spouse quite literally lacked conviction, according to the jurors, and the behavior of attorneys and judge reeked of bad theater, self-conscious and self-aggrandizing play. The jury, underwhelmed by bad acting, by characters "set beside their parts," acquitted, and acquitted itself.

McVeigh's trial showed no such lapses. The theater disappeared into itself, seemingly became one with itself. Bombast was displaced by an understated empathy and terror, and the performance (and its performative), tied to the narrative of terrorist ideology and history, played convincingly. Catharsis was effected, and the difference was lethal. McVeigh received the death penalty. Theater, it would seem, exerts the full force of its violence when it seems to vanish into its own seeming substance, into the seemingly authentic. Observers and critics made the mistake of thinking theatricality could be equated with, or submerged within, mere visibility or performativity. Both trials, in other words, were equally theatrical, both carefully rehearsed, and both in their own way oddly surreal. But the surreality of the McVeigh trial remained concealed beneath a seemingly authentic surface: not "reality" nor even an ideological realism, but rather an authentic that seemed uncontestably genuine in all of its features.

From the Standpoint of Form
(Theory as American Culture)

This ratification of the authentic through the very enactment of the theater of the courtroom, an authentic that is carefully documented in diaretic deposition and forensic performance, has its origins in the earliest scenarios of the American continent. In the Puritan culture of surveillance and correction, authenticity had to be gotten outside the possibilities of the real—a real shut off from the eyes of the faithful by the vicissitudes of sin.

This authenticity, which supplants the real in much current theory, is a central contention working beneath the surface of the present work. Others, of course, have noted this repression of the real by the authentic:

Gilles Deleuze notes in his prescient 1968 work, *Difference and Repetition,* that the virtual stands opposed not to the real, but to the actual (with an emphasis upon *act,* i.e., performativity). Deleuze suggests, somewhat tautologically that "[t]he virtual is fully real in so far as it is virtual," like the youth culture's immersion in the virtual that I noted above. The virtual's substance is real as long as it is taken simply as virtual, apart from the real, a critical distance or "cut" effected by the symbolic.[24]

Slavoj Žižek, on the other hand, sees a more or less epistemological opposition between the real and "reality." Here the real remains unsignifiable, but charged with *jouissance,* "a grey and formless mist, pulsing slowly as if with inchoate life," a quote he borrows from Robert Heinlein.[25] It is reality, according to Žižek, that informs this formlessness and provides the shapes that both indicate and conceal the real. The real, in any case, is not anything like "objectivity" or "concrete reality," but is, rather, more like the terror that precedes articulation and image, articulation and image forming, in Žižek's schema, real*ity.* Here is where I would situate art in modern Western culture, and most specifically, apropos image and articulation, the play-text. The play-text represents the third, and most highly scripted, performance scenario among the three discussed. In the play we have the appearance of the cultural subject onstage, caught in the act of theater, pulsing within the circle and the image of uncertainty, presenting, paradoxically, through her scriptedness, the unconscious in-substance of the cultural and political self. It is the stage, that closed and circumscribed space, that allows for an infinite play of meanings. It is the play that marks the location of failure, the failure that, Lacan suggests, is the true agent of historical causality. Thus while I might speak of theater in more abstruse terms—the theater of mind, the space of thought separating imaginary from symbolic, symbolic from real—I also most pointedly mean the doing of the play, the enactment of textual content. For what theater represents, contra Worthen's suggestion late in his article, is far more than what it encodes in its inflections and intonations. It is the space of thought, insight, revelation, ecstasy, despair, effected in part through the apprehension of the delicacy and power of the *word.*

Although theater, any theater, is the way it is because of the culture within which it appears, the reverse is also true: culture, any culture, is the way it is because of its theater. Theater as a phenomenon represents a historically situated critical feedback loop that moves from play to culture, from culture to culture's unconscious subject, and back again. It is a dialectical formulation, in other words, and an infinite regression of the theatrical that not only enmeshes the culture/subject, but the act of critique itself. The permeation of political culture by theater—a far more important hegemonic function than theater's permeation by the political—influences all aspects of cultural practice. Theater becomes, as I have suggested elsewhere, the equivalent of Derridean writing shifted to the registers of enunciation and gaze, articulating (disjointing) the real at each level of discourse. The problem, at each point of analysis, is, as the work of Herbert Blau so powerfully suggests, the nature of theater (and thus reality): the articulations of stage, mirroring the "grey, pulsing" preformations of reality, are, in the words of Beckett's stage directions in the Real trash-strewn landscapes of *Breath*, "all scattered and lying." They require a space of reflection, a theater, to be absorbed into thought, but a theater whose first and most necessary impulse is to show the veiling that makes it what it is: theater's Real.

But the real, long ago disposed of in the American philosophies of James and Dewey, has instead been transformed into the authentic, the practical, the effective—most explicitly, perhaps, in the rise of neopragmatism, specifically Richard Rorty's "postanalytical culture" (as if American culture were once analytical), but also in the various materialisms and historicisms that eschew the more abstract inheritance of Hegel and Kant for the seemingly more substantive approaches of multicultural and postcolonial theory. Thus many recent theoretical rejections of "essentialism," for example, actually spring from a long and deeply American suspicion of analytic thought that found the best expression of its anxieties about the authentic, ironically, onstage, in plays like Royall Tyler's *The Contrast* and Anna Cora Mowatt Ritchie's *Fashion*. This early concern with "the authentic American" continues in the contemporary Hollywood film, where the action hero has become the icon of American (previously exclusively male, and now, increasingly, female) identity, an icon with roots in the early American figures of George Washington, Tyler's Colonel Manley, and Ritchie's Adam Trueman.

More interesting, however, is the fact that so much of contemporary American theory is still deeply imprinted by this fascination with the pragmatic and the concomitant suspicion of "essentialism" and "metaphysics"—the very suspicion that has caused the substitution of the real by the seemingly authentic.[26] And yet the pragmatic and the "authentic" material are fraught with their own metaphysical problems: specifically problems of the theatrical. The appearance of the authentic and the material (i.e., the material conditions of cultural production) must be empirical, demonstrable; they must be, in other words, repeatable. In the case of the pragmatic, what works must work again in similar situations or under similar conditions. In the case of cultural materialism, the connections between attitudes and ideas and cultural production must be *shown*. The provability or authenticity, relies, in other words, on empirical verifiability, on a re-creation or replay, or, socially and psychically speaking, on theater.

One problem that arises here, obviously, is that in the realm of re-creation, the copy threatens to overtake the original in its claim to the authentic. The instant replay in sports, for example, calls into question the perceived circumstances of a given moment of play; in the infinite replayability of film and video the original moment of performance is refracted and buried beneath the wealth of detail that emerges in subsequent viewings (the Hitchcock effect). Or, in a reversal of the logic, a criminal trial is created as the authentic opposite of a previous trial that stank of inauthenticity. Here the authentic comes into being through the existence of an a priori "inauthentic"; seeming reality is not reflected in the theater but is, as has been much remarked recently, produced by it. This is what Hillel Schwartz, in his encyclopedic study of doubling and mimesis, calls "our habit of relying upon reenactment and repetition to establish the truth of events and the authenticity of people." He continues, "Despite the rhetoric of uniqueness[,] our culture of the copy mocks that romanticism [which] seeks out the irreproducible as the source of Truth."[27] This contradiction—that reenactment becomes the basis for establishing uniqueness—requires forgetting, the forgetting of re-presentation, the same amnesis that allows our culture to remain both blind and hostile to the theater that constructs it.

If the thematic of amnesis finds its uniquely American expression in the immensely popular play by Joseph Jefferson and Dion Boucicault, based on the American "tall tale," *Rip Van Winkle*, then amnesia's symptom, misprision (a kind of radical misapprehension), undergoes its own series of transformations within the contexts of the antebellum American South in Boucicault's *The Octoroon*. Meanwhile, the physical, *hysterical* manifestation of misprision in extremis, blindness, finds expression in the late-nineteenth-century play *Margaret Fleming*, by the realist playwright James Herne.

These plays, especially Herne's magnum opus, also help situate the recent arguments (in feminist performance theory, specifically) regarding theatrical realism and the mimetic, which are themselves often misperceptions of the real. The closer one comes to the seemingly real in theater, the more one is reminded that what one sees is not what one is seeing. I am, in other words, never fooled that what I am looking at is "real," or that it mimics the Real, but I *am* aware that what I am looking at is really happening. The actors, as Herbert Blau tells us, are dying in front of our eyes; the use of period costume, the use of idiom or reference to everyday life, never fool me into thinking that I am seeing that reality, or even a "reinscription" of it, but remind me instead that what I am seeing is real *theater*, like Deleuze's real virtuality—and that despite its realness, and most especially when that realness becomes nearly unbearable, as in some types of violent body art, what is "really" happening is never the substance of what I am "really" seeing. It is in this sense that we say theater always occurs elsewhere. The conventions only serve to remind me that behind or even within the costume, an actual event is taking place: the actors are acting in a play—whatever that might mean—that is, in the real, in perception/ memory, necessarily occurring someplace else. Moreover, the displacement of realism as a genre by "nonmimetic" modes,[28] far from rejecting the ethos of realism, re-creates it. All performance, I would argue, is representative; all is, in the richest sense of the word, mimetic. The difference is that some forms ("realism") foreground their mimetic strategies, while others ("performance") oftentimes do not. In that sense, as in the Simpson/McVeigh trial contrasts, the seemingly more authentic performance is often the more hiddenly theatrical.

Indeed, theater is the exacting demand upon consciousness that enforces these kinds of analytic speculations, these "cuts" or splittings. Theater (as opposed to performance or performativity, or even, as the term is often used, theatricality) shows, when it is most itself, that it is always occurring in "the other scene"—or rather, that theater is the scene that shows the other scene of violence and desire. Indeed, if, as I have said, American culture is the way it is because of its theater, theater is the way it is not merely or even primarily because of culture's function as vehicle for ideology, but because of culture's drive to performance through the structures of thought.

But even though, as I have suggested, the type of theatrical thought or theory that would find itself caught up in such issues has never appeared in the American traditions of theater, such ideas have found expression in American literature, most especially in the work of "European" authors like Melville, Hawthorne, and the "realist" Henry James (whose work I will not discuss). These writers were each caught up within the epistemologies of gaze and enunciation, albeit in quite different ways. It is, I believe, in American fiction and poetry that we have the best expression of performance theory throughout the nineteenth and twentieth century, from the psychotic, hieratic spectacles of Melville's *Moby-Dick*, to the troubled and troubling fracture of the gaze in Hawthorne's "The Minister's Black Veil." The "hauntology" of gaze and act and speech, absent from the stages of American theater, appears in the stories and novels that invoke it, while its most harrowing manifestation as *real theater*, Artaud's theater of cruelty, appears in the infinite plications of the minstrel show. Here the cultural, political issue is less the appearance of ideology than ideologies of appearance. Moreover, these ideologies of appearance, which have been largely unseen throughout American history, have deep roots in that history and culture and manifest themselves as demand for the oxymoronic mere appearance of the authentic— true salvation, an authentic American character and culture, the "true" historical archive, the eradication of "false consciousness," the theoretical certainty of uncertainty, and today, the preservation of "traditional" marginal cultural values. This is an authentic that can, ironically and tragically, only manifest itself through the performative and performance of culture(s) scripted as theater, what Ernesto Laclau refers to as the "essentially performative character of naming" that is "the precondition for all hegemony and politics."[29]

The "essentially performative character of naming," the theater of thought, is the condition of the theatrical that I have been discussing: "real" theater, differentiated from Artaud's theatrical double, exists in the space between the real and the Imaginary. Theater is the disappearing, continuously atomizing negotiation of the real, the act of thought or critique that bends rationality back upon itself in order, through critique, to show critique as mere pose, as mask. Theater is, in other words, like analysis, the space-time in which the unconscious—of both subject and culture—can appear. But today this function is undercut by theory's own "universalized reflexivity," to quote Žižek, "the loss of symbolic efficiency"[30] caused by a kind of "repressive desublimation" of theory's subject, which, in the postmodern game, is theory itself. Here theory mutates into endless recapitulations of itself, its practices and methodologies, its concealed enchantment by its own ideology and its repression of the cogito in favor of the hallucinatory dream of the utopian political collective. Indeed, French critic Alain Finkielkraut, speaking of the French abandonment of Enlightenment rationality for the seeming authenticity of the collective (culture) and its illusory "history," describes a situation redolent of today's academics who "had to . . . sink the cogito into the profound depths of the collectivity, renew broken ties with former generations, replace the quest for autonomy with one for authenticity, abandon a critical stance."[31] Finkielkraut sees in this the anticipation of a similar trend in contemporary American society, a displacement of analytic argument by "cultural criticism."

At the same time that authenticity has been "reinscribed" within cultural criticism and historicism, the decentered and multiple self has emerged with a vengeance. While I am in full sympathy with the understanding of the Lacanian "I" as fractured, empty at center, insubstantial to/at its core, the other problem, the weight of the self—guilt, both individual and collective—is, in the American academy, largely left unexplored. At the psychic level, this lack within the discourse of lack—the lack of any discussion of the self's gravity—shows as a complete avoidance of the problem of guilt. We see the avoidance not merely at the ethical, moral level, but at the experiential level, in which, when we most want the self to disappear, to become the very lack that composes it, it weighs on the mind as an intolerable mass of memory, pain, and remorse. Here we glimpse the psychotic mechanisms of mourning and melancholia, as Freud tells us, the very singularity of experience silenced by the Foucauldian paradigms of power, the singularity beyond the event horizon of the painful and ecstatic literary/artistic experience. The weight of the self, its gravity, is quite separate from the feeling of self as "genuine" or "stable." It is the state of self that may, in the poststructural world of indeterminacies, be the real problem: the phenomenon of multiple personality syndrome, a performative modality in which the anxieties about representation, the fears of self-disappearance, are adumbrated by the repressed terror that, although I may not in substance exist, existence is still killing me.

Thus the self as empty signifier in the modern period of American drama: here the strain between the sheer insubstance of a self that is fragmented into its constituent parts, and its agonizing recalcitrance, mirrors the very cultural/political history of American identity—pluribus or unum? It seems somehow curious that today, as the United States stands unchallenged as the single, heavyweight world power, the discourses of history and cultural materialism would be so vociferously negating the real of subject/nation. Moreover, at the exact moment of this American political ascendancy, and in the midst of theories of multiplicity and contingency, American youth are increasingly engaging in the most noncontingent action imaginable: multiple murder. The self's disappearance at the point of a gun becomes real at the very instant that that real is mediated and begins to disappear—the whole real business *there,* but unthinkable, the empty signifier of American culture and history. This empty signifier of the self's paradoxical disappearance and gravity, its zero-mass and infinite density, appears in the absent/present figure of the murdered child in modern American drama—a bastard child, the *infans* of a silenced cogito, either Symbolic in O'Neill's *Desire under the Elms,* Imaginary in Albee's *Who's Afraid of Virginia Woolf?* or rottenly Real in Sam Shepard's *Buried Child.* And in the end we rest at this present and final recursion; the performance scenarios of Karen Finley, and the plays of Tony Kushner and Suzan-Lori Parks, lead us back through the very themes of this American jeremiad. In Finley, we return to the diaretic and Enthusiastic excesses of Puritan American origins, the endless replay of the ecstasies of social and political violence. In Parks we see the reiteration of the anxieties about authenticity and the theaters of the Real, the multiplication of selves and their insubstantialities. In Kushner we confront the endless mutations of materialist desire and its bodies caught in the Mormon guise of Artaud's Plague. Each of these plays is a colophon to the central and empty location of the long history of the American other.[32] Each approaches the "positive" gap in memory, the split that gives access to a political and cultural unconscious, and within it the site of trauma, but then falters in the face of the American blindness to its theaters. Each contains a cicatrix hard and encapsulated, but ultimately leaves it unexamined. Each misses the hollow point, the fetish/phobic object of American culture and history that passes instead into the hands of a seemingly ever-increasing number of child psychopaths—children whose rifle scopes encircle and point back to the very institution of America as theater, whose crosshairs target the auricle in the brain[33] where thought literally and figuratively disappears, the hole in mind where theater ought to appear, but where, within American amnesis, it simply will not. Awash in the theatrical, infinitely refracted and splintered within the prismatics of a society of spectacle, we nonetheless still desperately need a *theater,* a viable theater effected through the textures and textualities of thought, to see it (thought), and to think and feel it through. A theater that examines, that feels the cruel intensities of its violence, but most importantly, that allows, in the speculations, "thought to remain hidden, even under the most intense scrutiny."[34]

Act I: Warning Signs

Television came over

on the Mayflower.

—Don DeLillo

1
Puritanism and the Early American Theaters of Cruelty

The Etiology

While it has become commonplace, following the work of Perry Miller and especially Sacvan Bercovitch, to see the Puritan "project" in terms of a progressive iconization of self as saint—the self as constructed hero emerging from the Puritan propensity "for epitome," to quote Bercovitch—this casting of self as principal player in a theologicopolitical drama has never been discussed specifically in terms of theater or theatrical ontology. The reasons might seem obvious. The Puritans vilified theater, often for reasons that were oddly prescient; the theater, like the Hollywood film of today, tended to demean women, and to focus undue attention on sex and violence. Theater, moreover, in its reliance on the false and the illusory, tended to coarsen sensibility, empathy, and even perception itself.[1] In this the Puritan attack on theater anticipated not only conservative Christian ideology of today, but also certain strains of feminism and cultural studies, as well.

I would like to suggest a reassessment of some of these early American Puritan texts, most particularly the diaries,[2] through the lens of mise-en-scène not only because these texts enact an uncanny grasp of theatrical consciousness, but because that consciousness represents the reemergence of the theater that Puritanism had seemingly repressed. This was a theater of mind that played out the growth of American culture as an increasing, and increasingly unacknowledged, theatricalization of itself.

Some see this theatricalization first emerging in modern American

society, a society of the image and the sound bite, the society of television, or for some even earlier, in the melodrama and social spectacle of
nineteenth-century America. But it had its roots in the very inception,
the very idea, of America. From the Puritan concerns with self-surveillance, through the Franklinesque focus on the mere appearance of propriety and prosperity, from the culture of the con man, the spectacles of
religious revival at Cane Ridge, Kentucky, and the Barnumesque
sideshows of nineteenth- and twentieth-century America, right up to
the inevitable discovery of television and the appearance of Ronald
Reagan, American actor as president, or Bill Clinton, president as actor,
American culture has been unknowingly immersed in and formulated
through theater, through the ontologies and strategies of seeing and
being seen, of revelation and concealment.

It is the unknowingness of that immersion, however, that is most
germane. For all of the professed hatred of sham and theatricality in
American culture, we are perhaps more than any other a society of the
spectacle. And yet in our demand for the authentic, the true beneath the
masks of sham and mere appearance, we demonstrate what is, I think,
a unique blindness to the nature of theatricality—a blindsight[3] that
finds its nascent expression in Puritan writing.

These texts describe the surveillance phenomenology of theater in
very different ways: watching and being watched in the Puritan style of
John Winthrop and Michael Wigglesworth, of course, but also the
awareness of watching oneself watch—seeing oneself through the
watcher's eye, the making of a seeming self through the insubstantiality of the seen—in the writings of Thomas Shepard. This was, in Puritan society, a long series of theatrical meditations that had no theater at
its conclusion, not unlike the long and tortured meditations of another
genius whose ruminations realized no theater, Antonin Artaud. In fact,
the writings of Artaud, also obsessed with self-surveillance, represent a
peculiar invagination of Puritan, and eventually American, ontology.
The cross-penetration of Artaud and Puritanism is illuminating, I think,
because both Artaud and the Puritans tried to invoke the impossible: a
theater that was not merely representational, a theater that was somehow more real than the world within which it appeared. While the
Puritans would never have named this impossibility theater, as did
Artaud, they seemed to have cultivated a consciousness that, like
Artaud's, both invoked and reviled theater and especially theatricality.
Taken together, Artaud's influence on modern theater, and Puritanism's influence on American identity into the modern period, desig-

nate the margin between theater and theater's double, a limit that generates desire and, in desiring, becomes the site of violence, excess, and duplicity, a desire that defines what we have come to call the theater of cruelty in the making of America.

The Plague

Artaud's *Second Manifesto for the Theater of Cruelty* is an anticolonial text that presents a scenario, *The Conquest of Mexico,* purporting to enact, from the viewpoint of his theater of cruelty, the defeat of Mexico (in the person of Montezuma) by Spain (in the person of Cortez), and the decimation of Mexico's inhabitants. This scenario was chosen, Artaud explains, in order to "pose the question of colonization"—most probably the French colonization of Algeria, and the attempted colonization of Indochina—and through it to foreground the moral and ideological scandal of racism.

Although he does not raise the issue directly, the scenario as it exists seems to suggest, in its violence and its excess, the concomitant issue of what has been called *endocolonization,* a term indicating the processes by which not only cultures, but the structures of thought that give shape to cultures, are themselves colonized by dominant ideologies. When dominant cultures take over and marginalize indigenous peoples, for example, they not only restructure culture itself, they restructure the very ways that indigenous peoples think, causing the colonized in some cases to desire their colonization. Furthermore, dominant culture perpetuates itself by endocolonizing itself, determining not merely what its own subjects think and believe, but how they think and how they believe. Thus dominant culture not only controls what is acceptable to think, but the possibilities of what can be thought.

As Gramsci points out, the structuring of hegemonic forces is quite a bit messier than I have presented it here; what constitutes "dominant culture," for example, is, in this scheme, often left unspecified. And while the concept of dominant culture remains more or less unquestioned, what of the effects of "subcultures?" Does membership in this or that ideological camp constitute dominance over the individual by a culture? Does that dominance produce its own endocolonizations? Is there thus *a* dominant culture, then, or is all culture and subculture—from the American middle class to cadres of Queer theorists—dominant and dominating to those who live within it? Is dominant culture itself as dominant as theorists think it is? Doesn't the Gramscian understanding of hegemonic forces allow, for example, new counterforces to emerge from within hegemony? Although questions like these very often remain not only unanswered but unposed, they are crucial because the "through-line" of endocolonization theory suggests that the endocolonized mind, because its thought strategies have been changed, remains blind to its own colonization, whether by middle-class ideology or theories from the margins. The endocolonized mind—and all minds are such—always thinks other than it thinks it thinks. The endocolonized mind, in other words, represents the creation and emergence of the unconscious, and, moreover, an unconscious that is at once individual and cultural/political.

Endocolonization, then, determines the edges of (political) consciousness and determines those edges through a theatrical reciprocity—a theater of mind that projects itself as culture, and a theatricalized culture that in turn infects the processes of perception. Thought, mind, and culture are thus as much the product of theater as theater is a "manifestation" of culture. Artaud is thus able to theatricalize Cortez's conquest not only because conquest is intrinsically theatrical, but also because the endocolonized mind thinks through the display and representation of power and dominance. Artaud's scenario, then, shows us theater recuperating colonization, but it also shows us thought colonized by/as theater.

The kind of power deployment Artaud suggests in this scenario works only in the absence of critical (Brechtian) distance—what we would term a theory of performance, but a theory that incorporates at its center the ontologic and epistemological problem of the theatrical as the condition of consciousness, a condition that, in the absence of such a theory, remains concealed to itself. The push toward thought—*critical* thought—that somehow moves through the coarser structures of the concealing mind and duplicitous consciousness and toward something both terrifying and sublime in Artaud's work, suggests his strong desire to identify that which is divine in consciousness and thought itself. Note that the issue is to identify, not identify with. Artaud's desire is to be the divine, not merely to lay himself subservient to it. There is, nonetheless, a pursuit of moral purity in Artaud, emanating from his Gnostic belief in the fallenness of flesh, that has strong Puritanical echoes.[4] For while Calvinism rejected this kind of Manichaeanism, the rejection was often not convincing. Thus while the intersection between Artaud's manifesto and the theatricalization of America, or even more problematically, the Puritan mind, may seem odd at first glance, the correlations are, I think, productive. The Puritans were, of course, both colonizers and colonized. I am suggesting that the colonization of America, like Cortez and Artaud's colonization of Mexico, appears first as theater. But while Artaud theatricalizes colonization through a performative cruelty that resists theatricalization in its search for life, in America colonization occurs through a cultural life that is both increasingly theatricalized and resistant to any attempts to distance or theorize it. This stage was set in the most unlikely of places, in the Puritan world of New England where theater itself was anathema—where in fact theater was repressed, was repression itself. The Puritan diary (among other surveillance techniques) took its place.[5]

Now, in order for theater to be "repressed" there must, obviously, be some sort of theater already in place. If, as was the case for the Puritans, there was no *established* theater, if theater existed only as a condition or possibility of mind, then theater becomes its own origin and end. The conscious mind, in other words, does not find its contours in an externalized structure, in (a) play, but only in yet another expression or representation of mind-play. This was certainly the case with Artaud, who created virtually no theater in his life, a situation that Michel Foucault cites as the root cause of his madness—a closed theatricalized consciousness that finds no escape through mise-en-scène to the "real" stage. In the case of the Puritans, theater, though absent as an institution, nonetheless acts in the interior as a kind of performance feedback loop that forms the very basis of morality. One is constantly assessing and reassessing *how one acts* in order to ascertain if one has *acted well*. In fact, even one's intentions are objectified as exhibition or *show* through the interior watching and are moved out of the realm of the merely intentional into the realm of the performative (how I present myself to myself), and into performance itself. I act, and I act well, but finally I realize that acting well reveals nothing about the condition or even the existence of my true self. Acting well might in fact be the best cover-up for a self that has denied God and his ways. My performance, in other words, finally refers to nothing but itself. It turns its back on life, as Augustine charges. The issue, ultimately, in the Puritan mind becomes the ability to construct one's own *character*, to construct oneself as a character, to construct character itself. Here is where the issue of the performative gives way, it seems to me, to theater. For performativity, as used, for example, by Judith Butler, denotes the conditions under which one becomes or "does" one's body/identity. In Butler, the process of performing the self, unlike the becoming or doing of theater, is largely unconscious and concealed, but influenced by any number of cultural norms and biases. Theater, on the other hand, seemingly brings into view the processes of enacting itself and in doing so largely ignores or forgets what is already in place—gender identity, for example. Theater becomes a kind of second-rate performativity, a fake performativity, while performativity itself becomes the more inclusive term because it exists a priori to theater. But this ignores, among other issues, the problem of *precession:* the theoretical notion of the performative, like the performative itself, is grounded in and emerges from the idea of theater. It is theater that in essence "gives birth" to the category of the performative, both historically and, as Jacques Derrida has pointed out, epistemologically as well.

Yet this theoretical quibble is no simple invocation to cultural constructivist views of theatricalization—that it is theater and not the performative that best describes the coming to being of identity. Butler herself seems to challenge such simple notions of constructivism, and indeed, the issue of cultural constructivism is itself challenged through the example of the Puritan diary. In New Canaan the cultural voices were loud and clear. It was obvious to the Puritans what they must be, what they must become, and why. They set about *consciously* to construct that self and yet lived in constant awareness of their failures. If the cultural definitions were so powerful, what are we to make of the fact that, try as they might, these diarists could *not* construct or reconstruct desire and will? It is, of course, unknowable if these men were as sinful as they say they were, or if they seemed or even acted so. To suggest that they "really" didn't want to be good and were just acting merely underscores my point—at one level at least the Puritan experience seems to suggest that one cannot change the lineaments of will or desire to conform to ideology (indeed, at some level this is one of the central issues in the history of Western drama). The failure, finally, to construct that life through an unrealized theatrical ontology links Artaud and Puritanism. In very different ways, both suffer the derangement of theater activated but unrealized. Both are left bereft by a theater operating only as consciousness. There is a strange affinity in the means to the presumed end—the purification of life and thought, "a meticulous and unremitting pulverization of every insufficiently fine, insufficiently matured form," a need to restrain the spirit from taking its leap "until it has passed through all the filters and foundations of existing matter," then redoubling its labor "at the incandescent edges of the future."[6] The words are, of course, Artaud's, but they seem imbued with the spirit of Puritanical desire, the desire for a salvation that was intense in its focus and purity, but never known for certain. Indeed, Artaud's whole notion of a theater of cruelty stands in strange and even harrowing relation to the Puritan ethos—the strict moral "athleticism," the activation of a theatricality that seeks "not theater but life itself," the powerful emphasis on a life delivered from delusion. "This cruelty," says Artaud, referring to theater itself, "can thus be identified with a kind of severe moral purity which is not afraid to pay life the price it must be paid."[7] Words that might have sprung, albeit with a certain moral subterfuge, from the pen of the pious Puritan Michael Wigglesworth himself.

The Puritan "theater of morals" also moves outside the more strictly theoretical ideas of Artaud. The self-observation and self-correction of the Puritans is employed by means of recollected memory and desire and is similar, in some respects, to Stanislavskian technique, and through it, to American Method acting. A theatricalized narrative is constructed on the basis of this recollection that allows the director/moralist to ascertain the status of his intentions. Were they pure (do not enter the theater with mud on your feet)? Was behavior seemly? Was righteousness observed? Yet at the moment that this theatricality emerges, it is repressed *as theater* and seemingly reemerges as "life," as the correction of false motive, false consciousness, or sinful desire. Theater thus becomes in Puritanism the repressed origin of life, the means by which one is saved or becomes righteous—becomes, in other words, an authentic human being, "a child of God."

"Theater is born in its own disappearance," writes Derrida, "and the offspring of this movement has a name: man."[8] While the Puritans sought "man"—their own personal identity and salvation in Christ—Artaud sought to erase man entirely, to create a theater that "sweeps away human individuality, and in which man is only a reflection."[9] Thus in both Artaud and Puritanism, "man," self, identity, is created through the very absence of "real" theater—in Artaud because he cannot realize his theater of cruelty, and in Puritanism because it remains blind and resistant to theater. Yet in both Artaud and Puritanism, the failure to activate this theater is the problem, whereas later on in American drama the problem is the failure to activate theatrical theory. In either case, one is consigned to blindness unless one sees the inevitable interplay between a consciousness formulated *as if* and its expression as theater. This theater is inevitably representational, perhaps even at some moments irresolutely real as *as if*.

The Diagnosis

In the chapter called "The Castaway" in Melville's *Moby-Dick*,[10] Pip the cabin boy falls overboard in the heat of the whale hunt. He manages to stay afloat, but as the ship disappears over the horizon and he finds himself bobbing in the undifferentiated sea, he goes mad, sees "the multitudinous God-omnipresent, coral insects, that out of the firmament of waters heaved the colossal orbs," sees "God's foot upon the treadle of the loom, and spoke it." He expresses that ineffable revelation, however, in a most distressing way:

> "This way comes Pip—poor boy! would he had died, or I; he's half horrible to me. He too has been watching all these interpreters—myself included—and look now, he comes to read, with that unearthly idiot face. Stand away again and hear him. Hark!"
> "I look, you look, he looks; we look, ye look, they look."
> "Upon my soul, he's been studying Murray's grammar."[11]

So also the earliest moments of the American experience as parable: the approach of the first band of Puritans led by John Winthrop writing his proclamation, he tells us, while they are still out on the Atlantic Ocean, the idea of civilization-as-theater formulating itself before civilization even takes root, emerging instead, like Pip's madness, on the undifferentiated sea, and finding its expression in the invocation to the seeing and being seen, to the interpreting and the seeing of interpretation; the proclamation ordains the new land "a city on a hill," an object of wonder, a dramatic melding of set and character, actors strutting against the backdrop of the New Canaan before the assembled gaze of the world: "I look, you look, he looks." The proclamation, in fact, bespeaks a man and a community already laboring under the watchful gaze of man and God. It is a community founded on watching—God watching them, they watching each other, each watching herself and watching herself watch:

So the ground of love is an apprehension of some resemblance in the things loved to that which affects it, this is the cause why the Lord loved the Creature, so far as it hath any of his Image in it, he loves his elect because they are like himself, he beholds them in his beloved son; so a mother loves her child, because she thoroughly conceives a resemblance of herself in it. Thus it is between the members of Christ, each discerns by the work of the spirit his own image and resemblance in another.[12]

In the mirroring projection of self-identity in otherness, one sees oneself in the other, in one's gaze upon the other, and sees in the other's gaze the projection of one's own guilt or glory—in the eyes of the other, the eyes I give to the other, I perceive my possibility and my failure:

The eyes of all people are upon us; so that if we shall deal falsely with our god in this work we have undertaken and so cause him to withdraw his present help from us, we shall be made a story and a by-word through the world, we shall open the mouths of enemies to speak evil of the ways of god.[13]

Succeeding or failing in the charge that God has given them, in other words, will turn their endeavor into a story, enacted even now before the eyes of the world. Thus the failure or success of the noble experiment is already being sealed in a grand play produced in the theater of humanity. The mechanism of the experiment—and the means by which we gauge its success or failure—lay in the eye of Puritan watchfulness, playing upon the actions of men. This was "a complex mimetic logic," in the words of Frederick Dolan, "a circular chain in which Winthrop's community mimes God's law (as revealed in the Bible), and the world, through miming the Puritan community, is brought to God; an endless chain of similitude, resemblance, and identification governs the colony's theologicopolitical strategy."[14] The similitude and search for resemblances, the captivation by mimesis that so distressed Artaud, means also, of course, that one is always alive to difference, to otherness as the sign and symptom of one's failure. This is held in check by the comfort of Imaginary sameness between self and other, the consolation of finding myself, my desire, in the Other, the pattern, in Lacanian thought, of narcissistic hysteria.

The founding move, then, the "primal repression" in the establishment of the American state, is a narcissism that becomes permanently inscribed in the Puritan/American consciousness. Moreover, Winthrop's description of the individual narcissistic movement between mother and child—in which the mother loves her child precisely because the child is seemingly *her*, or rather, she is the child—is transposed to the societal, in which God loves humanity because he sees himself in it. This sets up a correspondence between individual consciousness and social consciousness, and thus between the individual unconscious and its "socius." This narcissism, this self-absorbed and ironically egotistical activity of self-observation, is, as has often been observed, part and parcel of the Puritan mind-set. Indeed, in the earliest Puritan America watchfulness of all kinds was the key to salvation and even survival, from the "panoptical" Puritan concept of the village—central placement of the church, the village surrounding common pasture land, the very compactness of the village itself making all who lived within it visible to all—to the self-examination and preaching activities of ministers, to the public display of sinners, to the use of the diary as a means of objectifying a self that could then be measured against Puritan standards of behavior. As Everett Emerson writes,

> [P]ersonal documents reveal much about the nature of Puritanism. Self-examination by means of a diary had obvious virtues. The self that examines and the self examined could be distinguished as the diarist objectified his experiences, his feelings, his reasonings. What he learned about himself he recorded and by externalizing it felt a greater sense of control.[15]

The diary, then, helps the author narrativize his life and observations. He creates a true fiction, or what Jean Genet calls a "false spectacle born of a true illusion," through the form of the diary and uses it to *translate* his perceptions into "facts" that could be scrutinized over and over again. He utilizes, more than anything else, his memory of the day's events, and his memory turns those events into something like the fact of memory-identity. The diary thus represents the contents of memory, as well as what that memory could not contain. The Puritan diary, moreover, takes on historical interest for us—it provides a "glimpse into the Puritan mind." And yet the memory that the diary represents also resists historicization, just as any personal memory resists historicization unless it is ratified by others who can verify what memory gives over. Memory demands witness, in other words, to move into the domain of the historical. And it is the private and personal nature of the diaries that generates this resistance—how do we know that what they represent was in any way typical of the "Puritan mind," or even that such a thing as a Puritan mind existed?

And yet the form of the personal diary also resists the status of "mere" memory. In the diaries, after all, the observation of other selves (the Puritan village as institution) was shifted to the observation of self by self *through the eye of the other,* thus activating a consciousness that was grounded in mise-en-scène. The form and content of the diary, in other words, is generated through the very public (historical) eye of Puritan watchfulness—the spiritual and behavioral concerns, the Calvinist doctrine, the ethos of the diary itself were all shared communal experiences, as were, presumably, the experiences being recorded.

But this decidedly Brechtian distancing fails the Puritan imagination precisely because—though it is profoundly theatrical—it lacks an actual theater through which the personal vision of one's struggle can be assimilated into, or judged against, a communal consciousness. The repressive aspects of theater-as-social-control are here ameliorated when we see theater's lack in the neurotic consciousness of Puritan writing. Even though theater in some sense formulates (rather than "celebrates") communal attitudes and biases, it also provides an essential outlet through which those biases can be critiqued (leading, of course, to yet another round of formulated biases and attitudes). The earliest impulse toward theatrical consciousness in America and Americans' deep distrust of that very theatricality find their sources in the earliest days of the American experience, where such a formulated community might "rejoice together, mourne together, labor and suffer together, always having before our eyes our Commission and Community."[16]

Plague

For a people who formulated themselves so completely through the promiscuity of the other/self's voyeuristic eye, it is perhaps no surprise that through the past four hundred years this group of colonizers has itself undergone so many recolonizations. True to the theatrical ontology of absence that haunted them, the Puritans, through the rehearsals, revisions, and rewrites of history, have seemingly dissolved into an endless precession of dramatic images. For many years the butt of jokes and caricatures both in America and Europe, the Puritans early on were portrayed as stiff, pious busybodies, concerned not only with their own salvation, but with the salvation of all those with whom they lived, fearing sin in others as much as in themselves because sin in any part of the community could bring down God's wrath on the whole. Guilt and responsibility moved in the realm of the Imaginary. Sinners set out for public display in stocks, with their sins "writ full large" in signs about their necks, quickly became stereotypical of the Puritanical rage for guilt and punishment through, in part, the representations of sin and guilt. The caricatures of Puritanism, in fact, did much to help the literary careers of nineteenth-century artists. Most noteworthy perhaps, but not alone in his condemnation of Puritanism, was Nathaniel Hawthorne.

Later, in the middle and latter part of the twentieth century, thanks in large part to the work of Perry Miller, the Puritans were recuperated as a more human, less fanatical religious group. They drank, they liked sex and good food, they laughed and danced and read poetry, all with relative abandon, all seemingly without guilt or remorse. They were a people who valued progress and prosperity and linked the prosperity of the individual and community with righteousness and proper piety. This, along with their penchant for observation and exactitude, moved quite easily into the strictures of commerce and the empirical sciences. These Puritans were a focused and deliberate people, to be sure, but full of vigor and life, appreciative of what life offered them in the pleasures with which they surrounded themselves.

Then, seemingly swimming against this revisionism, there was Michael Wigglesworth,[17] a dyspeptic, nosy moralizer obsessed with guilt, "a poor, sinful worm" undeserving even of God's wrath. Whatever recuperation the Puritans might have undergone is undone the minute Wigglesworth's diaries are opened. Even his name seems a caricature of Puritanical ridiculousness that is quickly confirmed as one reads him, and reads about him.

Wigglesworth was a man without humor, "chief among sinners," with seemingly no appreciation for pleasure or any of the forms pleasure might take. At one point, early in his diary, he admonishes one of his students who had left Harvard College for a few days of fun in Ipswich, explicitly disobeying Wigglesworth's orders that he not go:

> I told him also of the dangers of pleasure and how they had like to have been my ruin. Knowing the danger of them therefore I dissuade both myself and others. And so I bade him farewell. But that very evening he was again at play I think among the students and when he saw me coming he slinked home and left his game

whereby I gather he is more afraid of me a poor, sinful worm than of God. (27)

Although we might appreciate the severity of an absence without leave, Wigglesworth's outrage at finding his charge playing a game with fellow students later that day is unintentionally funny, although, as the editor of his diaries points out, Wigglesworth seems not to appreciate the ridiculousness of his own tirades, or his overzealous response.

In typical Puritan diaretic style, Wigglesworth does not limit his observations to the students in his charge; he also inveighs against others in his community: "Lord in mercy heal, or I know not what will become of New England." At one point Wigglesworth launches into an extraordinarily obsessive meditation on his neighbor's gates, which swing back and forth at night in the wind:

> I cannot tell whether it were it my duty to give them some hint that owe them. When I think 'tis a common thing, and that 'tis impossible but that the owners should have seen them in that case, and heard them blow to and fro, and that it is but a trivial matter, and that I have given a hint to one that dwells in the house, and he maketh light of it; and that it would rather be a seeming to check others mindlessness of their own affairs . . . and I am troubled. (71).

He saves the great bulk of his observations, however, for himself, his vileness, his poor health, and most prominently, his sexuality. Indeed, Wigglesworth seems to be his own favorite subject. While he confesses again and again to the sins of pride and vanity and reminds himself (and his readers?) endlessly of his worthlessness, such castigations only serve to heighten the suspicion that Wigglesworth was in fact extraordinarily self-centered, even, perhaps, egomaniacal. His blindness to the double bind is remarkable: he castigates himself for pride but never suspects that his own self-obsessed self-observation might be vain or prideful. Moreover, the hide-and-seek style of the diary, especially when describing his sexual proclivities (which seem decidedly homoerotic) and guilts, takes on a voyeuristic theatricality beyond the conventional narcissism of the diary as self observed.

> ah Lord I am vile, I desire to abhor my self (o that I could) before the[e] for these things. I find such unresistable torments of carnal

lust or provocation unto the ejection of seed that I find myself
unable to read any thing to inform me about my distemper
because of the prevailing or rising of my lusts. (4)

The adolescent narcissism of the text is remarkable—it seems that
Wigglesworth is unable to read and learn about his sexual problems
because the words turn him on—and leads one to wonder if there was
in his mind an unseen audience, another reader. This is an unknowable
proposition, of course, but one that complicates the ontological cross-
reflections. There are moments, for example, when the diarist seems so
self-absorbed in his own physical and moral concerns, that he is oblivi-
ous even to his own conceit. When he asks his doctor if marriage is
advisable for him, it is not because he is afraid of infecting his wife with
the gonorrhea from which he suffers, but rather because he is afraid
marriage might further injure his health. When the doctor advises him
that marriage might offer physical comfort, the matter is more or less
settled in Wigglesworth's mind. The idea that someone might someday
read his words and be rightly appalled at such an egomaniacal after-
thought seems far from his mind. Yet, at another point, when he discusses his disease more intimately, he becomes evasive—he describes
the details of his affliction in Latin, "the excretio *(which happened in the
presence of such a friend)* seminis." (86)[18] The tantalizing, even seductive
timbre of the phrasing raises more questions than it answers. Who
might this friend be who witnesses the "excretio seminis," and under
what circumstances might he (she?) witness such an intimate occurrence? This is the reason, one might at first suppose, for the use of Latin,
but while such phrasing might elude the prying eyes of his fiancée or
other uneducated women or men, it would certainly not fool his audience of colleagues or students, who were required to converse in Latin
while at Harvard College. Finally, when he gets to the point of actually
naming the disease, he becomes almost coy and calls it "*Gon,*" suggesting in the word itself, *gone/Gon,* a Freudian *fort/da,* a double desire for
both concealment and revelation, or, in the *excretio seminis,* the hysterical desire to externalize the seminal, the primal repression.

What is interesting, in fact, about these evasions and sidesteps is
that they seem not to be intentionally tactical; that is, the Latin and the
abbreviations are easily deciphered and seem designed to protect Wigglesworth from his own self-revelations. This contrasts with other
places in the diary, where Wigglesworth actually writes in code, a kind
of shorthand developed by Thomas Shelton and quite elaborate

already, but complicated further by Wigglesworth, who added many of his own characters and abbreviations, rendering portions of the diary indecipherable.[19] While it is true that such shorthand might simply be shorthand, that is, a more efficient way of writing, one is impressed in the diary by the fact that most all of the shorthand sections deal with sexual matters, Wigglesworth's "filthy, carnal lusts."

One might also object that while Wigglesworth never intended his writings to be read, he feared they might. His refusal to write all of the seamy details in anything but the more elusive code indicates this. But then why use an accessible code like Shelton's that could be deciphered by an unknown reader? Why not use a private code that might more effectively prevent the private portions of his diary from being exposed? Perhaps because the issue was not merely to conceal the content of the writing. Indeed, even though portions remain occluded, the very idea of coded revelations suggest something else as well: that the desire might not be merely to conceal, nor merely to reveal—it might rather represent the desire to be seen concealing, to be seen concealed. The desire emerging out of this Sartrean voyeurism is the desire to be caught in the cross-reflected strategies of theater, revealing that one conceals, concealing the revelation, making sure the ruse is discovered, then covering up again, seducing the watcher in the shadows with the desire to be caught watching. It doesn't matter that Wigglesworth may not ever have imagined his diaries would one day be read by others, much less published; the ontologic desire of presentation and performance, finally of theater, animates his writing. There is a suggestion in the diary, I believe, that facts and observations are being concealed from potentially prying eyes. But there is a further sense or sensibility in the writing that Wigglesworth himself is the watcher in the shadows. He is the one from whom certain desires and lusts must be hidden. The very theatrical ontology that is developed is repressed—the unconscious as mise-en-scène.

But who, finally, in the cells of the repressed, might the watcher's object of desire have been? On the first page of his diary, in the first sentence, in fact, Wigglesworth first names the "unnatural, filthy lust" that arises in him as a result of a conversation with his pupils, all of whom are male, of course, and all of whom are "unloving . . . yet go so to my heart." His "fond affection," in fact, is often returned as ridicule and insult. He seems especially focused on one John Haines, the young man whom he castigates for being AWOL, and to whom he refers on several different occasions. Just what his feelings for this young man were, we may never know, but he appears upon the stage of Wigglesworth's meditations often, is privy to his intimate advice, and is even seemingly brought to tears by his abjurations.

The full effect of Wigglesworth's writing is, as I have suggested, very nearly a recapitulation of the Puritan stereotype. He is lust-driven and yet seems quite openly to detest the flesh and hovers dangerously close to Manichaeanism in his suspicion that the physical world is evil. His rejection of sexuality, and his fervent desire to have God relieve him of the temptations of the flesh, his constant physical pains and sickly constitution, his attraction, finally, to a kind of Calvinized Gnosticism, in which the stern, vengeful God of Sinai seems to threaten the obliteration of all flesh—suggests a man who, like Artaud, was possessed of a dramatic vision that was finally incapable of play. What is also noteworthy in Wigglesworth's diaries is his straight-ahead desire for constructedness, to be made as God would seemingly want him to be made, but finally to be rid of ego and desire along oddly egotistical, narcissistic lines, in which constructedness is perhaps the ego's way past the prototypical narcissistic stoppage.

It is, in fact, a kind of narcissistic masochism that probably best describes Wigglesworth's diaries. Indeed, it has often been noted within the psychoanalytic community that the diary is the expression par excellence of the narcissistic personality—recording all of the observed nuances and occurrences of the day in order to keep the self that is constantly in danger of fading into the image of the self-as-other, stable and self-possessed.

Consequently, in an extension of something like the Lacanian mirror stage, Wigglesworth is so preoccupied with his own self-image that he becomes entirely captivated by it. In his captivation, moreover, he projects that image onto the world around him, seeing in others the same masochistic abjection that fuels his ego. Ultimately he projects that image onto a potential love object, the above-mentioned John Haines, so that he may suffer the inevitable humiliation of ridicule, "meeting with some very disrespectful carriage," thus activating both a Freudian moral masochism and an erotogenic masochism that seems plainly homoerotic. In either case, Wigglesworth's captivation by his own image within the frame of a nearly infinite extension of the mirror stage suggests also his captivation by a theater that he never sees, but that sees him. We see in Wigglesworth the same Artaudian drive toward the divine, a divine that seems at every turn to reject and elude him—a drive that seems, in its pursuit of perfection, doomed to failure at the outset. There is in either case a desire to find the self as saved and purified, a desire that is aborted at each turn when the watcher watching the self watching finds only a sham identity, falsified papers.

The Catharsis

In the introduction to Thomas Shepard's collection of writings, *God's Plot*, the editor explains why he has used the phrase from Shepard's autobiography as the title of his work:

> Shepard and his people envisioned a divine scenario governing the living of their lives and the saving of their souls. They became actors with parts to play in a cosmic drama of redemption. God wrote the script, cast the parts, directed the staging; Christ took the starring role; religion explained each act and scene.[20]

Shepard indeed uses the phrase *god's plot* for the divine plan, but his writing reveals a theatrical ontology that moves well beyond such easy metaphors, into the seeing, and the doubled seeing, that characterizes so much of Western theater. On March 18, 1641, for example, Shepard writes in his diary,

> I saw if my mind acted it spun nothing but deceit and delusion; if my will and affections acted, nothing but dead works. Oh, how do I need Christ to live in me! Yet I saw if a man hath eyes and life he will not lean on another to lead him and carry him as when he wants both; so here. I saw the Lord made me live by faith by making me feel a want of both, to distrust myself and trust more unto the Lord. (87–88)

The incantatory use of the prophetic and quintessentially theatrical "I saw" (and even more compelling, "I saw if a man hath eyes") in this passage is typical of Shepard's style and occurs throughout his diaries. But this "I saw" expresses more than mere stylistic mannerism. The process of self-observation requires, or rather ratifies, the deep split within the self that allows for an observing self to monitor a self observed, and finally to observe the observing itself. The diarist, in other words, in watching his own watchfulness, activates and also represses that quality of consciousness qua consciousness which I have called the theatrical. Moreover, the process of observation that occurs in these diaries is not merely the idle action of mind that we so casually call "theatrical." Rather, this is a discipline that requires the individual to marshal a whole panoply of observational techniques. Sight lines must be opened. Emotional recall must be sharpened. Memory of part and dialogue must be recollected. In short, the Puritan technique of self-observation demands the realization of the field of illusion as illusion itself, the mise-en-scène.

The entry quoted above, for example, moves well beyond the discovery of the "primal wound" that is consciousness/theater. The observation enters quickly and quite unwittingly into the serpentine ontology that theater itself inhabits: for the very mind/self that observes is itself defined by its own "deceit and delusion." Consciousness, and that high consciousness which is theater, observes deceit and delusion as its own substance. But how can that observation be believed, made as it is by the deluded mind?

More than the mere riddling quality of such a statement, however, is the deep anxiety over appearances that runs throughout much Puritan theology and metaphysics, an anxiety well noted by those writing about Puritan culture. For the acute observations of Shepard the diarist are undercut by the realization that salvation can only be had by those who cannot observe, those who "want eyes and life"; salvation can only be had, in other words, by those capable of seeing the necessity of blindness, because those who want eyes and life are thrust into faith by their own distrust of themselves and their ability, thus inability, to see. And there is no reliance on "the wisdom of the body" either—both will and affection are as much to be distrusted as the mind.

This convolution of mind and desire, of consciousness and blindness, erupts in another passage by Shepard: "I saw that I was worthy to be left to myself and in my misery and sin, (1) not only because I had sinned, but (2) because of my very desires to come out of it" (97). Abandonment by God is deserved, Shepard seems to be saying, not only because I have sinned, but because I have desired to stop sinning, and thus come out of abandonment. This is the psychic conundrum of solipsism or tautology, similar in some respects to the convolutions one reads about in the practice of Zen meditation. As long as meditation is directed at "liberation," it is not true meditation; as long as the seeker seeks something through sitting, s/he is still lost. And yet obviously the reason one sits is because one wishes not to be lost, but wishing not to be lost renders it impossible to be any other way, and so on.

There is a similar conundrum in the Puritan attitude toward history. In Calvinist Christianity, and most pointedly in Puritanism, who we were in the past, and who we are now, is, in the doctrine of predestination, moot. Even though our fate has been cast in some divine past, that past is concealed from us. What matters is the future—either eternal life or eternal torment. But because that future depends on the hidden past, past is recast as future. Robert K. Merton, in his controversial essay "Motive Forces of the New Science," sees this recasting as leading to the Puritans' "fervent belief in progress," which induces them eventually to embrace science and empiricism as proper modes of thought. One can see in Shepard's diaries the intense mood of self-doubt intrinsic to much Puritan writing, an attitude of observational skepticism that could very well bolster an emergent empiricist and pragmatic search for "true causes." Indeed, out of the work of Merton and Sacvan Bercovitch one might see the insistence on materiality in theory and historicism as more properly Puritanical than more phenomenal or ontological approaches to performance theory.

I have suggested that the desire for salvation occupies a similar paradoxical niche as Zen Buddhism, that as long as one desires salvation, one is still too tied to self to attain it. The salient difference, however, between Calvinism and Zen and some other modes of spirituality is that in the Puritan mind the moral battle of blindness and insight plays itself out through a "self" that is seen as the origin, and not the product, of the wounded consciousness that observes it. The self appears to the Puritan writers as a lack, something that is at the moment of its appearance depraved and stunted. But in observing and trying to correct and recorrect the self, the diarists end up obsessed with the self, and so construct and reconstruct it again and again. The self, in other words, is for the Puritans real, but depraved, and so *causes* delusion and is not caused or generated by it, as is the case in Buddhism, for example. This confusion between cause and effect, or rather (in Wittgenstein's words) the confusion between causes and reasons, explains in part the confusion in Shepard's work between the necessity of, and desire for, blindness, and sin as the cause of blindness. Salvation necessitates sin, to be sure, as sin necessitates salvation. At some level of the Puritan mind, sin and salvation are the same:

> I saw that sin did blind, and God also for sin, three ways:
> (1) Sin blinds by driving God, the God of all wisdom, from the soul, and so there is nothing but darkness; a man sees no spiritual things.

(2) It spoils the understanding of all light also inherent in it that when the Lord opens the truth against it, cannot see it.

(3) The soul when it endeavors to conceive of spiritual things, it grows more blind. (113)

The passage is fairly straightforward until we recall that the author makes this observation having earlier sought blindness from God so that he might find faith. The "I saw" trope in Shepard is recapitulated again and again by the repetitive use of a thematics of blindness. The more intensely the self observes, the more it is led into blindness; the more the self seeks truth, the more it sees only delusion, until finally it sees seeing itself as merest delusion, but delusion well observed.

This observation of delusion also opens out into Shepard's ministerial work. In the confessions, we see an activation of a form of piety that comes tantalizingly close to theater itself. In the confessional displays,[21] would-be members of the congregation had to stand before those already accepted and tell of their sin and salvation. The speeches were carefully written and rehearsed again and again in order to straddle the fine dramatic line between humble admission of sinfulness, and glorification of God's power in one's life. If the speaker erred and suggested, for example, that salvation came because one had accepted God, or some such formula, one could easily seem to be taking credit for one's salvation. Thus the confessions were anxious affairs and sometimes provoked the audience to angry questioning of the confessor's sincerity and intent. In the language of Method acting, the confessor would be accused of "indicating" instead of experiencing. While the scenes unfolded, moreover, Shepard would sit to the side, quill in hand, and carefully record the script, stage directions and all, as it played itself out. But such displays and performances fall well short of anything like a morality or miracle play. Personal identity is still firmly, if problematically, attached to each subject, and the stories, even if carefully constructed, are still perceived to be true. The idea that American Puritan culture could take the step into theater, even sacred theater, remains unthinkable.

And it is small wonder that the Puritans could not make the break, finally into theater, a theater that would supply them with the paradigm by which they might find salvation from salvation, so to speak. For like Artaud, they could not carry the alienated self to its acting conclusion. They were caught in the ontological binarism of authenticity/falseness and were not able to find release in the rejection of the authentic and the tentative embrace of the mask. They were condemned to the lucid blindness of a theatricalized life devoid of theater, an inversion of Artaud's pain: the blind lucidity of a theater devoid of life.

At the level of the simply theatrical, it is not hard to imagine the Puritan penchant for observation and orchestration eventually mutating in other arenas of American society into an obsession for the spectacle. The critical *conversion* lay in the emergent traditions of American charismatic religion, what was once called Enthusiasm, a movement deeply embedded in American history and culture. The first major staging of this mode of performance occurred at Cane Ridge, Kentucky, in August 1801, where (and estimates vary) upwards of ten thousand people converged for a celebration of the spirit, a communion. That ten thousand people should gather for such a purpose in early American history is remarkable enough; that this number should appear in the near wilderness of central Kentucky in 1801 is astonishing. So is what occurred there.

Like the earlier Great Awakening, with which it is often, and somewhat erroneously, compared, Cane Ridge represents a profound rupture in the seemingly smooth contours of American Puritan culture and heritage. At Cane Ridge, American spiritual identity, American identity itself, was realigned along the axis of performance, and even more profoundly, along the axis of the theatrical. At Cane Ridge, this realignment was in essence an exteriorization, an *excretio seminis*, of an interior topography of soul that had earlier been the domain of the Puritan diary and Puritan modes of meditative spirituality. While the earlier Puritans certainly had their modes of the theatrical, as I have suggested, in the works of Thomas Shepard, none compared to the wild and wildly performed Dionysian excesses at Cane Ridge. Such a huge, orgiastic performance event had never occurred before. People chanted, sang, and prayed. They fell to the ground in coma, they laughed the holy laughter, cried, cried and laughed together, spoke exhortations, fell trembling to the ground.

> Sinners dropping down on every hand, shrieking, groaning, crying for mercy, convoluted; professors [of religion] praying, agonizing, fainting, falling down in distress, for sinners, or in raptures of joy! Some signing, some shouting, clapping their hands, hugging and even kissing, laughing; others talking to the distressed, to one another, and all this at once—no spectacle can excite a stronger

sensation. And with what is doing, the darkness of the night, the solemnity of the place, and of the occasion, and conscious guilt, all conspire to make terror thrill through every power of the soul, and rouse it to aweful attention.[22]

We have something like the ideal American participatory performance here, not unlike the Woodstock festival of 1970 (minus the guilty excess, perhaps, but not the bad trips), or the grand festivals of theatrical excess of the late sixties: happenings, love-ins, and even political demonstrations (Chicago 1968, minus the tear gas and batons, but not the tears and flagellations). Though in some ways an extension of it, this performance was quite unlike the earlier Great Awakenings, in which piety and inward rectitude were more emphasized than any wild display of psychoeroticism.[23]

In fact, the events at Cane Ridge verged on the chaotic. Revivalism careened toward demonic frenzy, and the organized event was very nearly derailed by the (somewhat) unexpected explosion of religiously theatrical fervor. And the event and its singular performances were theatrical. As Paul Conkin writes in *Cane Ridge:*

> What the exercises revealed were religiously serious people who, in a powerfully suggestive environment, chose, or were forced, to reenact the drama of Jesus' passion, and the ever-recurring drama of their own tortured quest for salvation. These mutually reinforcing dramas forced people toward experiential poles—on one hand the extreme of personal revulsion and self-doubt, on the other that of exaltation and joy.[24]

And apart from the overtly dramatic textures of the performance, was the performative itself; "the physical exercises at Cane Ridge were culturally conditioned," writes Conkin: "To some extent they were learned, even when they seemed completely involuntary."[25] But this performative, as the earlier quote suggests, was an emanation of the drama, of a theater in which a specific version of the tragic was being en-acted—the tragic torsions between self-doubt and self-revulsion that we see in Wigglesworth, and the desire for a liberating exaltation that we see leading up to Cane Ridge, and beyond. This phenomenon was, in fact, nothing less than the hysterical eruption of a peculiarly American symptomology, the externalization of Puritanism's fear of damnation, which is, in fact, the hidden fear of salvation, or pleasure without end. What, exactly, are we seeing in the theatrical excess of hystericism? An enacting of Puritanism's ideology *as* hysteria. Lacanian analyst Juan-David Nasio's description of the hysteric's mind-set leading to conversion aptly sums up the Puritan conversion to Evangelical excess:

> Gifted with a keen perceptiveness, he detects in the other the smallest fault, the least sign of weakness, the slightest indication of the other's desire. But his piercing eye is not content to penetrate the appearance of the other to find a point of strength or a chink in the armor, since the hysteric also invents and creates what he perceives. He installs in the other a new body, as libidinally intense and fantasmic as his own hysterical body. For the body of the hysteric is not his real one, but a body of pure sensation, opening outward like a living animal, a kind of ultra-voracious amoeba.[26]

What is the purpose of the hysterical conversion? The fear of "the danger of experiencing utmost pleasure," Nasio says, "a pleasure that, were he to experience it, would make him crazy, make him dissolve or disappear," a fear that clearly lurks beneath the surface of Wigglesworth's writing, at least. The hysteric conversion, then, ensures the repetition of practices, enthusiastic practices, that in turn ensure a continuous state of failure, a voracious dys-satisfaction[27] that finally invites the "ultra-voracious" hunger of unlimited consumption. The hysterical conversion at Cane Ridge represents a historical turning toward a society of the spectacle whose sole purpose is to both produce and reproduce spectacular consumption as the endless process of desiring that ensures dys-satisfaction. Thus, from the first Great Awakenings in the 1730s, through the spectacles of Cane Ridge, from the celebratory participation dramas of the Assemblies of God, to rock concerts and talk television, and finally, in the rhetorical excesses of theory itself, performance in America has been in some sense epitomized by the hysteric spectacles of enthusiasm: shaking and quaking, falling slain in the spirit, speaking in tongues, jerking and twitching, barking, moaning, shrieking and laughing. The Shakers and Quakers, of course, but also some of the Southern Baptist churches, Evangelicals, Jansenists, and other groups found and transformed an American culture that was particularly receptive to the kind of experiential, demonstrative, *performative* religion they preached and practiced. The concealing of theater in Puritanism was "repressively desublimated" or hysterically reproduced in these later spectacles of religious practice,[28] spectacles that represent the hysteric externalization of the interior gestures of Puritanism into an exterior, hysterical language of gest, the crucial movement of American religion into theater. The Puritan penchant for observation, for seeing, and seeing the seeing, moves into the spectacles of Enthusiastic performance and then to the conceptual space of the anathematized theater itself. In this series of translations all space becomes surface—the inner self, the soul, is worn like a mask, while external movement and gesture signify an inner salvation—the essence of spirituality enacted through the gestures and attitudes of the body. Soul in some sense becomes body, and spirit becomes gesture, all given over in performance for the congregation *to see.*

And indeed, if seeing, even seeing blindness, is the means to finding truth, what better truths than spectacles—tent revivals, Pentecostal possessions, circuses, Wild West shows, Barnum's freak shows, and Mardi Gras—whose entire truth lies purely in the seemingly seen. And what better protection from recognizing the emptiness of spectacle than a belief in an authentic behind it, an authentic constructed *through* the illusions of spectacle. What final way to solidify such a belief than through an enduring belief in the material, in the substance of the seen, the "ocular proof," as the means to truth. In response to the materialist captivation of current theory, Peggy Phelan, writing of the substance of the unseen and unseeable in cultural performance, issues a plea that might have flowed from the pen of Shepard himself, a prayer both moving and unnerving in its challenge to, and recapitulation of Puritan thought:

> At the limit of the physical body, at the limit of the blind eye, at the limit of the signifier, one sees both the knowledge of failure and the performance of belief propped up on all sides by serious and comic doubt. Certain of failure, I inscribe, again, my hope for blind (and forgiving) eyes.[29]

The recent dominance of the performative over theater, the tendency to relegate theater to but one form of performance and in doing so to erase the insubstantial substance of theater, is also to resuscitate the Puritan solipsism. In trying to find forms of performance that seemingly elude theater, we delude and finally lose sight of ourselves.

2
The Resistance to Theater in the Conquest of America

In the transition from the interiorized theaters of American Puritanism, through the exteriorized, performative "situations" like Cane Ridge, we see the birth of a peculiarly American ontology of appearances. The "hystorical"[1] quest is to locate beneath mere appearances the substance of an American self, or, rather, apropos hysteria, the birth of a symptom—Enthusiastic display—that masked a profound emptiness at the heart of American identity. Many recent critics have located the mechanism of this anxiety, and its concomitant symptomatologies, within the seemingly class-less structures of American culture and economics—labile structures generating infinite shades of difference in dress, deportment, and behavior in which the other could be anybody or nobody. The signifying elements of class and social rank that, in European societies, allowed one to *see* the other, even if only seemingly, had disappeared. In its place a society appeared whose excess of difference rendered difference meaningless.

The central thesis of Karen Halttunen's *Confidence Men and Painted Women*,[2] for example, is that the plasticity of American culture and cultural power in the nineteenth century was the locus of a deep-seated anxiety about identity, security (financial and psychic), and value. Halttunen finds deception, the "confidence game," to be the central moral concern in this country in the nineteenth century. Her very influential book speaks of the myriad ways that deception and subterfuge dominated the concerns of American moralists and thinkers, each of whom, it seems, wrote manuals warning young men away from the wiles and cons of big city life. Her concern, she says, is not so much with Victorians as "hypocrites," but rather with the fear of deception that these manuals represented. She thus avoids the strategy of earlier commentators who portray the Victorians as "pharisees," a class of people who abandoned sincerity for propriety, faith for churchgoing, and spoke of one set of sexual and political morals while practicing another.[3]

Halttunen's approach and conclusions, then, are concerned with the causes of an *anxiety* about appearances that is quite different from, but linked to, the Victorian *concern* with appearances. While the anxiety suggests uncertainty about the substance of appearances, the concern suggests an investment *in* appearances, an assumption of their worth. While by and large ignoring the issue of concern (cathexis), Halttunen focuses on the anxiety and locates its cause in the contemporary malleability of American culture, which was undergoing vast reorganizations of class and power. The standards and signs of stability of an earlier epoch were fast becoming blurred in a changing political and cultural climate. The democratic ideals of eighteenth-century America, emblematized in "the struggle between liberty and power, the danger of corruption and decay," represented "the ultimate threat of tyranny and enslavement" and were all too visible in the nineteenth-century culture of the confidence man and his gaming world.[4] The scams and ploys of the con men were later inverted in Victorian appearances or propriety. The con man thus by logical necessity precedes and formulates the man of substance. The very word *con man* suggests this transposition: a not-man, or man-as-negation-of-man. Halttunen goes on to suggest the depths to which the anxiety over "false" appearances sounded. The party system of politics, which relied on a certain charisma on the part of the candidate, was linked in many people's minds with the snake-oil pitch of the charlatan:

> The dangerous direction of American politics seemed equally clear: hypnotic, charismatic demagogues were rising up to enslave a generation of American youth for selfish, unprincipled gain. Through the art of the confidence game, they were usurping the prerogative of local authorities to shape the character of the rising generation, and in doing so were threatening to destroy the American republic.[5]

Halttunen suggests, but does not say, that the appearance of American-style stump politics *required* the earlier appearance of the con man on the landscape. Just as the empiric, or scam artist, precedes the scientist, so the con man sets the stage for politics and ideology.

Halttunen also notes the character of American capital and cites writers who compare playing the stock market to games of confidence. The interesting point here is that the whole confidence enterprise—both licit and not—is predicated on *speculation:* "[A] Speculator on the exchange, and a Gambler at his table, follow one vocation, only with different instruments."[6] The speculation is always a specularity; it always requires, in other words, a consciousness that is divided against itself, a consciousness that in its very structure is *duplicitous* (literally doubled) and given to subterfuge—an *Ichspaltung,*[7] to use Freud's term, a theatricalized consciousness, to use my own. Halttunen thus places the "problem" of the con man in Victorian America, but, as I have already suggested, it clearly begins much earlier and is, in fact, part of American Puritanism itself. What she sees as causal is merely the exacerbation of a more primal trauma.[8]

Although Halttunen and other critics differ somewhat in their respective takes on the con in American history and culture, they tend to agree that its appearance was due to the economic and political exigencies of the period. But I am suggesting something more, something that goes well beyond the merely political, or is, perhaps, more properly the shadow or inversion of it: the Puritanical need to produce self and identity within the theaters of culture, and the concomitant desire to have that self/identity exceed the illusory reality of the very theater that created it, the desire for a "surplus value" of self—a desire to fill the Lacanian lack.[9] Thus the Puritans staged an interiorized surveillance and later enacted that script in the exteriorized performances of salvation, making visible and visual what had been seemingly hidden, creating an excess (in sanctimonious behavior, possession by the Spirit, etc.) or "surplus value" through theater.

So, too, the emergence of the "con man culture" and its anxieties: the self in the con was produced through a clear theatricality, following as it often did a tightly scripted performance. The source of pleasure here, however, lay outside the possibilities of financial gain: the pleasure lay in an excess of the real that the con produced, for within the theatricality of the con it was the threat of violence that gave pleasure and substance to the scam. The scam/con was a gamble, in other words, and the compensation, as it is for compulsive gamblers, was not merely or even primarily monetary, but the psychic and libidinal thrill of risking it all.

The con, then, had an existential payoff for the con man: the threat of violence, and the deliverance from it. An excellent example of the psychic mechanism of the con is the autobiography of the "notorious Stephen Burroughs" published in 1798, in which he depicts himself as a con man and counterfeiter, an alchemist, in fact,[10] who goes from village to village in New England and "becomes" whatever the townspeople need, a character who transmutes not only gold, but himself as well,[11] and who on occasion barely escapes with his life.[12] Burroughs represents a key transitional figure in an increasingly theatrical American culture: a man who embodies a fully cognizant realization of his duplicitous nature, and who still believes himself to be, at some real level, a man of substance. He is, as Robert Frost recognized, the perfect realization of the Franklinesque American.

Burroughs's confidence games, then, are far more complex than they at first seem, more than mere performance, and combine concealment with an almost obsessive desire to reveal the scam. During one con, he learns that the good citizens of Pelham, Massachusetts, are in desperate need of a minister, and so he sets out to present himself as such. He preaches a sermon he has stolen from his father and is nearly discovered, but regains his standing after delivering a homily he has been directed to write on the phrase "old shoes and clouted [patched] on their feet" (Josh. 9:5). His exhortations are quite surprising, however, dealing as they do with the con itself, with persons who "had recourse to patching and clouting themselves over with false and feigned pretenses." What's more, in the course of his preaching and con games he is himself seemingly taken in by his own exhortations and presents himself, finally, as a decent, even honest God-fearing man. In his writings the line between con man and genuine citizen becomes hopelessly blurred, even erased. Stephen Burroughs, like Franklin himself, seems to find his substance to be precisely mere appearance, and this does not trouble him in the least.

The inauguration of the culture of the con man thus precedes Haltunnen's scope by at least some fifty years and is born within a theater of the authentic that ironically and tragically gave birth to illusion and deception. This quest for the authentic, however, masks a broader anxiety and contradiction. The search for authenticity was, in this nascent democracy, a search for identity—both individual and national—but an identity whose genuine substance could somehow be externalized and enacted. The writing of the Constitution, for example, set into motion a double movement: on the one hand, the basis of democratic *idealism* was the desire to create a nation founded upon individual human rights and liberties; on the other hand was a desire to escape from the burden and terror of this responsibility by constructing a nationalistic group identity—the American—who was at heart a rugged individual, clear-eyed, square-shouldered, straight-shooting, et cetera, ad nauseum. In Lacanian terms, we might see this as a split between a national ego ideal and the fantasy of collective American identity. This split accounts for the peculiar "cut" in American consciousness that both embraces and denies the mask—the embracing and denying of the very drive that defines us *in/as* contradiction. The individual hides from the profound terror of responsibility that democratic action demands by masking and cloaking her vulnerable, individual self within a political collective that protects her against pain, grief, and death. This vulnerability then reemerges in the poststructural repressive desublimation as a preoccupation with (false) contingencies, and the hallucination of the decentered self.

Not exactly the stuff of comedy, perhaps, but anxieties that return out of tragedy as farce in the American theater. They underscore in the form *of* farce the profound historical anxiety of the Return they represent: the return of the repressed terror upon which the country was forged—the call for individual human rights that was and is derailed at every turn by the subsumption of individual thought into the collective, utopian, and pragmatic mind.

The plays in question emerge over a period of some sixty formative years of American history, from 1789 to 1850. The texts are a subset of a much larger collection of American comedies-of-manner whose plotlines and characterizations are quite similar, presenting the issue of violence and critique[13] within the cruel theaters of wit.[14] The persistence of theatrical wit as critique in American culture speaks to the continuing anxiety about mere appearance over and against the authentic. This is an anxiety perhaps best understood through the language of the plays themselves, which moves vertiginously between the poles of the authentic and the false. This linguistic movement—oscillating as it does within the realms of Being—always carries with it the threat of violence, as "authentic" speech tries to silence false speech, and genuine identity (presence) tries to unmask duplicity (absence). Violence attends these plays within the texts themselves, but also, in a more hidden and sinister way, in the relation between the plays and the culture within which they appear, culminating at crucial moments in the complete crossover between the representations of violence in the plays, and actual harrowing and historical moments of real violence onstage, turning the stage at those instants into the Real.[15]

In Contrast

Royall Tyler's play *The Contrast* was first published in 1787 and represents a rather straightforward continuation of the earlier English tradition of the comedy of manners. This play is perhaps also the first to name the divided mind[16] that still articulates the American political and social landscape—the *contrast* between the values of shallow, self-serving, and unpatriotic characters, and the sentimental, sincere, and patriotic character of "real" Americans. What makes this contrast particularly American, however, is the peculiar critique of theatricality inherent in Tyler's play—a critique that proclaims (ironically or not, the point is the same) theatricality to be inimical to American society, indeed the handiwork of Satan, while suggesting at the same time that it is theatricality itself that constitutes American culture.

The Contrast exhibits this dual consciousness of the authentic against the theatrical and inauthentic in the work's doubled form. Although the play is a comedy, it contains all of the earmarks of an emergent melodrama—virtue battles duplicity, chastity and faithfulness are upheld, and villainy is exposed. Indeed, as David Grimsted points out,[17] the structural differences between comedy and "serious" melodrama are often difficult to ascertain throughout this period. The main differences, according to Grimsted, lie in the loftier qualities of hero and heroine in the more serious plays, and in the more "interior", and "personal" nature of their moral struggles.

Indeed, the problem of teasing apart the differences between these two forms—comedy and melodrama—exposes at once a peculiarity at the heart of American drama and culture at this point in history—*the problem of contrast or difference itself,* or more precisely, the difficulty in *telling* the difference. The indeterminate middle ground between melodrama proper and comedy recapitulates the thematic of illegibility that seemingly recurs again and again in every play: the count that is not a count but a scoundrel, the "woman of fashion" who is generally ill-bred and crude, the rich businessman who is in reality facing financial ruin. Characters such as these populate many of the plays in this era and represent a more widespread anxiety in American life, an anxiety, as I mentioned above, over the *social* illegibility of class structure and identity in an emergent American culture. And while such plot and character subterfuges were common in other European traditions (most notably, of course, British theater), there is nothing like the enduring desire for the authentic that so characterizes the American oeuvre. The comedies of Sheridan and Goldsmith, for example, which are roughly contemporaneous with *The Contrast*, show a decidedly more cynical and jaded view of "the authentic," which is acknowledged in those plays only as merest theater. The reason for America's need for belief in authenticity is thus linked to its substance as (mere) theater. The need for authenticity, in other words, is generated by repressed theatricality itself, or again, the need for the authentic would logically arise precisely where there is a *lack* of authenticity.

Indeed, as American theater progresses through the early part of the century, the belief in the authentic seems to grow stronger, as a growing nationalism would demand. This is not to dismiss the widespread appearance of sentiment in both American and European theater, but it is to suggest, rather, that sentiment in American theater was, and is, more strongly aligned with social ideology. The masculine and sentimental cult of the American hero, for example, the natural extension of the traditions of the American tall tale, was itself the repository of nationalist critique.

Consequently, while one might initially object that the comedies of nineteenth-century America can hardly be expected to bear the weight of serious critique, it is nonetheless true that most of these plays are themselves explicitly engaged in critique. *The Contrast*'s social commentary begins in the opening lines of the play, with a conversation between two shallow and insincere young women, Charlotte and Letitia, who are discussing the comparative merits of the pocket hoop skirt and the "luxurious, jaunty, flowing, bell-hoop." The former, Charlotte tells us, is adequate for visits to grandmama's home or a Quakers' meeting, but the latter is to be preferred for traversing the social whirl of "well-dressed beaux." She describes a scene that exemplifies the virtues of such costume:

> I was dangling o'er the battery with Billy Dimple; a knot of young fellows were upon the platform; as I passed them I faultered with one of the most bewitching false steps you ever saw, and then recovered myself with such a pretty confusion, flirting my hoop to discover a jet black shoe and brilliant buckle. Gad! To hear the confused raptures of —

> "Demme, Jack, what a delicate foot!" "Ha! General, what a well-
> turn'd—"
>
> LETITIA: Fie! Fie! Charlotte, *(stopping her mouth)* I protest you are
> quite a libertine.[18]

This scene, apart from outlining the social frivolity that the author is
critiquing, also uses many of the tropes and conventions of the English
comedy of manners: the nearly cabalistic preoccupation with the
nuances of dress, a later reference to the long, tortured hours spent
before the dressing mirror, the intimation of sexual play and intrigue,
and most importantly here, the practiced theatrical astuteness of the
participants. The entire opening is suffused with an invocation to theatrical preparation and execution—the "knot of young fellows . . . upon
the platform," the concern with proper costume and makeup, the carefully blocked staging and well-executed false step, and even the re-creation of dialogue and voice, "Demme, Jack, what a delicate . . ." Indeed,
in the remembered dialogue of the night in question, repeated as dialogue within the dialogue of the play, the cross-permeation of theater
and theatricalized life is seemingly completed.

Such crass frippery is contrasted in the very next scene with Maria,
who is seemingly pure and true-hearted and demonstrates depth of
thought and emotion proper to a young woman of the period: she
appears genuine, authentic. She reveals this the first time we see her, as
she sits among her books, alone:

> How inconsistent! That man should be leagued to destroy that
> honor, upon which, solely rests his respect and esteem. Ten thou-
> sand temptations allure us, ten thousand passions betray us; yet
> the smallest deviation from the path of rectitude is followed by the
> contempt and insult of man, and the more remorseless pity of
> women. (54)

This is a typical melodramatic set scene, which contrasts nicely with the
opening scene in its invocation to solitude and inwardness wherein, it
is supposed, theater does not enter. But of course the moment is in
many ways more theatrical than the opening. Whereas Charlotte's and
Letitia's frivolity is obvious, Maria's deep and worried soul is only
seemingly private; her emotions need the large arc of theatrical gesture
to make them apparent to herself and to her audience. The difference or
contrast, then, is really quite empty, and the playwright seems to be

commenting on precisely this difference that is not a difference. Maria and Manley, the heroine and hero, are really quite ridiculous, whereas Charlotte and Letitia, though shallow, are at least canny. At any rate, the seeming contrast—both in and out of the theater—between the appearance of the authentic and the trivial demands a theater in which to appear, or so the play suggests.

In a similar contradiction, Maria seems concerned about potential temptations only because they will bring on the well-rehearsed and very public contempt of men and women in the theaters of reputation. The contrast so eagerly sought after in the play's opening almost immediately begins to dissolve, a dissolution that is enforced by an explicit threat of violence—the ridicule and contempt of society that one endures as a result of "the smallest deviation from the path of rectitude."[19]

Maria's "moral purity" notwithstanding, she falls rather too quickly in love with the honest and clear-eyed Colonel Manley, a superpatriot with a stiff, moralizing manner who spends his time "humbly imitat[ing] our illustrious WASHINGTON" (58). He, like Maria, decries the current obsession with fashion—"In America, the cry is, what is the fashion? and we follow it, indiscriminately, because it is so" (59)—yet blindly follows the fashion of mimicry, a kind of American Thomas à Kempis, a reincarnation of Bercovitch's "epitome."

Finally, though not a major character, we meet Jonathan, the naive but shrewd country servant, a popular character who becomes the base and prototype for a long series of low-comedy characters that continue to stream across the American stage and screen. One of his more recent appearances is Forrest Gump in the Oscar-winning film of the same name, whose title character's "mental simplicity [comes] to imply a kind of superior wisdom," a description Grimsted applies to the Jonathan character in *The Contrast*.[20]

And yet, as we shall see, Jonathan's pragmatic "superior wisdom" is wholly insufficient before the theatrical spectacle. The other, insincere characters are far more astute when faced with the ephemeral hide-and-seek of the stage. Charlotte, for example, does not merely see things in a theatrical light; she is all too keenly aware of the doubling of theater in "the side box at the play":

[T]he curtain arises, then our sensibility is all awake, and then by the mere force of apprehension, we torture some harmless expression into a double meaning, which the poor author never dreamed of, and then we have recourse to our fans, and then we blush, and then the gentlemen jog one another, peep under the fan, and make the prettiest remarks; and then we giggle and they simper, and they giggle and we simper, and then the curtain drops . . . and then we bow . . . and then the curtain rises again, and then we blush and giggle, and simper, and bow all over again. Oh! the sentimental charms of a side-box conversation. (58)

What is notable here—apart from the intrinsic suspicion of critique itself, "torturing some harmless expression into a double meaning, which the poor author never dreamed of"—is not only the indication toward the theatrical in affairs of the heart, but the ontological reflections as well. The curtain going up, then down, then up again, suggests not only the rhythms of sexual arousal, but a growing illegibility between stage and life. By the time the final curtain comes down, we can no longer tell for whom it is rising and falling: the actors onstage, or the lovers in the side-boxes. Thus while the play shows its British roots in its worldly cynicism, it also demonstrates an emerging American suspicion of fashion and pretense (as expressed by Manley, for example) that appears as but another kind of role to be played—just as ephemeral and thin as the first, but backed by a certain status quo nationalism that gives it seeming substance.

Of course, for this antitheatricality to work, keepers of sentiment like Manley and Maria need a certain blindness. As Frederick Dolan comments in his discussion of the anti-Federalist critique that fulminated during this period: "Unmasking the duplicities of others . . . entails its own duplicities and self-delusions: the strenuous attempt not to be duped, to sharpen one's vision so as to penetrate all masks and disguises, does not succeed without its own epistemological costs."[21] Seeing the parts played, the citizen must never see his own participation in the play within, or the value of Americanism becomes relativized. It is crucial to keep the theater displaced and hidden in society. We see this blindness, of course, most clearly in Jonathan, who goes to a whorehouse thinking it a church, and more telling yet, goes to a theater thinking it someone's home:

JONATHAN: Why, I vow, as I was looking out . . . they lifted up a great green cloth, and let us look right into the next neighbor's house. Have you a good many houses in New York made so in that 'ere way?

JENNY: Not many: but did you see the family?

JONATHAN: Yes, swamp it; I see'd the family.

JENNY: Well, and how did you like them?

JONATHAN: Why, I vow they were pretty much like other families;—there was a poor, good-natured, curse of a husband, and
a sad rantipole of a wife. . . . but of all the cute folk I saw, I liked
one little fellow—

JENNY: Aye! who was he?

JONATHAN: Why he had red hair, and a little round plump face
like mine.

Jonathan, then, a character in a play, sees himself a character in the play
within the play (the very recapitulation of the Puritan narcissism now
transposed into theater) but is unaware of it:

JENNY: Well, Mr. Jonathan, you were certainly at the play-house.

JONATHAN: I at the play-house? Why didn't I see the play then?

(65)

The very absurdity of the conceit underscores the blindness of the critical eye to the theatrical, for Jonathan is nothing if not critical. While
Dimple the poet knows enough to despise the theater because it fails to
convince him—he only goes to watch women—Jonathan despises the
theater because at base it is the substance of evil, indeed the dwelling
place of Satan, *because* it takes him in its illusion and threatens the substance of the real.[22]

Jonathan (and to a lesser degree Manley) despises theater, then,
because it underscores the illegibility of his own identity. The inability
to separate theater from life, the smearing of the contrast between the
two realms, causes them both distress because they don't understand,
as do the Dimples and Letitias of the play-world, that the two are at
some profound level inseparable—that true identity or reality does not
appear in *contrast* with theater and role-playing but is constituted by
them. Jonathan's and Manley's repugnance for the theater, that it is
"the devil's drawing room," is born not merely of a suspicion of players and playing houses, but is redolent of *epistemological* misperception,
a dialectical opposition between authenticity and illusion that wants its
synthesis—a truth born of illusion, an illusion born of truth. The problem is not that good needs to be contrasted with evil, the authentic with
theater, but that such a contrast can be established *only in and as theater*
because the critical contrast, or contrast itself, rises from the sociospec-

ular realm, the realm of the theatrical. And yet contrast, like difference, also implies a kind of invisibility. Contrast, like difference, cannot be perceived in itself. It exists here as a lapse between the authentic and the presumed false. Contrast is difference shifted to the registers of the specular. Moreover, contrast—like rupture, the crack, discontinuity, and all the other tropes of (dis)articulation bequeathed to us from Foucauldian and Deleuzean thought—presupposes similarity or continuity against which contrast becomes legible. Contrast, in other words, is a type of critique. But it is critique immediately bound to a theatrical ontology, an ontology that it constantly tries to elude, inasmuch as theatrical ontology and the threat of the false are precisely what critique seeks out and also attempts to avoid. Tyler's play, tinged as it is with the cynical eye of its European roots, expresses, nonetheless, a rising American ethic of the authentic in the invocation to contrast and, in contrast, the seeds of American nationalist critique. The critical epistemology fails, however, because it lacks the broader contours of philosophy, here the power of analytical thought. The contrast, then, between American and European culture is (in the American mind) a contrast between an authentic and inauthentic set of cultural values, a contrast that European theatrical tradition recognizes as nonexistent. Lacking the requisite self-scrutiny, American culture still, I think, believes in an authentic identity at its core.

In Fashion

Fashion, written by Anna Cora Mowatt Ritchie in 1845, is a further development of this type of American drama, the nationalist comedy of manners designed to showcase something of the perceived nature of "true" Americans and America. The apparent retranscription of Tyler's play into Ritchie's is more interesting for transformations in character than changes in plot. A character like Letitia in *The Contrast*, for example, is apparently transformed from a canny player of the social set into a character like Seraphina Tiffany, a dull-witted victim of social pretense in Ritchie's play. The shift from a "Jeffersonian" to a "Jacksonian" mind-set is signaled in such a transformation, and in the transformation of other characters as well: the Washington-like Colonel Manley is displaced as the hero by the Jacksonian Trueman who takes on some of the earthy qualities of Jonathan, while Jonathan's dimwitted aspects are transmuted into the racist figure of Zeke, a Negro butler played, ironically, in blackface. Later on in the century, of course, this transmutation is rerouted back into the figures of urban romantic violence in characters like Mose the Fireboy. In Ritchie's play, however, the "plain citizen" of Jacksonian America has finally taken the moral high ground from the neoclassical Jeffersonian thinkers of the Revolutionary period.[23]

These rather obvious historical shifts, are, I think, interesting in what they demonstrate about the changing face of American social and political tastes. They are also suggestive of a nineteenth-century attempt at theatrical social engineering, what Jeffrey Mason calls "theater as strategy." I, however, am more interested here in what has been lost in the transformation. In *Fashion*, this transformation suggests critique that takes the form of a latent aphasia, a speech or language void of content, a critique that exists only as force, lacking significance. This critical failure—here the failure of signification—is both the symptom and cause of social decay: psychosis[24] as critique. *Fashion*, in a more focused and uniquely American way, places us in the midst of the excesses of New York social life of the mid–nineteenth century and makes definitive comments about what constitutes true culture and political sensibility. Mrs. Tiffany, the focus of the play's attack, is a shallow, incompetent mimic of French manners. She hires Millinette, a French maid, who, ironically, will teach her the ways of the latest aristocratic French fashions from the "subject position" of the hired help. Meanwhile Mrs. Tiffany fawns and frets over the imposter Count Jolimaitre, hoping to marry off her daughter, Seraphina, into apparent nobility, while Mr. Tiffany, driven to embezzling by his free-spending wife, is blackmailed by Snobson, his clerk, who hopes to gain the hand of the daughter as well. Against this background of chicanery and pretense stand the figures of Adam Trueman, a rich, rough-cut farmer and self-made man despising of falsehoods, Gertrude, his (as we learn later) true-hearted granddaughter, and Colonel Howard, the clear-eyed man who loves her. As is usual in this genre, the various machinations are foiled by the noble Trueman, whose plain-speaking ways and hatred of lies finally ferrets out the scams and misalliances before real harm comes to chez Tiffany. A chief tactic in this endeavor is coercion and physical violence. Trueman threatens and then later beats the false count with his cane, threatens Snobson with prison, and assaults Zeke because he is a "grinning nigger."[25] The play ends, nonetheless, with the requisite happy alliances, with Trueman promising to square Tiffany's debts, as long as he and his family move to the country, where they will be insulated from the falsities and temptations of rapacious city life.

The play begins, significantly, with a speech by Zeke the butler, the butt of racist insult throughout the play. He is admiring his new livery:

> Dere's a coat to take the eyes ob all Broadway! Ah! Missy, it am de fix-in's dat make de natural *born* gemman. A libery for ever! Dere's a pair ob insuppressibles to 'stonish de colored population.[26]

Zeke speaks a white version of Black English, a form of speech that is incomprehensible to Millinette, a French-born servant. "Oh, *oui* Monsieur Zeke," she responds in her own thick accent, and then follows by admitting, in a polite aside, that she cannot "*comprend* one word he say!" There follow several more exchanges between Zeke and Millinette. Zeke's speech is composed of malapropisms and broken speech patterns, and, though he is "natural born," his words are at times barely intelligible, while Millinette's, though more accessible, are nonetheless also filled with mispronounced words, alien phrases, and fractured English grammar. When Mrs. Tiffany, an upper-middle-class American, enters the scene, we expect a character who will speak clearly, but she also quickly lapses into linguistic casualties as she tries to lace her English with very badly pronounced French:

> MRS. TIFFANY: . . . Millinette, how do you say *armchair* in French?
> MILLINETTE: *Fauteuil*, Madame.
> MRS. TIFFANY: *Fo-tool!* That has a foreign—an out-of-the-wayish sound that is perfectly charming—and so genteel. There is something about our American words decidedly vulgar. *Fow-tool!* how refined. (284)

Indeed, Mrs. Tiffany not only massacres the French tongue, but her mispronunciations undergo further shifts. "Fo-tool" becomes "fow-tool" becomes "fow tool." The split that appears in this single word signifies the problematic status of the speech-act itself throughout the play. Meanings, beginning with pronunciation, are broken, unstable, multiple. And here, in a challenge to the Deleuzean validation of rhizomatic multiplicities, the fracturing of language represents a kind of powerlessness and psychic injury. Indeed, Mrs. Tiffany's speech is so tortured that Count Jolimaitre, a con man poseur who is fluent in both English and French, cannot understand her at all. "She's not talking

English, nor French, but I suppose its American" (288). Indeed, the failure of American speech seems to be a structural principle in the play: even the more marginal characters suffer from various forms of aphasia. The poet Mr. Twinkle is interrupted some five times as he begins his recitative. After the sixth attempt, he is once again interrupted by Zeke's introducing the ineffable Mr. Fogg, who, with Mrs. Tiffany, finally silences the young man for good. Mr. Fogg, an enigmatic member of Mrs. Tiffany's circle, appears to be nearly autistic, for through the course of the play "he never takes the trouble to talk, and he never notices anything or anybody" (286). His very name suggests the fog of miscommunication and miasmic thought that envelops the play.

The aphasia that characterizes the play does not signify mere miscommunication. Everyone seems to speak a strange language because every character is a foreigner. Not only the foreign maidservant and her expatriate con man boyfriend, but the Americans themselves, speak in alien tongues. Zeke, of course, will always be a foreigner in his own land, while Trueman, the true-blooded American and racist, is described as a foreigner amid the mannered culture of New York City, which is itself foreign to "true Americanism." "Where did you say you belonged my friend?" asks Jolimaitre. "Dug out of the ruins of Pompey, eh?" (289). A few lines later, he describes Trueman as a "barbarian," and Trueman is correspondingly characterized in Mrs. Tiffany's bad French as "owtray," *autre*, other. Mrs. Tiffany, in the meantime, can't seem to fit into any of the cultural niches available to her. Indeed, the sheer emptiness of her character is signified through her continual (and incorrect) invocation of the *abîme*, the word she uses again and again to describe her distress at the situations in which she finds herself. It is Mrs. Tiffany, in fact, who probably best describes the ontologic condition of the play itself: a *mise en abîme*, the infinitely framed abyss at the mirrored heart of meaning, memory existing as absence, like Twinkle's unremembered verses, the radical alterity of identity in the play characterized in the scene of/as absence. Indeed, Mr. Tiffany, in some sense the most mysterious of the characters in the play, is described by Trueman in these terms:

> [Greed] has made your counting-house a penitentiary, and your home a fashionable *museum* where there is no niche for you! You have spent so much time *ciphering* in the one that you find yourself at last a very *cipher* in the other. (290)

Tiffany, like the others in the play, is driven by a desire (greed) that floats like a cipher in a linguistic play of Otherness. While the action of the play emerges within the field of a seemingly foreign speech, it is not merely a speech that comes from beyond the ocean, or across borders, but is alien to itself. It lacks the proper difference of the linguistic order, it lacks *contrast.* Here the spoken word is not true or false but functions as aphasic silence, a silence that challenges: aphasia as the unconscious, the speech of the Other that emerges as "something that is radically unmappable, namely, *He is saying this to me, but what does he want?*"[27]

Throughout *Fashion* the play of false appearances operates within a violent field of signification that is itself seemingly damaged and deluded. As in *The Contrast,* characters cannot construct themselves in or through appearances, but here language does not work either. Although, as Lacan points out, memory and so history require the symbolic order—the order of language—this order fails within the play. When Mrs. Tiffany says we must "forget what we *have* been, it is enough to remember that we *are* of the upper ten thousand," she is not merely attempting to *fashion* herself, but describing a kind of forced amnesia whose *symptom* is the failure of the signifying order. Moreover, the once fashionable theories of failed signification are themselves critiqued by Mr. Tiffany, who might be addressing the shifting fortunes of Derridean and Lacanian thought itself:

> TIFFANY: But now you have grown so fashionable, forsooth, that you have forgotten how to speak your mother tongue!
> MRS. TIFFANY: Mr. Tiffany, Mr. Tiffany! Nothing is so positively vulgarian—more *unaristocratic* than any allusion to the past!
> (295)

He suggests that her inability to control the signifying systems, or, more precisely, her linguistic amnesia, is symptomatic of a radical mis-remembrance of history. "Why I thought, my dear," says her husband, "that *aristocrats* lived principally in the past, and traded in the market of fashion with the bones of their ancestors for capital?" (295).

Now Marx and Lacan, and more recently Slavoj Žižek, have pointed out that such symptomatologies are far from trivial, for the symptom is precisely the point of heterogeneity, the moment of difference or contrast (or in Lacan, failure), that allows the constitution of identity. It is the symptom, the sign of contra-diction that splits open the seemingly seamless contours of political ideology. The problem here and in the political sphere is deciding who is reading the sign/symptom when the sign/symptom is precisely what constitutes the reader reading it (the sign/symptom). How will the watcher in/of the play read false appearances and failed language when these are what constitute the eye and tongue of the watcher? How can Trueman critique false manners when false manners are what fashion him? How, in other words, can Trueman escape his own endocolonization by a theatricalized ideology? Here the separation—the contrast between critic and object of critique, between performance critic, if you will, and the theater of authenticity—disappears. But while Mrs. Tiffany would rather forget the past, Adam Trueman is the one character in the play who is explicitly forced to remember. Late in the fifth act he recalls through a long narrative the death of his daughter Ruth, Gertrude's mother. Trueman's speech thus represents a doubled maternal death— his own late wife, Ruth's mother, is never even mentioned. She exists as pure absence, while Ruth, Trueman's daughter, dies. What Žižek refers to as the *maternal superego,* the functions of a social superego in a patriarchal society, thus disappear into the patriarchal figure of Trueman. He represents, in this sense, a melding of phallogocentrism and a false *femme écriture:* although he speaks with authority, his recollections break down in an excess of grief, in mourning and melancholia. We see here a doubled mask, feminine writing masquerading as phallogocentrism and phallic speech masquerading as *la femme écriture.*

Ruth, the child of this peculiar marriage of masks, is born within the warp and weft of these duplicities: "None ever saw her to forget her," Trueman says. He goes on to describe her fate as "an object of speculation" by virtue of Trueman's wealth. Indeed, she is more than a mere object of speculation. She is the unsignifiable, the empty placeholder of desire within the play. Ruth represents, in her female persona, death's representation and abeyance—the mother's absence, the *matrilineal* absence—that has set the play into motion. Moreover, this unsignifiable, *unspeakable* death is brought about by a young woman's seeming inability to perceive the desire of the Other. Ruth dies, Trueman tells us, because she is unable to see beneath the duplicitous exterior of the nameless man who courts, weds, impregnates, and leaves her. She is, in a melding of the linguistic crises of *Fashion* and the ocular crises of *The Contrast,* seemingly led astray by her inability to read words and appearances, for it is his "fine words and fair looks" that deceive her.

While the women in the play seem especially prone to misrecognizing duplicity, it is finally Trueman himself who refuses meaning: he misrecognizes Ruth's death as a death in the Other, a death caused by the Other man, the Con man. But it is Trueman who has caused his daughter's death: only after Trueman refuses to will his fortune over to the nameless young man—Ruth's husband, after all, Trueman's son-in-law—does he leave Ruth, causing her to pine away and die. Trueman is at least in part responsible for his daughter's death, but he is blind and will not see it. His blindness is converted into a psychotic-hysteric fixation on Gertrude, the "apple of his eye." He has, in Juan-David Nasio's formula, "lost sight of the image of the other" and instead "focuses his unconscious gaze on one sole thing: the other's libidinal charm. He loses his sight but preserves the intensity of his gaze."[28] After Ruth dies, Trueman sends the infant Gertrude to stay with relatives. She ends up in New York unaware that Trueman is her grandfather—unaware that she even has a father *or* a grandfather. The mother-grandmother's doubled absence is here reinscribed in the father-grandfather's doubled, and unknown, absence. Trueman's "straightforward" narrative thus represents something other than itself, not recollection but rather the intensity of a violent and perverse memory—a narrative that, like the aphasic, broken speech of the others, is a mask through which he tries to speak, a mask that might allow him to justify his actions, which have led (perhaps) to his wife's disappearance, his daughter's death, and Gertrude's exile. His speech, in other words, both masks and activates the unconscious.

What is notable here is the *sense* of Trueman's speech, which seems the only *true* speech in the play set apart from the aphasic, duplicitous talk of the other characters. But his story really amounts to an abandonment of the real that appears around him in the whirling, pulsing interplay of performative forces and desires. The duplicitous nature of Trueman's story resides precisely in its disavowal of the theatrical real and his withdrawal into a symbolic *seems*: more the calcified speech of the psychotic (a speech that *pretends* speech), however, than an engagement and negotiation with the real.

Gertrude thus appears as an other child, an enfant terrible. She is the sign of death, loss, and grief that allows Trueman to set into motion the creation of this long phantasia, which covers over the in-substance of American identity represented not by the fakers and con men, but by Trueman himself. As Nasio says, describing the peculiar melancholy characteristic of one type of hysteric:

They create a conflictual situation, set dramas in motion, get mixed up in disputes, and once the curtain has fallen they become aware that everything was merely a game from which they have been left out. . . . the hysteric is no longer a man, no longer a woman; he is now the pain of dissatisfaction. . . . the sadness of the hysterical ego corresponds to the emptiness and the uncertainty of his sexual identity.[29]

Trueman is an ideological phantasia. He seemingly enters the play as a neutral and pragmatic observer, securing his position at the perimeter, a type of theoretician convinced of his ability to make *material* judgments about belief, behavior, and the authentic removed from the ambience of performance in which he finds himself. It is Trueman's belief in authenticity born of materiality, his belief in empirical veracity set up against false appearances, that puts him in this position and ultimately puts us in that position as well. In fact, we ourselves are called upon to subsume the position of critic and critique in the final words of the epilogue:

GERTRUDE: *(to the audience)* But ere we close the scene a word with
    you—

We charge you answer—Is this picture true?
Some little mercy to our efforts show
Then let the world your honest verdict know
Here let it see its ruling passion,
And learn to prize at its just value—*Fashion.*

We are asked to subsume a position, it would seem, conjunctive with Trueman's own problematic vision, which seems the perfect embodiment of American pragmatic critique that Tocqueville so aptly observed.

Yet in the process of disarticulating the empty center of *Fashion* and its play of appearances, Trueman "forgets" his own false play. He comes, after all, to spy on his granddaughter. He deceives her again and again, hiding his identity, covering up his actions in order to get at the "truth," all the while chastising her and everyone else in the play against lying and deceit.[30] His critique and appearance is, to say the least, doubly suspect and is redolent of the theatrical concealings and revealings of self-loathing that we saw in the earlier Puritan writings.

Trueman is, further, aiming his critique at those within the play who themselves are busily critiquing culture. Mrs. Tiffany certainly has very strong notions of what constitutes real cultural value, going so far as to embrace a kind of proto-multiculturalism, and Trueman's criticism of her is really a critique of critique—as my criticism becomes a critique of *that* critique, and so forth. Critique, as a matter of fact, becomes an infinite nesting of "subject positions," an other *mise en abîme*, each position *seemingly* more acute than the position it holds, each trying to escape the proscenium of theatricalized thought. The stagings of critique, each nested within an other, enfold each other seamlessly, but not seemlessly. For each staging is presenting that vision *as* vision, as *speculation*, and so inhabits an exquisitely theatrical site.

Similarly, when the cultural critic speaks from the position of ideology, she speaks from the very site of assumed identity—as woman, as lesbian, as African American or Latina. Such positions necessarily cast the critic in the role of ideological mouthpiece. Once again, the ideal of antagonistic human thought (the cogito) is displaced by the shared assumption of belief (ideology). To speak polemically—contra dialectically—from a defined (named) political position is to assume the role of Mrs. Tiffany, or Trueman himself. The important point here is that Trueman's inability to see his own captivation in the web of critique and performance keeps him from recognizing that what he critiques makes him who he is—the guardian of the authentic, the preserver of presence and true consciousness. Indeed, there is a deep irony in the fact that what Americans (at least onstage) apparently rejected as the false theatricalities of other, European, cultures—manners, aristocratic behavior, fashions—became the basis for their own anxious attempts to construct, out of nothing, "nontheatrical" identities. In trying to rid itself of what it perceived to be the false and theatrical bases for identity, American culture had no option but to adopt Other, opposite, and oftentimes far more ridiculous theatricalities: the blustering braggadocio of the Davie Crockett character in James Paulding's *The Lion of the West*, for example, or Trueman's own overbearing, rustic swagger.

Trueman, then, occupies the position of the American who has always hated pretence, the theatrical, but is curiously and willfully blind to it when it appears. This citizen would elect Ronald Reagan or would believe the performance scenarios of Rush Limbaugh or Jerry Springer, or even more telling, would claim not to.[31] This is the odd combination of self-fashioning and its concomitant self-suspicion (the suspicion of inauthenticity) that Jonas Barish called the antitheatrical prejudice. It is Trueman's friend Mr. Tiffany who perhaps best describes this paradoxical situation when he interrupts his wife's proclamations concerning fashion. "All women of fashion . . ." Mrs. Tiffany begins, only to be preempted by Mr. Tiffany:

> In this land are *self-constituted,* like you Madam and *fashion* is the cloak for more sins than charity ever covered! It was for *fashion's* sake that you insisted upon my purchasing this expensive house— it was for *fashion's* sake that you ran me into debt. (295)

This is an apt and powerful response to notions of self-fashioning, or (performative) self-constitution. The paradox is that Mr. Tiffany attacks his wife precisely because she is attempting to do what Trueman has himself done and abjures others to do—he constructs himself according to a specific set of cultural values. Trueman is nothing if not the model of the self-made man. The crucial difference, of course, is that True- man's self-construction is seemingly authentic and Mrs. Tiffany's is not. But the evidence for Trueman's claim to true consciousness and his rejection of Mrs. Tiffany's false consciousness resides in a maddeningly tautological moral high ground that he constructs entirely upon his rejection of Mrs. Tiffany's world of fashion: he is authentic because he perceives that she is false. She is false, as a consequence, because he per- ceives himself to be authentic, and so on. In another *mise en abîme* of critical positions, Frederick Dolan quotes Slavoj Žižek quoting Lacan:

> "The final deception," according to Lacanian theory, "is that social appearance is deceitful, for in the social-symbolic reality things ultimately *are* precisely what they *pretend* to be," Žižek concludes. The symbolic order in which one's public identity is constructed is *not* unreal; to assume that it is, or that there is a "real" identity hid- den behind it, are equally pernicious errors.[32]

The problem, finally, is not that Mrs. Tiffany is merely acting, it is that she doesn't act well enough. Trueman, on the other hand, also acts—he shows up in the heart of New York City in farmer's costume complete with a literal prop, his cane. He, however, acts quite convincingly. It is, oddly, the seamlessness of his role-playing that gives the lie to his implied claims of authenticity. This seamlessness is born of Trueman's belief in the act; it is generated by his capitulation to the very theatricality of his appearance in the play and his forced, even violent, forgetting of that theatrical role. It is Trueman's ability to "saturate the void that keeps open the space for symbolic fiction,"[33] his closing of the critical distance that allows him, like Stanley Kowalski, to seemingly "become one" with his role. This saturation, this closing of the distance between the symbolic and the real, is what allows Trueman, again like Stanley Kowalski, to avoid pleasure, the pleasure of mere acting for acting's sake, the unrepentant immersion in the theatrical necessities of critical thought.

As a consequence of this avoidance, Trueman's critique of false appearances activates an entirely different level of the inauthentic, a profound and radical bad faith, the inability at some level to account for the critique of presence and disappearance—pleasure and grief—within the realist/materialist project. Trueman's unquestioned belief in the authentic, and his belief in the ability to *critique and thus perform* the authentic, mark a profound contradiction both in him and in American culture at large. Trueman, the "epitome" or paradigmatic American, becomes the cipher that will not be read even as he fails to understand his own tenuous placement in the reflex between vision and what is not seen, between language and what cannot, or will not, be spoken.

In Fact

This last, finally, is mere footnote. Footnote, and perhaps hyperbole, but an inkling nonetheless of a disturbing relationship between violence and blindness to the philosophical and ontological conundrums of theater, culture, and critique. *Our American Cousin,* written by an Englishman, Tom Taylor, was first produced in 1858 in America and follows the main character, Asa Trenchard, yet another Trueman-type farmer-Yankee, to England, where he serves, once again, as the critical eye through which American audiences could view scornfully the frippery of English manners. He, and to a lesser degree his cousin Florence Trenchard, exposes the treacheries, foibles, and falsities of aristocratic pretense and restores the foolish character's fortunes to them.[34] The play re-creates many of the conventions of the genre: the rustic dress and ways of the farmer-Yankee, his plain-speaking but boastful speech, "I'm Asa Trenchard, about the tallest gunner, the slickest dancer, and generally the loudest critter in the state," and his almost immediate grasp that "a queer lot of fixins" are afoot.[35]

This "threadbare" (in the words of one commentator) comedy of American manners, however, is well known for more than its continuation of the genre's Anglo-American tradition. For the most famous production of this play was also the scene of America's first presidential assassination, its first scene of domestic terrorism—a performance that would leap the threshold from theater to life, rendering national tragedy as performance in a way that would guide the darker side of American political history for the next century and a half.

The entire disposition of the scene that night in Ford's Theater depicts a grotesque chiasm of theater as theater, theater as American life, and life as theater. The Civil War was ending—the same war that saw its opening battle at Bull Run attended by men and women with picnic baskets, who sat high upon the hills to watch the shooting commence. The same war that saw that first battle re-created on a stage in New York City some three weeks after its occurrence, complete with real horses and cannon-fire. But now in Washington it was Good Friday, the Christian remembrance of a divine concealing preparatory to revelation. The Lincolns had decided on a lighthearted comedy to forget the agony of national crises: a peculiarly apt repressive tactic soon to be undone. The presidential box, specially prepared, hung not over the pit, as is usual, but over the stage itself. This afforded those seated in the box, hidden from the view of the audience, a view of the stage and backstage areas and also kept the president and his entourage both continuously present and hidden to the audience. The president occupied this odd panopticon, itself a kind of black-box theater or camera, hung with presidential bunting and flags—a *kammerspiel* suspended within the theater, the center of attention, revealing and concealing all and nothing, the space within which the real—and unsignifiable—drama would occur. Lincoln arrived to the strains of "Hail to the Chief," stepped from the shadows into the frame of the booth, and gave brief audience. The play itself was given new lines in honor of Lincoln's presence.

Meanwhile, a famous actor in a family of great actors, John Wilkes Booth, haunted the corridors and passageways beneath and behind the theater in preparation for the act, like Kafka's creature of the Burrow, moving and feinting in a seemingly endless ballet of anxious self-subterfuge and self-revelation, both beneath and behind the stage, and, we might surmise, within his own mind. He finally positioned himself outside the box and then entered the concealed stage within, gun drawn. He chose the opportune moment in the play, apparently the line in the script wherein Asa Trenchard, the reapparition of Adam Trueman

(A.T.), refers to another character as a "sockdologizing old man-trap."[36] A sockdologer is, apparently, a deliverer of heavy blows, one who gives doxology (ideology) as beating, but also, perhaps, one who wears the sock or buskin (buckskin?), that is, one who acts upon the stage. At the utterance, as an utterance, Booth pulls the trigger, shattering the utterance into aphasic noise. Utterance and gunshot become one. He then leaps to the stage, turns to the audience, and delivers—in the Latin of Michael Wigglesworth—his last and most famous line, "Sic semper tyrannis," articulating the persistent and continuous theatrics of American domestic terrorism, from Booth to McVeigh: "Thus always to tyrants."

Death to liars, pretenders, death to the inauthentic American, the politician, the traitor, the speaker of alien tongues. Booth becomes Trueman, or, rather, Trueman becomes Booth, an actor who leaves behind the trappings of pretense for authentic action. A true man. A patriot. A terrorist. He then disappears through the wings,[37] setting into motion the great national production of grief and mourning that followed America's first presidential assassination, the theater of abjection with which Americans are now so familiar—the caisson bearing the casket, the riderless horse, boots backward in the stirrups, the little boy saluting, the arms pointing up from the balcony, the bloody hands holding the rosary, the firing of the volley, "Taps." The stage translating through our history comedy to comedy, comedy to tragedy, tragedy to life, life back to the theaters of memory and grief.

ct II: Confession

In a strange way, Americans are
looking for authenticity—among
actors. This is like choosing *ER*'s
George Clooney for your
pediatrician.

—Ellen Goodman, *Boston Globe*

3
Ripping Good Time: History, Blindsight, and Amnesic Thought

History as Disappearance

The correspondence and tension in the subject between present perception (what some philosophers term *qualia*) and memory as past or history suggests a kind of ontogenetic recapitulation of consciousness at the phylogenic level of American culture. The American subject and her culture tend to focus on the present and future instead of the past, and concomitantly to forget or repress what is other—and so in some sense most us—in our own individual and cultural history. The paradigmatic play about memory and its vicissitudes in the nineteenth century's historical archive might well be Joseph Jefferson's *Rip Van Winkle*, while the prototypical play about the problematics of perception and ocularity may very well be Dion Boucicault's *The Octoroon*. But whereas Boucicault's play deals with a serious topic through a serious form (tragedy), Jefferson's play seems little more than a bit of humorous American fluff. I would like to suggest, however, as I did in my discussion of the American comedies of manner, that the immense popularity of this play suggests that something in its theme and structure was deeply appealing to American sensibilities. Jefferson's play, which is thematically about the redistribution of memory, struck a resonant chord with an emerging world power that experienced its own truncated history in similar fashion: American history as amnesia, American cultural identity as absence, memory as forgetting, history as disappearance, what Homi Bhabha terms the "Janus-faced discourse of the nation."[1] Similarly, in *The Octoroon*, a play written during a period of American history that was constructing the idea of race through a binarism of whiteness opposed, and superior, to blackness, refines the difference into virtual disappearance, recasting perception as identical with mis-perception. Finally, appearing in the insufficiency of the perceptual lacuna, we have the seeming realism of James Herne's *Margaret Fleming*, the virtual ensign of an emergent American dramatic realism that, like the real it invokes, existed only as illusion.

The story of Rip Van Winkle first appears in the American canon through the work of Washington Irving. Irving wrote *Rip Van Winkle* in 1819 as part of *The Sketch Book of Geoffrey Crayon, Gent.*, a collection of character sketches, tales, and essays that, for the most part, dealt with English life and manners (Irving was living in England at the time). Two of the sketches, however—*The Legend of Sleepy Hollow* and *Rip Van Winkle*—portray life in the Hudson River Valley of colonial America. What is notable about these stories—and especially *Rip*—is the peculiar staging with which Irving presents the stories; although *Rip* is based on an older German folk-tale, Irving presents the story in a side-note as the work of one Diedrich Knickerbocker, a "fictitious historian" who, Irving tells us, has gotten the tale from the mouths of the actual inhabitants of the Hudson Valley region. Not only are claims made to actual eyewitness accounts, but those accounts themselves, Irving claims, are remarkable for their "scrupulous accuracy." The conclusion of the story, moreover, assures the reader of the veracity of the account because the author has ocular proof—he has himself "seen a certificate on the subject, taken before a country justice, and signed with a cross in the justice's own handwriting. The story, therefore is beyond the possibility of doubt."[2] The obvious ironies aside, this strategic and conventional appeal to veracity is quite interesting, applied as it is to a story about faulty memory, about forgetting—a story, in fact, about a drug-induced *amnesia*, one of the enduring plot devices in Western drama, and especially so in American culture (we need only note its ubiquitous presence in contemporary soap opera as a device and motif). Few dramas or films, however, present amnesia as a structural principle within the drama or film itself.

The particulars of the story are worth noting. Riddled with hints of various performative strategies, the narrative suggests its later success as a stage play. The story itself is the narrated retelling of a recollection, for example and, like all theatrical performance, is the remembering of a memory lost, or at least displaced, and unfolds much as the style of memoir might, with invocation of an emotionally laden place in time past, the Hudson River Valley of the mid–eighteenth century. The opening is almost cinematic in its invocation of the scenic majesty of the Catskill Mountains, "a dismembered branch of the great Appalachian family," "fairy mountains" within whose valleys is nestled the picturesque village of Rip and his family—his children (including a son, also named Rip, who is the image of his father), a "termagant wife," a loving daughter, and his faithful dog, Wolf (2–3). Together they live a simple and dysfunctional life, Dame Van Winkle having as her chief occupation the belittling of Rip's lazy, but good-natured, character. Rip, in fact, is content to do little in the way of work and spends his time with his cronies in the tavern "telling endless sleepy stories about nothing" (5), re-creating in the telling the story of *Rip Van Winkle* itself, also and literally a "sleepy little story about nothing," in this case, the nothingness of forgetting.

Rip continues in his usual bucolic mode, idling, telling stories, drinking, until his nagging wife strains him to the breaking point: he takes gun and dog and traipses off into the woods to escape his family duties and the abuse of his wife. And here is where the story "turns," so to speak. What had been a rustic and humorous reminiscence now becomes almost surreal, even hallucinatory: Rip hears a voice calling his name from deep in the darkening glen but sees no one. The schizoid auditory hallucination is soon compounded by the appearance of a strange figure dressed "in the antique Dutch manner," a Pilgrim-like creature, strangely daemonic, a silent emanation from the historical unconscious who, dreamlike, "makes signs," but owns no speech. This figure beckons him farther into the mountains, through a "cleft, between rocky lofts" and into something like the theater of dream consciousness, "an amphitheater, surrounded by perpendicular precipices," a place compelling but "strange and incomprehensible," and peopled by odd, Ensor-like apparitions:

> On entering the amphitheater, new objects of wonder presented themselves. On a level spot in the centre was a company of odd-looking personages playing at nine-pins. They were dressed in quaint, outlandish fashion. . . . Their visages, too, were peculiar: one had a large head, broad face, and small piggish eyes: The face of another seemed to consist entirely of nose, and was surmounted by a white sugar-loaf hat, set off with a little red cock's tail. . . . [T]he commander . . . wore a laced doublet, broad belt and hangar,

high crowned hat and feather, red stockings, and high heeled-
shoes with roses in them. (6–7)

When Rip enters the midst of this strange and polymorphous group—
the ghostly crew of Henry Hudson's *Halfmoon*,[3] as it turns out, and led
by the great Hudson himself, transformed in the logic of dream economy from the English Henry to the Dutch Hendrick (the real Hudson
was, in fact, in Dutch pay)—he is struck by their grave faces and "most
mysterious silence," a silence broken only by the pealing thunder of the
nine-pin balls as they roll. The phantomlike figures bid him to drink
from a keg, and Rip, though filled with terror, complies, and soon his
head swims with the strange liquor and he falls into a deep sleep.
Within the scene as dream, however, Rip's sleep is an awakening from
hallucinatory dream into consciousness as amnesia—the Lacanian-like
béance of sleep.

The next movement is, of course, the most familiar: Rip wakes after
what seems like a single night's sleep and finds the world familiar, but
forever changed. He leaves the valleys and mountains, the sulci and
gyri of dreamscape, and his return is very much like the moving of
unconscious thought back through neural tissue into consciousness: a
stream fills the glen "with babbling murmurs," and he toils his way
"through thickets of birch and sassafras, and witch hazel, and sometimes tripped up or entangled by wild grape-vines that twisted their
coils or tendrils from tree to tree, and spread a kind of network in his
path" (8–9). He finds that the amphitheater has vanished behind a wall
of stone, and, confused and hungry, he heads back to his village, where
he both appears as, and sees before him, the Other, for of course he has
slept twenty years and has grown old, his clothes out of date, his beard
long and white, while his village, though familiar, is also uncannily
changed.

Here the story explicitly engages with its own mimetic doubling;
just as the tale itself is a kind of double of an earlier, dimly remembered
narrative, so doubling itself becomes the leitmotif of the final movement of Rip's story. As he enters the village, for example, he is met by
villagers who, assessing Rip's startling appearance, begin to stroke
their chins in skeptical wonder. But "the constant recurrence of this
gesture induced Rip, involuntarily, to do the same." The whole action
that follows—Rip trying to negotiate sameness and difference in the
aspect of the village and villagers, the villagers trying to make the same
negotiation in the person of Rip—appears an attempt to rediscover

similitude beneath difference, a reminder of the excruciating confusion of mere difference detached from continuity—in some sense an enactment of the dislocating terrors of Alzheimer's disease. Rip finds his way to his home, for example, but though it remains familiar, it has also become *unheimlich*, "empty, forlorn, and apparently abandoned." Similarly the inn where he spent so much idle time is displaced by an odd and slightly absurd building whose broken windows are covered over with old hats and petticoats—not unlike the Lacanian foreclusion, a kind of mismatched "patch" covering over the holes in psychotic remembrance. And stranger still, the great tree that had stood outside is now replaced by a naked, ludicrously phallic pole, from which hangs a flag, the impenetrable archival document, covered over with strange symbols, "a singular assemblage of stars and stripes . . . strange and incomprehensible." Even the seemingly familiar face on the village sign has "singularly metamorphosed" from an image of King George, into George Washington—the shifting position of the *Nom du Père* an interesting linguistic mutation from the registers of the monarchic into the registers of the paternal/patriarchal through which scepter is transformed into sword (10).

Rip then learns that the Oedipal construct has found a kind of completion through his absence as father: his son, who appears as "the ditto of himself," has overtaken him in the paternal role of idler and dreamer, while Dame Van Winkle, Rip's termagant wife and de facto patriarch of the family Van Winkle, has died of an apparent stroke— that Other malicious disease of the amnesic—in an ambiguous "fit of passion at a New England peddler" (12). Rip, finally recognized and certified by another old inhabitant of the village, resumes his languid ways, now blessed in that laziness by old age, which is reckoned to be just such a time of idleness by the others in the village. The story then ends with the aforementioned "ocular proof," the presence of the affidavit "signed with a cross," which determines the authenticity of the story and its retelling. This signature, as we will see, takes an interesting turn in Jefferson's dramatic version of the story.

The invocation of remembrance, the emphasis on recollection, the transformations and duplicity of appearances, the emphasis on costume and the scenic shifts in time and place all suggest a deeper theatrical sensibility in Irving's story (a sensibility that, as I will suggest in the next chapter, is not uncommon in American fiction, replacing, as it does, a kind of "missing" theoretical understanding of theater and theatricality). We might recall at this point that Irving was himself an avid theatergoer and wrote extensively on the theater. This, along with the story's preoccupations with memory, history, and forgetfulness, may very well account for the story's success as a stage play—not only in Jefferson's version, but also in the numerous versions that preceded it. Indeed, both story and play seem at some primal level to be about acting and forgetting, forgetting one is acting, acting as if one has forgotten, aligning acting and forgetting with the well-known Nietzschean dictum, "All acting requires forgetting." "A man who wanted to feel everything historically would resemble someone forced to refrain from sleeping," writes Nietzsche.[4] Indeed, at the center of human experience, creating the very rhythms of life, lies the forgetfulness of sleep, and within that sleep, punctuating forgetfulness, the hyperconscious recurrence of dream, and encoded within that dream, the eternal nagging forgetfulness that so characterizes, and even articulates, the dream state: memory and forgetting as *mise en abîme*, framing memory within forgetting, forgetting as the core of remembrance, a *mise en abîme* that describes quite faithfully the structure of Joseph Jefferson's version of the play.

Although not much is known about Jefferson's contribution to Dion Boucicault's adaptation of Irving's text, the thematics of consciousness and amnesia seem peculiarly close to Jefferson's own concerns as a stage artist. Jefferson, who was so thoroughly identified with a character who sleeps his life away that some of his admirers thought he *was* Rip Van Winkle, showed a kind of hyperconsciousness when it came to the art of acting. While recognizing that the dramatic impulse is deeply grounded in human consciousness and society, and in some sense is the natural state of consciousness,[5] Jefferson was also very careful to admonish aspiring actors to memorize their parts first and not trust mere "instinct," spontaneity, or inspiration. At the same time, Jefferson recognized the radical evanescence of theater, which determines that each performance "not only dies with [the actor], but, through his different moods, may vary from night to night."[6] Every true performance, as Artaud would suggest some forty years later, is unique, is not representation but presentation. In struggling to master the script, the actor must be careful not to overmemorize or over-rehearse, lest the lines become stale and empty. The art of memory, in Jefferson's view, was to trust in memory, but at the same time to realize that memory is in some sense an illusion: to truly memorize a part is to maintain the sense that the lines have never before been spoken. The "truest" memory, then, is remembrance of that which has seemingly never before happened. Simply put, one must recall that in repeating one's lines, it is also impossible to repeat them: this is acting (as) amnesia, certainly, but amnesia with its own political content: "[T]he most adaptive state of mind," writes Herbert Blau, is "alternately known as selective inattention."[7]

Specific structures in *Rip Van Winkle* replicate this thematic concern with memory, both in Jefferson's acting commentary and in the play itself. Jefferson's *Rip*, for example, like its earlier incarnations, is a story about doubling, as I've already suggested, about mimesis *as* memory, or the appearance of memory *as double*. Moreover, not only is the central issue in the play the remembrance of things past, remembrance is itself divided: *Rip*, as I've said, is a story that is, through its recollection of other, older sources, literally remembered twice. As a dramatic text, Rip is split along similar lines: in Jefferson's version, the play falls quite neatly into two parts, what occurs before Rip's sleep and what occurs after. Past and present are held apart by the twenty-year sleep, a Nietzschean forgetting that, of course, does not actually appear in the play (performances producing the sleep state itself, or following it through to its conclusion, must wait until the endurance works of Andy Warhol and Robert Wilson in the latter part of this century). The very events, in other words, that give the play its impact and shape, the events that give the play meaning—what has occurred during Rip's sleep—are missing or forgotten within the structure of the play itself. The play forgets the forgetting. This amnesis is what allows Jefferson as Rip *to act*, a forgetting—again following Nietzsche—that allows history to appear, as when *in* the play Rip pieces together the events of the American Revolution through the signs and recollections of the townspeople, while outside of the play the motif and image of forgetting in Irving's original story quite literally gives Jefferson the material he needs to construct his drama.

But the play is not only about forgetting, it is also about remembering. Not only is the *performance* of the play a re-membering (as any play must be), it is a play that through its status and thematic of and as remembrance focuses attention on memory itself, or "remembers remembering" (as I am doing right now). Moreover, while *Rip* is a story precisely about remembering memory, it is also a play that remembers what has not happened: the substance of the play, again, is about what has and has not occurred during Rip's amnesic, comalike sleep, what is seemingly concealed within sleep: the dream of the mountain, the hallucinations in the amphitheater, "the nightmare of history from which we are trying to awake." It is within these cross-reflections that memory and forgetting, seemingly Other, also begin to seem the Same. It is also from within these theatrical conundrums that the numerous stage versions emerge that again double, multiply, and replicate the original story. This space of multiple re-memberings is the space of history.

As I have suggested above, these many earlier versions of the play differ structurally from Boucicault/Jefferson's interpretation in one very important respect: other versions of the play typically began with Rip's awakening from his sleep and his subsequent reassimilation into the life of his family and village. Jefferson's version, however, is truer to Irving's original story: it begins with Rip as a young man. The characters are developed from this perspective, and so Rip's awakening and his (and the audience's) shock at what has gone by in his absence are more poignant and have more visual impact—Rip suddenly grown old and gray. More importantly in terms of the thematic of memory and its loss, Jefferson's play, like Irving's story, lacks substance at its center. As I have elaborated, Jefferson's version has, quite literally, a hole or *rip* at its core. Rip names and is named by his own insubstance, his own forgetting. And when Rip enters the amphitheater through (in Irving's story) "a cleft, between rocky lofts," he is doing just that—entering the cleft or rip in consciousness-memory that at once contains and disavows meaning. Rip enters the unconscious, in other words, but a decidedly political unconscious, and one that seems somehow to take on the contours of traumatic amnesia. This is quite literally the space of theater.

The immense popularity of the story itself bespeaks a culture in resonance with the amnesic, willing to believe a political reality coming into existence "from nowhere." This is a fitting description of the American desire to turn its back on the past, or perhaps more exactly in terms of Jefferson's play, in tune with an amnesic leap through a double bifurcation of time—the leap forward within the play from pre- to post-Revolutionary America, and the leap backward of the play itself, set in antebellum (both pre-Revolution and pre–Civil War) America, but appearing in the theaters of postbellum culture. In either case, history in the play—both as a kind of fiction, and in its status as traumatic performance—is absent. Similarly, the most painful episodes of early American history are excised from political consciousness. The bloody Revolution, the enormity of slavery, the war crimes against the indigenous nations and tribes, the huge body-count of the Civil War, the assassination of a president, are effectively repressed into a merely *political*, historicist unconscious. Or as Homi Bhabha would have it, discourse turns Janus, the two-faced god, "into a figure of prodigious doubling that investigates the nation space in the *process* of the articulation of its elements," where history may in fact be only "half made because it is in the process of being made,"[8] or in the case of historicism, possibly unmade in its repressed, traumatic content.

This suggestion of trauma is, like dream consciousness itself, ethereally present in the play beyond Rip's difficult family life and his consternation at waking up an old man. In Irving's story, for example, no storm threatens, only the rumbling of the surreal nine-pin balls that *simulate* thunder. In Jefferson's play, however, "a furious storm can be seen raging, with thunder, lightning, and rain."[9] The storm is the mimetic image of the turbulence in Rip's home and in the nation's past and present: "Not into the storm, Rip! Hark how it thunders!" cries the young Hendrick (who is himself a nominal double of the ghostly Hendrick who appears later). "Yah, my boy, but not as bad to me as the storm in my home."[10] With this, Rip staggers drunkenly off into the mountains to defy, like Lear, the tempest, and like Lear, sees his wits begin to turn during his confrontation with the elements.

The confluence here between Rip and Lear is not an overarching observation: in his autobiography, Jefferson specifically states that the reunion scene between Rip and his daughter is modeled upon the scene between Lear and Cordelia.[11] The similarities move beyond this one scene, however. Both Rip and Lear are cast out, and both are or become Other: Lear in his madness, Rip in his immigrant accents and later in his antique appearance. Both leave behind loving daughters who fear for their safety in the storm, and perhaps most importantly, both suffer a kind of psychotic episode during the storm's peak. Indeed, Lear's famous speech upon the heath, when he addresses the "sulph'rous and thought-executing fires," carries accents of Rip's coming condition. Both characters, as a result of their exposure to a chaos that might be the chaos of insanity, lose themselves and lose memory of themselves. Rip's first line upon awakening is, "I wonder where I was," echoing Lear's after he wakes: "Where have I been? Where am I?"

In the Environs of the Hole: The Repressed and the Occluded

The issue here of psychosis, of the "approach to the environs of the hole," to paraphrase Lacan, is central to both versions of *Rip Van*

Winkle. The ghostly lost seamen with the phallic features that Irving's Rip confronts in the mountains eerily echo the "the little men" in the hallucinations of that most famous of psychotics, Daniel Schreber. Lacan equates these "little men" with a kind of Derridean dissemination (dispersed spermatozoa/lost semen), with Schreber's desire to repopulate the world with himself. This repopulation is the exact equivalent of the American political agenda during this period—decimating Native Americans and repopulating the continent with "real Americans,"[12] a situation that reached a pinnacle of brutality barely twenty-five years before the appearance of Jefferson's play—the Trail of Tears in 1831–32, and the Great Removal of 1838, which together epitomized the "ethnic cleansing" of the American continent.[13]

But this real hallucination of decimation and repopulation that drove the nation ends in this play in a form of dispersal, dissemination as *mis*semination, the *excretio seminis* again. Rip not only sleeps through his fatherhood and thus abandons the procreative function of patriarch, but also spends all of the family's money on drink, even assenting to the sale of his home to pay off his drinking debts—a missemination that is doubly ironic because Rip fails to sign the document of forfeiture and carries it in his pocket into the mountains. As a result, when Rip returns, his enemy Derrick, who thinks he now owns Rip's properties, finds he does not: Rip shows (again the ocular proof) that he never signed the agreement. Rip's power thus resides in an absence once again—the absence of his name, a peculiarly "pere-verse" *Non du Père*, recapitulated in his name itself—the rip, the *béance* or hole in consciousness.[14] Rip's initial missemination is now born into an economy of such, dispersals passed along like currency, leading to the false stewardship of Rip's property by Derrick, a doubled image of the false stewardship of America's "settling" of the West, the dissemination and dispersal of the American mythos of democracy, rule without king, power as dissipation, history as psychosis.

In so artfully leaping over the historical traumas of an emerging nationalism, however, *Rip,* like so many other plays in the American canon, indicates the place of its interment as a deficiency or *want* in the structure of the play, characterized in this case by the main character himself. The simple response at this point would be to reiterate the substance of the repressed as political crimes against humanity; the appearance of this space of the repressed on the American stage indicates, in the larger political scope of things, the very traumas that were visited upon others in the formation of the nation. The attitudes of the middle class to which the plays appealed were formulated upon the hidden corpses of slaves, indigenous tribes and nations. And, though the point is somewhat simplistic, I generally believe this to be the case.

But the more difficult analysis of the rip or hole in the American theater would align itself with the repression of America and its history as a primal signifier, the *excretio seminis* of the political unconscious. A nation dedicated to the proposition that all are created equal, constructed on the backs of slaves and fed with the flesh of Native Americans and poor immigrant workers, to be sure, was also a nation condemned to play out its own image of itself continuously in order to fend off the terror that it may not exist after all. American identity, American authenticity, is precisely the absent center within which our still unrealized history exists, as Lacan might say, as "a historical scar: a page of shame that is forgotten or undone," and out of which theater, and now film and television, emerge, rife with their wish-fulfillments, egoistic nationalist defenses, and self-eradicating violence. This is also the empty space of analysis or theory, the theory that did not exist in American letters until quite recently, and now with a historicist and materialist vengeance—a theory of the theater. Such theory has been lacking in our history because that history itself exists as a lack or emptiness concealed within the immense theatricalization that is American culture. But cultural materialist theories that attempt to get at the documentable reality of this scarified past may be missing the point of this history-as-disappearance: the recovery of history is, as Lacan says, "not a matter of reality, but of truth." The newer cultural materialisms must eventually confront this issue: that in some profound sense the reality of what it studies does not exist, only its ghostly outlines, its specters, to use Derrida's term, or its ghostings, following Herbert Blau—like the phantoms of Hudson's crew, or Hudson himself, set adrift to die and vanish by his mutinous shipmates in the bay that bears his name. Like Rip's own history in theater/as theater, theater history, like all history, exists as lack and seeming truth. And in the theater, Blau tells us, the seeming search for that truth is very often the worst deception of all:

> From the vantage point of that truth, I know the evasion when I see it, the hedged bets, the alibis, the cheats, the things you can get away with, the unexamined propositions. . . . What I have been suggesting is that in the approach to meaning any [ideological] position is necessarily an illusion.[15]

Theater history, however necessary and admirable an undertaking, can
never approach the real of its historical vision, a real whose substance
is disappearance within the lacuna that is history. The dawning recognition that this real is forever denied us, makes the pursuit of materialist histories even more tempting.[16]

Telling the Difference: Color and the Lacunic Eye

In the *Octoroon*, Dion Boucicault explores this illusory history from a
slightly different perspective. The play, first performed in 1859, deals
thematically with the "slavery question" of its time. While we may
argue over the inadequacy of its vision and the narrowness of its political insights, it is, nonetheless, one of the first successful plays[17] to deal
with the gnawing question of slavery and racism, and as such is useful
in what it might show us about the reception of that issue in American
culture at the time.

In a broader sense, however, the play deals with more than slavery. Racial difference, and the roots of racism in particular, are explored
in startling ways. But while the play raises the issue of black differentiated from white according to the dictates of liberal, abolitionist morality, the "slavery question" quickly and unconsciously folds into the
issue of perception itself. The categories of black and white seem not
only to dissolve into one another—the obvious deconstructive tack—
but threaten the dissolution of consciousness itself. The divisions of
perception become negated not only in their opposites, but in their own
self-identity: black is not black, white is not white, red blood is not
red.[18] This moves beyond deconstructive revelation of privileged bina-
ries and toward the abolition, not only of slavery, but of categorical
thought itself, a threatened erasure of self/consciousness, or death. In
this threat, perhaps, lies the existential terror of the racist, but also the
terror of the theorist who must confront in the erasure the abolition of
ideology, a kind of "thought slavery," and the concomitant death that
that erasure seemingly entails.

Thus while black and white is in some sense a "primal binarism,"
the prototype of binary thinking (as different as black and white, night
and day), and arguably the main determiner of the character of life and
death in American society, the categories themselves become increasingly problematic, not merely as, we might expect, social truth, but as
representations of all mental categories. While the issue is of grave

importance to the characters in the play—whether one is perceived to be black or white—whiteness or blackness is determined, in the case of the Octoroon, at least, by that which is enormous but even in the Imaginary very nearly imperceptible, and in the Symbolic not existent at all, the faint blue tinge that separates black from white, that appears in the *béance* or blank space of the unconscious. "[T]here is a gulf between us," says Zoe, the Octoroon, to her white lover George.

> ZOE: . . . Do you see that hand you hold? look at these fingers; do
>   you see the nails are of a bluish tinge?
> GEORGE: Yes, near the quick there is a faint blue mark.
> ZOE: Look in my eyes; is not the same color in the white?
> GEORGE: It is their beauty.[19]

That gulf is seemingly uncrossable; it is the breach between the races, a breach constructed through the cultural opposition between black and white. But it is also the appearance of the fundamental lacuna of perception—the empirical lack in the observing eye, the blind spot, or "eye's navel," so to speak, where meaning goes out of sight, or conversely where meaning appears in the Lacanian *béance,* in the caesura, as hallucination. The slight, bluish tinge of the nail and eye, seemingly seen but merely imagined, seems the determining mark, but it is a myth, a fiction, one of numerous illusory "racial markers" that were used at the time to determine the potential scandal of one's (invisible) racial heritage. As Werner Sollers remarks, "Such descriptions of fingernails appear in texts set in India, Germany, France, Britain, and—most frequently—the United States; they can be found in short stories, novellas, novels, autobiographies, plays, and nonfiction, and are particularly prevalent in popular literature."[20] The perceived need to create these markers in order to prevent a miscegenated state is, of course, obvious. The need to locate these seemingly empirical markers within the Imaginary, beyond the reach of Symbolic discourse, is also rather predictable. What is perhaps most compelling beyond these very important issues, though, is the fault line demarcated within the architecture of sight itself. Three recent articles have, in very different ways, approached this site of the perceptual in Boucicault's play.

Harley Erdman, in a 1993 *Theater Journal* essay,[21] reads *The Octoroon* quite literally through the lens of the photographic eye, citing the appearance of the camera as the empirical ground upon which the discussion of racial difference occurs. Erdman suggests that the camera—the apparatus that establishes the ocular and forensic proof of guilt in the play—is the image or reference point for the empirical truth of racial difference signified by the "bluish tinge": "The apparatus can't mistake. . . . the machine can't err—you may mistake your phiz but the apparatus don't."[22] Erdman then goes on, rightly, to demonstrate the false empirical bias of this assumption by delineating the ways in which neither the intent of the photographer nor the significance of the subject photographed is transparent. Neither "proves" anything about reality or truth, and neither can be interpreted with any degree of certainty. The photograph, that seemingly neutral and dispassionate document, is in fact every bit as complex and duplicitous as the written text or the theatrical scene; it merely appears not to be so. In the photograph, once again, a kind of theatricality disappears into itself. As proof of the interpretive malleability of the photographic image, Erdman cites the testimony surrounding the Rodney King trial, in which every frame of the now famous videotape was subject to diametrically opposed interpretations by prosecution and defense—King's retracted leg, for example, was seen as a defensive action and as an aggressive attempt to kick at the officers.

It is Boucicault's attempt to neutralize the ambiguity of the photographic image that aligns itself with the appearance of the nonexistent "bluish-tinge"; both seemingly demonstrate an empirical and rational proof that in both cases is radically uncertain, even hallucinatory. The problem is not that "the apparatus don't lie" and thus must tell the truth, but that the eye that sees—whether photograph, a nonexistent color, a theatrical scene, or life—is infused with desire and must, to some extent, always lie. At any rate, for Erdman Boucicault's attempt to present this ocular "proof" as immutable and irrefutable is the spectacular means through which the social order is preserved, in spite of Boucicault's attempt to change it through the abolitionist sentiments in the play.

In Joseph Roach's article "Slave Spectacles and Tragic Octoroons: A Cultural Genealogy of Antebellum Performance,"[23] this preservation of status quo attitudes about slavery is framed within a larger cultural theatricalization, a different sort of "ocular proof," the spectacle of the slave market of the mid-1800s, which forms the central scene/image in *The Octoroon*, as well as the central image of New Orleans culture of the mid–nineteen hundreds. This scene in *The Octoroon* is described by Roach as a recapitulation of a "real" cultural theater that manipulated the spectacle of the trading block upon which the distinctions of race were maintained. For Roach, culture is produced through such spectacles and reproduced through theater. Here critique—the dissemination of racial markers and their meanings—becomes spectacle as well.

The focus in Werner Sollers's article, to which I have already alluded, is this marking system itself, the falsely constructed delusional system of empirical proof and its deployment as a means of maintaining racial distinctions. Sollers includes the interesting anecdote that Francis Galton, the inventor of fingerprinting techniques, made his discovery while attempting to find an irrefutable racial marking system. It is, of course, ironic that Galton, who begins by searching for a system to establish a sameness of race, ends by discovering pure difference—a technique to identify that which is irreducibly unique to each subject, perhaps the only objective marker of absolute subjectivity that existed until the discovery of DNA profiling, a technique that still has a margin of error greater than the singularity of fingerprints.[24]

Still, in all of the aforementioned articles, the problem of the seen lies elsewhere than in the seeing itself. The camera as a model of objective proof fails, of course. But it is not merely because the image is infinitely interpretable, it is because the eye sees what it wishes to see. Nor is the ideologically driven act of framing certain cultural formations as theater in order to reap the power of the performative isolatable from the plethora of other desires that infect the seeing: desires that may or may not be political. Finally, the sign system itself—whether the markers are seen or merely imagined—is not only redolent of the social need to keep certain classes of people subservient or apart, but also indicative of a wider propensity for vision to fail. What is important in Boucicault's play, it seems to me, is not that this or that aspect of the visual is prone to political/ideological bias, but that all seeing is infected by desire. All seeing is seeing what one wants to see, a desire to which ideology is especially prone.

Certainly in Zoe's eye the seen is excruciatingly complex. In the faint blue blush of the eye one sees the difference seeing, eye reflecting upon eye reflecting back again, another *mise en abîme*, the difference between black and white determined by the bluish tinge of the eye itself, and the "blackness" of the red blood:

[D]o you *see* the hand that you hold? *look* at these fingers; do you *see* the nails. . . . *Look in my eyes;* is not the same color in the white?

> . . . That is the *ineffaceable* curse of Cain. Of the blood that feeds my
> heart, one drop in eight is black . . . and that one drop poisons all
> the flood. (383; emphasis added)

This scene, in which Zoe reveals herself to be black and not white, as
she appears, is itself very nearly overdetermined—like the diaries of
Thomas Shepard—by the invocations to sight, to the visual. At the
same time, Zoe's invocation to the visual is necessary because she
thinks she is other than what she appears to be: her whiteness is an illusion, her color is not to be believed. Her "true color" is rather indicated
by the Other color that appears in the half-moons, the roots of her hair,
the tint of the eye—the hallucinated "blue tinge" that is not there.

In *The Octoroon* the visual, perhaps the most powerful determiner
of cultural difference, is the only means by which one can be certain of
one's identity—even if one *appears* to be other than what one is. At the
same time, outside the play, visual certainty is itself undermined by the
empirical fact that the blue tinge simply doesn't exist. And yet this, too,
is a visual, empirical judgment. The audience, like the characters in the
play, is being asked to reject the evidence presented before its eyes
(Zoe's apparently white skin) on the basis of a color that is invisible to
them. They (we) are being told that the visible should be rejected as
false based upon the truth of an other visible that also remains hidden
from us, a visible that is paradoxically invisible: here vision disarticulates itself. This is very close in disposition to Shepard's invocation to
blindness, another recapitulation of the desire in American culture for
philosophical and empirical benightedness.

The deadly blue color, which seems so full of significance, then, is
really empty of meaning; it seemingly exists only within a circular, tautological chain of signification: red is really black, black is signified by
blue, white is signified by the absence of blue, and, of course, by blackness itself, while blackness (or whiteness) is determined by the substance of red blood that is indicated by the color blue, and so on. Like
the shifting significations of language, there appears to be no color that
is not merely an indication of another color; the significance of any
color is always other than itself. The invocation to the visible in Zoe's
speech is thus also an invocation to the invisible, to what Peggy Phelan
has called the unmarked, and what Merleau-Ponty addresses in his
final, unfinished work, *The Visible and the Invisible*. In chapter 4 of that
work, he discusses the indeterminacy of the seen in terms of color, and

coincidentally the absent color red seen in contradistinction to the present blue of the sea:

> Claudel has a phrase saying that a certain blue of the sea is so blue that only blood would be more red. The color is yet a variant in another dimension of variation, that of its relations with the surroundings: this red is what it is only by connecting up from its place with other reds about it, with which it forms a constellation. . . . And its red literally is not the same as it appears in one constellation or in the other.[25]

Color, then, is never an inert, stable characteristic, according to Merleau-Ponty, but changes according to alterations in its contexts, the contexts of the visual, but also the contexts of memory, texture, and a nearly infinite range of other possible "constellations." It is not merely that color exists in a continuum, that every color exists in an infinite series of gradations, it is that color itself is seen through the filters of whatever contextualizes it. The red of a satin dress, for example, might be nearly identical to the red of flowing blood, yet because of the radically different contexts, the reds are utterly different.[26]

In *The Octoroon*, the color that occupies this site of shifting visibility is, ironically, white. The white man, for instance, is contrasted with both the black man (the African American slave), and with the red man (the Native American). While whiteness in these instances might usually connote superiority, civilization, and culture, here it indicates depravity, racism, and murder. The villain M'Closkey, for example, who is white, abjures Salem Scudder, another white man, when Scudder abandons M'Closkey after learning he has murdered a Native American child: "You are a white man; you'l [sic] not leave one of your own blood to be butchered by the red-skin?" (396).

Similarly, whiteness, the color of Southern gentility, is also the color that signifies violence and fury. When M'Closkey attempts to seduce Zoe, he promises her a share of his wealth that will so infuriate the Southern aristocratic Peyton family that "their white skins will shrivel up with hate and rage" (380).[27] Whiteness later comes to represent both the savagery of culture and its duplicitous appearance. When Scudder tries to resist a lynch mob intent on hanging the innocent Wahnotee, he characterizes the situation in these terms: "Here's a *pictur'* for a civilized community to afford; yonder, a poor, ignorant savage, and round him a circle of hearts, *white* with revenge and hate, thirsting for his *blood*" (393; emphasis added). Finally, the color white (white—both the lack of color and the plenitude of color) comes to signify decease, as Zoe's lips turn white at the approach of her death, and her eyes after it. "Her eyes have changed color," says Dora, Zoe's friend who attends her in death (397). In fact Zoe's changing eye color is foreshadowed earlier in the play when Dora's father comments on her eyes, red from crying. "Why Dora, what's the matter," he asks her. "Your eyes are red." "Are they?" she replies. "I don't care, they were blue this morning, *but it don't signify now*" (389–90). Blue eyes turn red from blood-engorged capillaries, blue eyes turn white as blood ceases to circulate, blood/colors transposed. In their transposition, meaning is seemingly canceled.

The contrasts, then, are throughout composed as difference and not opposition. Black and white are not opposed but mediated and differentiated through the faintest hue or mark of blue. Boucicault is in fact trying to disarticulate racial oppositions through the oxymoronic presentation of the invisible: Zoe, after all, looks white, but isn't. The radical difference between black and white is, as I've said, invisible, or is, rather, only visible through a secondary, *imagined* sign, the blue nails and eyes. This echoes the many references in the play to the sameness of blacks and whites beneath their skin colors, a sameness that is annihilated by the fatal marker; despite his championing of racial sameness, Boucicault maintains racial opposition through the hallucinatory blue tinge: blacks and whites may be equal, and they may even appear to be the same, but they are still different, and that difference is visible if one can but read the (nonexistent) critical signs. Finally, racial difference becomes, in the context of the Octoroon's trauma of misrecognition, as deadly as opposition.[28] This colonial authority of white over black turns, in Homi Bhabha's words, "from mimicry—a difference that is almost nothing but not quite—to *menace*—a difference that is almost total but not quite."[29] Colonial racism, then, turns upon the axis of perceptual crisis set within narrative: a theater.

And the context of the play is trauma, is crisis: the crisis of perception by which one is unable to determine truth, in which one's vision is skewed, paralyzed, unable to discern, or to discern only according to the lineaments of desire, of seems, the seam of the half-moon in the nail, the indigo glint in the eye. The crisis is a crisis of seeing, the crisis that is seeing, and is negotiated, concomitantly, by seeing the crisis (or not). This crisis is engendered in the very act of looking upon the world, as Oedipus, at the inception of the Western dramatic tradition, already knew. But seeing is "always already" a crisis state not merely because what one sees is questionable or ambiguous, but, in Merleau-Ponty's words, "because vision is a palpation with the look, it must also be inscribed in the order of being that it discloses to us; he who looks must not himself be foreign to the world that he looks at."[30] In other words, vision, at the moment of its inception, is infected by theatrical, even narcissistic desire. But Boucicault's consciously theatrical play, at the moment of its inception, is also infected by an other theater that he does not see: the appearance of the invisible as the substance of identity. This play, infused as it is with a clear ideological agenda, is captivated by the very theater that it attempts to deploy.

Boucicault is certainly not suggesting that difference ought to define racial opposition—indeed, he seems to be suggesting that what separates races in America is a difference almost too small to be noticed, a difference that is magnified in the bigoted hearts of Americans to near epic opposition. And yet that difference is (in Boucicault's play) real (indeed, in the Lacanian scheme the faint blue blush is the Real because it is experienced as such). The categorical structure that is responsible for the politics of opposition remains intact, and remains intact *through and because of the politics of difference that frames it*. Difference and opposition, in other words, are not opposites in Boucicault's play, as they are in deconstructive thought. Here difference and opposition as one of the binarisms upon which deconstruction is founded collapses upon itself. The meaning of difference (and *différance*) is erased in sameness. Of course, the nature of difference has been defined in deconstruction by its difference from opposition. But when *that* difference is erased, the categorical opposition upon which deconstruction is based disappears. Difference, because it is the "privileged" side of the equation, seemingly becomes opposition, as opposition becomes seeming difference in the slight bluish tinge. This issue, of course, is another way of defining the perceptual conundrum that we would call theater, and the appearance of that theater through mise-en-scène.

Seen a different way: the influence of Michel Foucault has led to the production of countless historical rereadings in literature, law, history, and even the sciences. These studies tend, by and large, to emphasize difference as rupture. Seeing local histories instead of relying on the narratives of previous "large" histories, they tend to emphasize various aspects of marginality—homosexuality, racial minority, women's histories, and so forth. The work has been crucial in opening up new ways of understanding the hiddenness and disenfranchisement of various social and political groups. It has led to useful rereadings of canonical and noncanonical texts and has led finally to its own series of repressions.

The emphasis on rupture has all but obliterated cultural and theatrical studies of *persistence,* or the reappearance of the same (no matter that that sameness is illusory; it seems and so is Real to those upon whom it impinges). History as rupture has likewise erased the historical continuity that underlies any notion of rupture or difference, while homogenizing the uniqueness of individual discourses has eradicated their differences. This has had concrete political effects: the ethos of difference, for example, has repressed the pain of the seemingly insoluble problem of marginality versus assimilation. These repressions tend to blunt the impact of the tragic or deny it altogether. I would argue against the domination of Foucauldian thought along primarily two lines: by privileging rupture or difference over continuity, we have come to believe that rupture and discontinuity are somehow more authentic, less constructed than continuity. Second, and more importantly, by repressing the same (continuity, persistence), we are miscasting difference itself as mimesis, or as a crucial aspect of it. Bhabha, for example, says this about the mimetic underpinnings of racial difference:

> *Almost the same but not white:* the visibility of mimicry is always produced at the site of interdiction. It is a form of colonial discourse that is uttered *inter dicta:* a discourse at the cross-roads of what is known and permissible and that which is known but must be kept concealed.[31]

Mimicry, in other words, that primary tool of colonialism that seeks to reproduce the other as the Same, *interdicts itself,* exposes its own internal split between Same and Other. It is a "discourse uttered between the lines and as such both against the rules and within them." Mimicry, seeking to reproduce the same as other, also must reserve within itself the sign or mark of difference by which the Same can also be undone: "Almost the same, but not white." Mimicry, then, is "always already" undone by difference, just as difference itself is supported and ratified by an unspoken Same beneath it. Bhabha puts it that "the question of the representation of difference is therefore always also a problem of authority," an authority marked by persistence and continuity.[32] Mimicry, far from the patriarchal reinscription of cultural value within art, is really a self-deconstructing category. It seeks to remind the cultural other that—though she must "toe the line" of colonial sameness, must reproduce seemly behavior, must *act well*—that action is immediately interdicted by the impossibility of Sameness: "You act, dress, believe as we do, but it is clear, nonetheless, that you are forever different; the mark upon your body shows it." Mimicry, in other words, shows its own impossibility, and that is its sole purpose. Here, then, I disagree with Elin Diamond, who sees mimicry as a more or less successful cover-up of realism's patriarchal agendas, an enforcement of Sameness and homogeneity. While that may be mimicry's most superficial appearance, its gravity rests in its function as the site of the impossible. The myriad refractions of this site of the impossible are the presumed stages of realism.

Realism

The logic of visibility and visibility's seeming truth—predecessor, perhaps, to today's visibility politics—is arguably most present in American realism, which became the dominant American theatrical epistemology of the latter half of the nineteenth century, and into the twentieth. But realism's legacy has from the beginning been suspect: at least since the work of Warner Berthoff in the 1950s and 1960s, through the work of Walter Benn Michaels and more recently Michael Davitt Bell and Brook Thomas,[33] the dominant voices in nineteenth- and twentieth-century American literary criticism have proclaimed, in one way or another, that American realism, though loudly championed among its supposed practitioners and condemned by some of today's feminists, has never really existed. Berthoff, commenting on writers as diverse as Howells, Henry James, and Twain, states the issue: "What do they all have in common? Not form, certainly, and not theme either, in any ordinary sense: to attempt to define American 'realism' by classifying the particular books written in its name according to form and theme is to sink into a mire of inconsequential distinctions and details."[34] Similarly, Michaels suggests that American naturalism, an extension of realist dogma, aligns itself logically with the appearance of the gold standard as the seeming foundation of American economy: both naturalism and the gold standard promised a kind of bedrock stability through the consistency of form and content, but both were, in essence, illusions designed to create the effect of stability where none in fact existed.

More recently, Bell has reopened the debate by suggesting that while the term "realism" (which he suggests ought only be used in quotes) may not specifically refer to a particular type of literature, the term itself, as Berthoff's work also suggested, indicates a kind of artistic position, a literary ideology, as it were, based on pragmatic action and a belief in certain "American" values. Bell's project is to rediscover the ways in which the term "realism" was used in the nineteenth century and first part of the twentieth to promulgate certain political positions, including social reform, certainly, but also rejection of effeminacy and homosexuality, and a "reinscription" of notions of masculine strength. But in much recent performance theory, most notably the work of Jill Dolan and Elin Diamond, the questionable historical status of American realism has been largely ignored or misperceived: American realism as a *literary* movement was not, as it sometimes was in the theater, simply a drive toward verisimilitude, a reconstruction and "reinscription" of bourgeois life. It was not a literary or dramatic *form*, but an *ethos*, an ethos that, in the words of a standard literary handbook, sought

> to find and express a relativistic and pluralistic truth, associated by discernible consequences and verifiable by experience. . . . [R]ealists are unusually interested in the effect of their work on the audience and its life. . . . Realists eschew the traditional patterns. . . . Life, they feel, lacks symmetry and plot; fiction truthfully reflecting life should, therefore, avoid symmetry and plot.[35]

This baseline reading of the realist project seems quite similar to Dolan's own feminist project, which is heavily invested in women's experience as the basis of performance, along with the predictable poststructural emphasis on decenteredness (lack of symmetry) and pluralism, and the rejection of traditional theatrical patterns (ironically, realism itself).[36]

And Dolan is not alone in her misprision of realism's lack. A number of recent essays acknowledge the "problem" of defining the realism they seek to illuminate, all the while studiously avoiding any such attempt at definition.[37] Apart from the occasional reference to "real" props, and idiomatic dialogue, no one set of features, conventions, attitudes, or structures is held to be the defining term of realist drama. The import of the various debates in terms of the present study is this: realism, the seemingly dominant literary form in our culture from the last century to the present, has seemingly never existed. It is an illusion, a theatrical and theoretical cover-up. The question among American realists was never, as it was in France with novelists like Zola or Flaubert, a matter of analyzing literary form and its relationship to life. Rather realism was an attempt to invoke certain political ideas—and through those ideas, a measure of notoriety and fame—through the term itself. As Berthoff suggests: "Insofar as it constituted a literary movement at all, American literary realism was concerned less with problems of artistic definition and discovery than with clearing the way to a more profitable exercise of individual ambition."[38] This goes well beyond anything like the bracketing of the Real in Lacanian thought. American realists did not problematize the real or debate the possibilities of the real and its representations in realism: American theorists of realism invoked the term specifically to conceal (and thus inadvertently to reveal) the disappearance of the real beneath the cloak of pragmatism and hidden ideology.

American realism as a term, then, is an empty signifier: a lack engendered by the absence of epistemological and analytical thought about the nature and representations of the real that realism presumably articulates—indeed, a lack of debate about whether the real might even exist. Any reference to realism in American culture, then, is a reference to double illusion: the illusion that supposedly constitutes realism's reinscription of patriarchal power, and superseding this, the illusion that such a thing as realism exists historically. The very term itself, then, as a doubled illusion, represents something like the space of theater unrecognized, or repressed.

To complicate the issue even further, American *theatrical* realism was at an even further remove from the problem of realism in American literature. The illusions of realism—the supposedly gritty portrayal of experience within the social dynamics of power politics in the work of William Dean Howells or Stephen Crane or Ambrose Bierce, for example, or later on in the toughened, realist/naturalist works of Theodore Dreiser—were displaced by a realism that meant, in essence, visual and acting verisimilitude. Realism stood as a kind of visibility politics, once again, the assumption of visibility's seeming truth. Plays might be melodramatic in nature, ignoring the registers of the political or social, and still be thought of as examples of realism because of "realistic" set, costume, and acting technique. Thus the real onstage was *rep-*

resented by pure seeming. Realism was like theater disappearing into itself once again, theater and the real becoming the Same.

This fascination with the theatricality of the real is a revisitation of what I earlier invoked as a kind of "theater of the authentic" in the work of Tyler and Mowatt. But whereas that theater sought or assumed truth beneath the mask of manners and conceit, the reformulation of the authentic in realism deflected the seeming substance of the real into the empirical—the reproducible delineations of experience. As has been often remarked, American culture was moving headlong into full-blown industrial capitalism during this period, a capitalism that was more reproductive than productive. This economic reproduction, in fact, was a replication of the desire that the myth of theatrical realism represented: the reproduction of "real" locations, costumes, and actions, the ability, as in Joseph Jefferson's acting theory, to reproduce the Same as difference—the capitalist euphoria. In the desire for supposed verisimilitude, however, mise-en-scène would presumably seek the highest level of sameness or reproducibility in each instance of performance, while trying at the same time to "seem" unique. Here mimesis, even in its most conservative guise, demanded a *seeming difference.* In a kind of final irony, the anxiety and fascination represented by realism in the theater were the anxiety over, and fascination with, reproduction or doubling, in which the false or difference becomes the dominant threat, becomes the Real.

In fact, many of the current debates about theatrical realism in the nineteenth century overlook that the anxious drive toward "realism" and verisimilitude was concomitant with a widespread captivation with devices that mimicked "the real." Kinetoscopes, zoetropes, phenakistiscope, stereoscopes, the camera, and finally film were wildly popular throughout the nineteenth century.[39] Counter to the claim that audiences were "reinscribed" by realist portrayals of their worlds, the nineteenth-century audience was being introduced to the profoundly illusory quality of their seemingly "real" world. Indeed, those audiences, supposedly anxiously trying to stabilize the "real" in realism, were thoroughly entranced by the very illusions that presumably threatened their perceptions. Steele Mackaye, perhaps the most interesting figure during this period from a theoretical standpoint, brought the illusions of stagecraft most closely to the illusive realism of life. In one theatrical rendering of something like a Wild West show (anticipating the recently constructed venue "Twister" at Universal Studios theme park) he created a realistic tornado and cattle stampede. Similarly, P. T. Barnum himself conjured his emissaries from the frontiered edge of American consciousness itself (such edges Lacan called the Unconscious): Pony Express riders; "Indian fighters"; and the demons of discord themselves, the warriors Little Heart, Yellow Buffalo, War Bonnet, and others. These reproductions were, then, double reproductions. The Wild West show was, after all, a highly theatricalized rendering of a frontier life that was already busily theatricalizing itself. Mackaye's realism, as well as the Wild West shows of Barnum and Buffalo Bill Cody, presented the reproduction of the reproduced, literal plays within plays, or, like *Fashion*, an infinite nesting of mise-en-scènes. Mackaye also recognized, *avant le lettre*, something like Robert Wilson's appreciation of the possibilities of theatrical space, organizing, for example, a huge "Spectatorium" with twenty-five stages on which the epic journey of Columbus to the New World was reproduced as the scene of multiplicity

Instead of the more common reading—that audiences sought reassurance of the world's substance in realist drama—the drive to realism and its popularity might rather be read as an anxious symptomology of the world's realized unreality, an unreality or unprovable reality apprehended by American philosophical pragmatism. Realism expressed a dawning knowledge that what seemed real in the world was merest illusion. It might, as is the case in many realist plays of the period, disappear in a single revelation. The drive toward verisimilitude onstage betrayed a repressed understanding that the *illusion* of real life constructed upon the stage *was a reproduction of life's own seemingly unreality*. Realism, then, was mimicry, but mimicry that sought to find in the theater some indication of what the real world itself concealed. In the words of Lacan, "The effect of mimicry is camouflage in the technical sense. It is not a question of harmonizing with the background, but against a mottled background, of becoming mottled—exactly like the technique of camouflage practiced in human warfare." In the words of Joan Copjec, "[T]he effect of representation ('mimicry,' in an older, idealist vocabulary) is not a subject who will harmonize with, or adapt to, its environment." Rather, "the effect of representation is, instead, the suspicion that some reality is being camouflaged, that we are being deceived as to the exact nature of the thing-in-itself that lies behind representation."[40] In this sense, the real does not appear in the pretense of showing reality onstage, but rather in the indices of a theater that suggests there exists a real behind it. Seen this way the "reinscription" of the seemingly real is often more powerfully written

as the "beyond," or the indicated, of experimental or avant-garde performance. Conversely, realism could just as easily be read not as a reinscription of a bourgeois status quo, but as the anxious desire to be rid of
the weight of self/perception, the desire to disappear into the mimicry
of a camouflaged subjectivity, to vanish, in other words, into "subject
position." American materialism and pragmatism, then, from James to
Rorty, represents less a commonsensical assessment of the material
conditions of life ("what works") than a reinscription of an authentic
that, in the political unconscious, seeks in the reification of realism its
own desire: escape both from the terror of ephemerality and the
oppressive weight of an alienated, individuated consciousness.

Arguably, the American anxiety about, and fascination with, stasis
and reproduction during the latter nineteenth century found its most
enduring expression in the work of James Herne. Herne was, of course,
a seminal figure in the development of American theatrical realism,
recognized by many theater historians and critics as the "father of
American realism" (patriarchal intonation intended), the "American
Ibsen," and the primary proselytizer in America of the "well-made
play."

Margaret Fleming,[41] the most well known and widely anthologized
of Herne's plays, was written in 1890 and describes the bourgeois life of
an affable but rapacious upper-class mill owner, Philip Fleming, and
his loyal and saintly wife, Margaret. As the play unfolds, we learn that
Philip has sired a child out of wedlock with the sister of one of his ser-
vants, and that the mother of this illegitimate child dies shortly after
childbirth (yet another dead and absent mother) but not before naming
Philip as the father. Margaret, who though vibrant and charismatic, is
apparently in frail health, goes blind at the shock of the revelation.
Philip in guilt and despair disappears for a time. When he returns, he
begs his wife's forgiveness, and she gives it. She also adopts the illegitimate child, indeed breast-feeds it after its mother's death, and brings it
into their home, placing it beside their daughter. The play ends with the
blind Margaret, seemingly joyous at the reunion of their family, looking rapturously into the darkness, seeing nothing in two distinct
senses: her visual field is a blank space, and that blankness itself covers
over the hopelessness of her hysterical cul-de-sac. The reproduction of
blindness is once again doubled, as it was in the writings of Thomas
Shepard. But not only is blindness split, the two children themselves
suggest a reproduction that is at once true (Margaret's daughter) and
false (Philip's bastard son). Reproduction, though conjugal and sacred,

has a dark and anxious side: a potential missemination that produces the false, the illusory, the con man.

In fact, the play conceals its reproductive strategies from itself. Although perhaps the best example of a "well-made" play in Herne's repertoire, *Margaret Fleming* feels more like melodrama than the realist theater of Ibsen, for example. Lacking the stark dichotomies of good and evil, poverty and wealth, purity and depravity that mark much of the melodramatic canon, *Margaret Fleming* is nonetheless saturated with the sentiment of that genre. When Margaret first takes the bastard child in her arms and quiets him by breast-feeding him with the milk produced by her own child, she is already blind—she does not see her husband standing broken before her. The scene is very nearly over the top for melodrama, and certainly so for Ibsenesque realism. Similarly, when Philip finally returns and Margaret confronts him in her remarkable saintly composure, the scene, though tinged with realist scandal and social moralism, lapses into sentiment:

> PHILIP: *(With urgency)* You say you want to forget—that you for-
>   give! Will you—?
> MARGARET: Can't you understand? It is not a question of forget-
>   ting, or of forgiving— *(For a moment she is at a loss how to con-*
>   *vince him)* Can't you understand? Philip! *(Then suddenly)* Sup-
>   pose—I—had been unfaithful to you?
> PHILIP: *(With a cry of repugnance)* Oh, Margaret!
> MARGARET: *(Brokenly)* There! You see! You are a man, and you
>   have your ideals of—the sanctity—of—the thing you love.
>   Well, I am a woman—and perhaps—I, too, cry "pollution." *(She*
>   *is deeply moved)*.[42]

Gradually the scene moves toward Margaret's acceptance of Philip, and his growing manliness in the face of that acceptance. The moralist-realist proclamation that marital fidelity ought to be as important to men as it is to women is submerged beneath the mawkish timbres of the scene. In fact, one would be hard pressed to find a more dead-on example of clinical hysteria than Margaret's blindness as she comes to "see" her husband's moral turpitude. The onset of blindness here, as in the case of Adam Trueman's blindness, entails a dissolving of gender and refusal of pleasure, inasmuch as the hysteric's object of desire, either as omnipotent, or in the case of Philip, horrifically weak, becomes the other unsexed. In Juan-David Nasio's words:

> In the hysteric's eyes, then, the Other's genital is neither the penis
> nor the vagina, but his flaw as revealed by too much weakness or
> too much power. What moves a hysteric is not sexual charm (in the
> sense of the genital) but the charm that derives from the strength,
> or on the contrary, the fragility of the partner.[43]

This hysteria is thus a kind of narcissism, but also paradoxically a social
exchange, an illness not "affecting an individual, but rather the
unhealthy state of a human relationship that subjects one person to
another."[44] It is a master-slave relation, in other words, in which the
blind eye becomes the phallus itself, or rather the place the phallus
would occupy were it not dissolved in the impasses of power, the blind
eye as the locus of seduction, a locus (the eye), that in the words of
Bataille is "more attractive in the bodies of animals and men" than any
other part, yet a locus whose attractiveness rests in an "extreme seduc-
tiveness" that is "probably at the boundary of horror . . . the cutting
edge."[45] The blind eye here is thus a critical eye, the demarcation of a
cutting edge, the castrating blade at the center of the action, so to speak,
assessing power and its absence, but blind, finally, to its own desire
denied.

Seen another way, the purely aesthetic weakness of the play, when
compared with Ibsen's contemporaneous plays, lay not in an obdurate
realism, taking in the audience with its portrayal of authentic emotion
and thus reestablishing middle-class values, but rather in its own
intrinsic blindness, its lack of realist striving. The play simply does not
go far enough, or as far as Ibsen would have, in its investigation of marital hypocrisy (which Ibsen seems to locate in the rank and pervasive
theatricalization of family life). In Herne's case, the realist project fails,
not as Dolan suggests, "because its ideology is so determined to vali-
date dominant culture," but rather because it must always remain blind
to the forces that constitute it—the ghostings of theater.

But my argument here is not a defense of realism. It is rather an
attempt to draw my own isomorphism between Herne's "classical"
realist play and the critique against realist drama, not in defense of that
drama, but rather as a cautionary point to theory itself. The problem of
American realism as an ethos is the problem of any approach to truth in
theory—its captivation by (an) illusion. When Margaret first cries out
the doubled invocation, "Blind! Blind!" it is in some sense a recapitulation of the doubled lack implied in the American materialist position:
as the seemingly real (or rather the authentic, the material) is

approached, sight fails. Indeed the failure of sight in realism becomes the principal truth of the seen. Once again, the issue is not that the play is perceived to be real and thus some notion of reality becomes "reinscribed." Rather, the problem in realism, oftentimes seen by European realism, is that *any* seeing of the world/theater operates out of the implacable anxiety (and often the conviction) that there is no real to be seen: it is not so much that hegemony constructs the observer, but rather that the observer—realist or not, socially constructed or not, actual or not—constructs the scene through a relentless blindness and remains blind to her own blindness, as Margaret is. Thus the original ideal of realism as a conservative corrective vision becomes nullified in the recognition that the seeing subject is radically alienated by her own sight—is blind. The vision of social in/justice is displaced by the nightmare of the watcher, like Margaret, tragically and solipsistically cut off from the social entirely, struggling with the insubstance of the seen, struggling with the weight of the self and its guilt, mocked by a phantasm (realism) that instantiates her own antirealist dogma but does not in fact exist.[46] Theory is tragedy, the tragedy of phantasmic necessity.

This, it seems to me, echoes the tragic timbres of Herne's play in its recognition that things will not simply "work out in the end" but will instead remain damaged and scarred. The cicatrix will forever be visible at the skin's surface of the Fleming's marriage. Even though Margaret bravely tells her husband, in yet another formulation of American rejection of history, "The past is dead. We must face the future," the sentiment is overshadowed by her later comment, delivered in a kind of schizoid detachment to Philip's claim, "I know I shall be able to win you back to me all over again":

> MARGARET: *(Smiling sadly)* I don't know. That would be a wonderful thing *(She weeps silently)* A very wonderful thing. *(Then suddenly she springs to her feet)* Ah, Dreams! Philip! Dreams! And we must get to work.[47]

The chilling recognition is that the substance of their life together will only be recovered as illusion, as dream—or, even more painfully, that dream and reality will both be erased in the hysterical delusion. Margaret now blind, will regain her sight only to enter another kind of blindness.[48] It seems to me that "realist" drama is ensnared by these recognitions. It is not mere reproduction of bourgeois mores, but a recapitulation of the real problem in the genre of the problem play itself:

what is crucial in interpretation is what will always remain unseen, my desire in the play, the desire that allows me to bypass the real stratum of terror—that life and its meanings are constituted by phantasms, unknowability, by blindness and death, and that there may be no understanding to be had, nothing to be done. This is, and is not, a theoretical issue.

Indeed, in a final beguilement matching the hysterical beguilement of Margaret's own blindness, the play itself cuts away the issue of its own theatricality. As Philip prepares to go back to his job, after a ritual cleansing and recostuming, he says to Margaret, "I'd like to see Lucy," his daughter. Margaret, in a terse reminder to Philip that he is now the father of two children, replies, "They are both out there. In the garden." This final scene underscores Philip's repressed desire to obliterate the Other, male, child in an act of castration, cutting him off, rendering him an orphan, a "floating signifier" that reenters the unconscious of the American drama and reemerges from that drama onto the cultural stages of American life: the enfant terrible again, the child born within absence, through blindness and foreclusion, a child that reappears on the cultural landscape as the horrific Other, conceived between theater and theater's denial, delivered from the constricting, suffocating space of symbolic closure.

4

Excursus: The Thought of an American Theater

> Between me and the other world there is ever an unasked ques-
> tion: unasked by some through feelings of delicacy; by others
> through the difficulty of rightly framing it. How does it feel to be
> a problem? . . . Leaving, then, the white world, I have stepped
> within the Veil, raising it that you may view faintly its deeper
> recesses—the meaning of its religion, the passion of its human
> sorrow, and the struggle of its greater souls.
> —W. E. B. DuBois

Veil and Vel: Hawthorne's Hidden Theaters

If we read in the canonical plays of the mid–nineteenth century an
unresolved confluence of the amnesic, the "unmarked," and the lineations of hysterical blindness, we find in the fiction of this same period
something quite different: an articulation of the theatrical that far out-
strips American theater's misunderstanding of its own peculiar hide-
and-seek, *fort/da* ontology. The subtlety and complexity of fiction's contestations with the theatrical nearly overwrite the near blindness of
American theater's "insight" into its own impulses. We can, for example, often locate in a single character the very nearly overdetermined
complexity of theatrical presence and absence: the figure of the Reverend Mr. Hooper, the self as Other in Hawthorne's "The Minister's
Black Veil,"[1] appears as epitome of theatrical mask. Here the black veil,
like theatrical space itself, both externalizes and conceals the blank
space of the other, invoking something like the aphanic Lacanian *vel*,[2]
the reciprocating split in perception that engenders the Other engen-
dering the self.[3] In this unique figuration, the undertow of socially engi-

neered blindness and amnesia is cast backward through time, set, like much of Hawthorne's fiction, in Puritan New England.

But here, the blinding enigma, unlike Zoe's body in *The Octoroon*, acts less like a (white) screen upon which desire is cast, than the (black) curtain that conceals desire and in doing so foregrounds it. As in the case of G. G. Clerambault, Lacan's "only master" and collector of countless numbers of photographs of draped Moroccan subjects, the "colonial cloth" that covers body and face seems less an evasion of "the gaze of power" than its elicitation: the very act of "covering up" creates the desire and illusion for that which was never hidden. Desire here becomes the mask that covers its own substance.[4]

The entire disposition of Hawthorne's story—from the opening sentences, in which children "mimicked [the] graver gait" of their parents on their way to church, and "spruce bachelors looked sidelong at the pretty maidens" (872), to the Black Veil itself that is the cipher or syntagma of the story—is set within colonial surveillance, but surveillance that is absorbed and refracted back into the surveilling eye.

When the Reverend Hooper emerges from behind his door that Sunday morning wearing the black crape veil that covers his face but for his mouth and chin, the effect upon his congregation is fearsome. "He has changed himself into something awful, only by hiding his face . . . Our parson has gone mad!" (873). Yet the fear is struck not merely by the possible reasons behind the masking—which might suggest mental aberration—but by the sheer effect of the blank space itself. We are reminded of Lacan's history as the traumatic blank space of desire, the visage-as-hole that now signifies the minister both to his parishioners and to himself, for he is as horrified by the veil he wears as they are. Far from allowing him to exercise a kind of panoptical "gaze of power" unseen, unreturned, and thus unchallenged from behind the mask that conceals his eyes, his black crape renders "the pale faced congregation . . . almost as fearful a sight to the minister, as his black veil to them" (874). The hole in the gaze, in other words, operates on both sides of the curtain—within the panoptical theatricality of the Puritan village that Hawthorne evokes, but also within the theatricality of the act of reading the story itself. For the veil not only gave "a darkened aspect to all living and inanimate things," it also "threw its obscurity between him and the holy pages" of Scripture (874, 873), very like the obscurity the story casts between the reader and the pages of Hawthorne's text. In both cases—within the conceit of the story, and in the act of critical reading—the fundamental and compelling "fact" seems to be the thing that is not there. This "thing not there" is the meaning, the *phantasmic* meaning, that accrues to an empty space. This space, however, is not mere negation, but, is, paradoxically, a sign that represents both an emptiness and a plenitude. It is the impenetrable veil, after all, and it functions as the "darkness of blackness" that locates, in fact creates, the narrative desire of the story and its interpretative enactment. The veil, like the theatrical curtain, the costume, and the mask, conceals in its materiality the disappearances that we associate with theater, rendering the bleeding, suffering body merest shade: "But the strangest part of the affair is the effect of the vagary, even on a sober-minded man like myself. The black veil, though it covers only our pastor's face, throws its influence over his whole person, and makes him ghost-like from head to foot" (875). Indeed, when Hooper bends to give a last farewell to a dead parishioner, it seems as if the corpse—in death seemingly the only one able to see his face—shudders at his empty countenance. And when those dying, clambering for Hooper's presence in their death-throes, actually see him, they seem more horrified by the veil than by the aspect of death itself.

Early on Hawthorne offers a possible, if tepid and moralistic, reason behind Hooper's wearing of the veil, that it was meant to represent some "secret sin," not unlike that letter from the unconscious in his most famous novel. But clearly the issue is not so simple. While there is, of course, the Hawthornian residue of contempt for Puritanical hypocrisies that infuses much of his writing, here there is something else and something more. Here we see an elaboration of a theatrical ontology that melds, in the panoptical effect of the theatrical curtain as experienced on both sides of the proscenium, both seer and seen: "They sat a considerable time, speechless, confused, and shrinking uneasily from Mr. Hooper's eye, which they felt to be fixed upon them with an invisible glance" (877). This is a formulation that speaks both of the actor's plight as object of the audience's gaze and of the audience's secret pleasure and anxiety as voyeur, "caught in the act" within the circle of the Other's eye, the circle of theater's gaze that runs, as Lacan suggests, both directions: the eye eyeing the curtain/screen, the curtain/screen, in turn, concealing the gaze of its own baleful eye.

Finally, then, the parishioners see dread in the very curtain as curtain—it is not what the veil conceals, or even what it might mean or reveal, it is the veiling itself that is fearful, and the workings of consciousness that are suggested in the veil as "a type and symbol" (878). But the curtain also locates the repressed desire and horror constructed

around an unsignifiable space, the Other's body, the indeterminate surface upon which the phantasy of the ego-ideal or love-object is drawn,
for though the veil seems "only a material emblem . . . the horrors,
which it shadowed forth, must be drawn darkly between the fondest of
lovers" (879).

The horror of the veil, which Hooper reveals in death, is the horror
of its indeterminacies. While he wears the black crape and evokes terror in all those who look upon him—terrors born of the veil's suggestion of horrible, concealed crimes—the abjection of the minister is born
of the realization that the Others, too, wear veils but *cannot see them*.
Here the literal replication of the veil, the "two folds of crape" (873),
erases its own presence. While Hooper's own veil conceals his countenance, the veil the others wear conceals itself. The veil is itself veiled,
the axis of a theater disappearing into itself, like the spectacle of the
black-veiled axle in the Oklahoma City trial. The result is horrific—the
villagers, bereft of the theater's space of reflection in which they might
see concealment itself, live instead within concealed tragic theaters of
guilt and black crime, of theatrical pretense and stunted critical judgment. They do not see their own performance upon the cultural and
theatrical stages of consciousness. They die thinking themselves real—
an anxious, but collectively reinforced, virtual community that dies
each alone, as mere actors orphaned onstage.

The deep horror, then, is not that the citizens find themselves
"merely actors," mere performative entities, "socially constructed."
Rather, the horror is that the curtain is the very site of separation and
nothingness that constitutes them. Then, as if to mock the insubstantiality of it all, the curtain doubles, and so doubles the insubstance: first,
the multifarious watching audience is composed through its own
observations of the minister as actor, and second, the minister as actor
is himself constituted in the gaze-absorbing blackness of the veil *as seen
by the audience*, all composed within the virtual frame separating stage
from audience. Here we have something like a Genetic theatrical perception, in which the substance of life, "socially constructed" or not,
shows itself to be far more insubstantial than what appears, or disappears, onstage. Desiring beyond desire the Yeatsian folding of this veil
in the making of theater, Derrida writes:

What I am entertaining doubts about, supposing it is of interest to
anyone at all, would be the extent to which that scene [the scene of
desire] betrays me. . . . Beyond memory and time lost. I am not

even speaking of an ultimate unveiling, but of what will have remained alien, for all time, to the veiled figure, to the very figure of the veil.

This desire and promise let all my spectres loose. A desire without a horizon, for that is its luck or its condition. And a promise that no longer expects what it waits for: there where, striving for what is to come, I finally know how not to have to distinguish any longer between promise and terror.[5]

And as if in direct response, Joan Copjec writes, following Lacan, "The subject is the effect of the impossibility of seeing what is lacking in the representation"—here the veil itself: "The veil of representation actually conceals nothing: there is nothing behind representation."[6] Nothing, and, we might add, the literal and ponderous nothingness that is death.

Shuffling Off the Mortal Coil: Black/Face/Face/Off

The point of this rereading of Hawthorne's well-known story is not merely to underscore the black veil's peculiar affinity with theatrical theory—the scripting of theater's disappearances. It is, rather, to extrude the central image of the veil as both broad and abstract, and absolutely particular in its reflection and absorption of what is also perhaps most broad and particular about American society: its racism, and, moreover, its racism as the manifestation of an inability to see the very difference upon which racism is founded. Hooper's veil, then, presents an unsettling possibility. It clearly represents something like the repression of blackness in American culture, both the continued repression of African American culture and the concomitant repression of the memories of slavery and genocide, the hidden "sins of the community." There is also something in the image of the veil that suggests, through the jaundiced eye of American history-as-theater, the necessity of American slavery *avant le lettre* in the creation of white American identity. The ocularity and its occlusion, the theatricality of America born on Winthrop's *Mayflower*, required the Otherness of Blackness— the theatrical curtain, so to speak, in place before the audience arrived—to complete itself. This is an Otherness both hidden and blatant, an *unconscious* that, ironically, gave birth to an American society that is today differentiated from its European etymon only through the imprint of "colored" cultures. The difference, in other words, that defines American culture is precisely its history of repressed race, a difference that, in the registers of racism, masquerades in yet another permutation of its theater, *as* difference (that is, the pseudodifference of literary theory). The very blackness that white American culture has despised represents the substance of that culture: both the blackness of perceived skin color, and the blackness of a psychotic *béance* that denies the racism—and thus itself—predicated on color. The formulation of skin color as a "racial marker," a marker in some sense as indeterminate and Imaginary as the "blue tinge in the halfmoons," has been the subject of much research in the recent past, none it more apropos to the present study than the excellent work done on blackface minstrelsy.

Minstrelsy[7] was a unique American institution that found its roots in the search for a "true" American culture, a popular culture, whose lineations appeared in earnest after the War of 1812. In part the result of a desire to infuse art and culture with what was most "truly American," minstrelsy, throughout its history, walked a fine line between nostalgia and ridicule. "Traditional" songs and stories, often written specifically for the minstrel show and thus not traditional at all, were mixed with skits and bits that played directly to the audiences' anxious racism. From its earliest impulses in the 1820s and 1830s, when T. D. Rice began to collect his minstrel "materials," through the period of its highest popularity in the mid-1840s, minstrelsy represented what was perhaps most American in America: its racism, of course, but beyond this an increasing propensity to construct itself theatrically—and not merely "performatively"—within the unformulated space of its own desire. It was, as we shall see, as *theater* that the minstrel show created its own peculiar vision of American culture. Minstrelsy did not merely represent black culture, or what whites thought black culture was, it created both cultures *onstage* as purely staged events. This was no mere instance of performance or performativity percolating up through culture, no mere "repetition of stylized acts," to quote Judith Butler,[8] but the very double-bound perceptual conundrum that Hawthorne saw so clearly, the theatricality of consciousness given script and form. Indeed, it was the very scriptedness of the minstrel shows, their appearance as institutional theater, that created the illusion that there was a "real" racial history behind them.

Beyond its uniqueness as an American institution, minstrelsy is peculiar as a theatrical form because it represents a "top down" parody of black culture. Although the carnivalesque traditions of ridicule aimed at dominant institutions are quite common in Euro-American history, and although we may see in some established theatrical traditions comic or "low" character types being ridiculed by dominant culture (the working-class in English drama, Zeke the butler in early American drama), we seldom see entire theatrical forms emerge whose raison d'être seems to be gratification through the ridicule of a specific underclass. Despite recent studies' attempt to either recuperate blackface minstrelsy as purely carnivalesque,[9] or to emphasize its roots in working-class culture,[10] the fact that minstrelsy attained such a level of influence on American stages attests to the magnitude of the threat white America saw in African American culture, even well before the Abolitionist movements of midcentury.

But minstrelsy was also not merely parodic attack on African American culture (although it certainly was that); it was also the expression of a peculiar longing for "simpler" bucolic and agrarian times—the "old folks at home" melancholia that was particularly attractive to the American working class of midcentury (white and black), who found themselves bound to the increasingly brutal and filthy labor conditions of nineteenth-century American culture: indeed, even though minstrelsy was apparently born and flourished in urban America, its images were those of the rural South. And finally, minstrelsy was not merely the exploitation of black culture by white theatrical entrepreneurs. As Eric Lott explains:

> It is . . . crucial to acknowledge the intricacies of the process by which black performative practices were recruited into blackface minstrelsy, a process that is only partly accounted for in the notion of a static reified "black culture's" removal into the pocketbooks of white imitators. Black performance itself, first of all, was precisely "performative," a cultural invention, not some precious essence installed in black bodies; and for better or worse it was often a product of self-commodification, a way of getting along in a constricted world. Black people, that is to say, not only exercised a certain amount of control over such practices but perforce sometimes developed them in tandem with white spectators.[11]

There was in minstrelsy, in other words, as in Hawthorne's story, a mutual construction of blackness and whiteness, but a construction that ironically ended up *erasing the difference*. There could be no way of telling which were the black cultural formations of a given performance and which the white. Thus the doubling or folding of identities, one into the other, was, like Hooper's veil, itself doubled: black performers performing, white imitators imitating, black performers borrowing from those imitations and introjecting them back into their own unconscious cultural practices, whites appropriating those changes, and so on. Moreover, this blurring of distinctions came about at the specific moment that minstrelsy was being used by white culture as the means of inscribing the distinctions between white and black performance as a set of racial markers. There is, then, in the minstrel show no mere imitation of black culture by whites, but an elaborate and unconscious cultural con-game in which everyone was gulled—a con with no "outside," no shill or charlatan manipulating the deception, but rather a theater in which everyone—black and white—was onstage. As Lott says, the performances of minstrel groups "were fed into an exchange system of cultural signifiers that both produced and continually marked the inauthenticity of their 'blackness'; their ridicule asserted the difference between counterfeit and currency even as they disseminated what most audiences believed were black music, dance, and gesture."[12] Even though audiences knew the performers were "really" white, in other words, even though they knew they were seeing mere mimicry, they believed that what they were seeing was at the same time authentically "black." The perfect con, in a sense: tell the gulls you're going to con them, and then do it without their (or your) knowledge. This scam "opened to view the culture of the dispossessed while simultaneously refusing the social legitimacy of its members," to quote Lott, but it also threatened to obliterate the white culture within which it appeared. With a psychoanalytic sensibility more acute than many of the commentators on minstrelsy, Ralph Ellison perhaps said it best:

> When the white man steps behind the mask of the [blackface] trickster his freedom is circumscribed by the fear that he is not simply miming a personification of his disorder and chaos but that he will become in fact that which he intends only to symbolize; that he will be trapped somewhere in the mystery of hell . . . and thus lose that freedom which, in the fluid, "traditionless," "classless" and rapidly changing society, he would recognize as the white man's alone.[13]

Minstrelsy, in other words, apart from its expropriations, its cruelties, its anxious portrayals of black potency and anger, was more about whiteness than about blackness. While in *The Octoroon*, blackfaced performers presented racial anxiety within the frame of whiteness in the figure of Zoe (who is "really" black though she appears to be white), blackface minstrelsy presented a seeming inversion, a "black" frame within which "real" whiteness appeared as blackness. Moreover, whereas the fear of hidden blackness played as sentimental tragedy in Boucicault's play, hiding one's whiteness safely behind the mere mask of black paint or burned cork played as farce or farcical romance in blackface minstrelsy. This farce was and is a far more brutal and coercive theatrical form, one that attests to the level of cruelty inherent in this odd species of prototypical performance art:[14] "Sentiment is a simple common-place business; But cutting a Joke is the most serious undertaking this side of the grave."[15]

We see in the split and inversion between inner/outer, blackness/whiteness something like a hysterical conversion once again, but here the hysterical impulse is decidedly phobic; by externalizing the hidden white anxiety over race, placing it quite literally on the skin surface, blackface and its admirers gained an Imaginary control over the vicissitudes of race and identity—both blackness and whiteness. This was a twofold proposition: not only could the performer/audience "control" the presentation of blackness, they could also hide the terrible insubstance of whiteness behind the mask; thus while the fear of African American presence in America was and is certainly born of racist guilt and power-madness, it also, and perhaps more primally, was and is a fear of whiteness: the fear of nothingness seemingly concealed by the black veil, a blankness constituting white America's lack of being and identity. Far from the anxious "mystery" of blackness, both exotic and fearful, whiteness—sheer emptiness—appeared as the very nonsubstantial substance of the Lacanian phobic hole.

But what are we to make of this minstrel history, apart from the social and historical dynamic of racism and classism it represents? Lott relates a revealing *Atlantic Monthly* story,[16] written in 1867, describing an actual event in the development of T. D. Rice's blackface persona. It seems that Rice met a poor African American named Cuff, an "exquisite specimen of his sort," and persuaded him to come along to the theater where Rice was performing. When they arrived, Rice took the man's clothing, put it on, and proceeded to, in essence, "become" Cuff, while the latter sat backstage naked. It happened, however, that Cuff had to leave to return to work during Rice's performance and called to him to return his clothes. Rice apparently couldn't hear (or didn't want to) and Cuff was forced to go out onstage and beg his own clothing back, a moment of high hilarity as far as the audience was concerned. Lott reads this very interesting story as a "master text of the racial economy encoded in blackface performance."[17] The story itself uses minstrel devices like black dialect ("Massa Rice, Massa Rice, gi' me nigga's hat"), to narrate the origins of blackface and its economy, and the story also relates in all of its duality the anxious deprecation of, and fear of, the naked black male body. What Lott doesn't pick up on, however, is the sheer theatricality of the play within the play. The *real* scene of theater, hidden backstage within the circumscription of Cuff's cruel humiliation, erupts through the theatrical double itself, Rice's minstrel show. This, again, is a doubling of the double—as Rice creates a seeming replication of black American culture, a real denizen of that culture strikes through the pasteboard mask. But when he does, the Real does not appear; rather the real is masked and neutralized, and his frustration and humiliation is taken to be part of the theatrical performance itself. The real becomes theater at the precise moment that theater becomes real. This story, and its profound and literal theatricality, frame Lott's larger argument that minstrelsy was no simple thing, no easy racist appropriation, but was rather the site of an immensely complicated series of contestations that only appeared to be simple and straightforward.[18] The moment of performance, in essence, pointed away from itself to some Other site, the unconscious, the place in which theater always appears in reality. Said another way, race *is* theater: seeing and being seen, but behind the seeing of black skin and ragged costume is the blank stage of whiteness itself in the struggle to become, and behind that the dark space of audience that appears only as other— an other theater of cruelty. Blackface theater, then, is not the *product* of the sociopolitical struggles of race, it constitutes them. Or even more radically, it *is* those struggles. It is the substance of racism's appearance *as* mere appearance. Minstrelsy, then, is not a representation or embodiment of racism's contestations, but is in its very theater racism itself, inasmuch as racism, operating along the contours of the seen, is nonetheless the enactment of the unseen, the site of invisibility, the site of fear and terror that, in the theater, is always other than where it seems to be.

The circle closes on this peculiar blindness and forgetfulness later in the traditions of minstrelsy when Rice "blacks up" for the role of Uncle Tom in Harriet Beecher Stowe's *Uncle Tom's Cabin*.[19] A blackface minstrel stars as the literal Uncle Tom in abolitionist theater, and no one, no one, sees irony or absurdity in such an appearance. We see, once again, that the political issue is not theater per se, or even racist theater per se. It is, rather, a theater unaware of its problematic placement within the reflexes of sight and thought, a theater untheorized, or theorized within the very veils and subterfuges of the theatrical itself, a theory blind to the theatricalities of its own presentations. In America the issue is a theater theory existing as merest absence, an absence that, in this period, renders the very idea of race meaningless, or rather, places race outside the very culture within which it seemingly exists.

The "outside" of race, then, is very much like the "outside" of gender or sexuality. If there is, following feminist/Lacanian notions of contingency, "no sexual relation" because, in part, woman-as-other resides forever "outside" the social constructions of gender, does it not follow that, in terms of dominant white culture, there is also no racial relation, no class relation, no Queer relation, and so on? Isn't, in fact, Queerness itself the expression of a nonrelation, a hollowing out of heterosexuality's presumed "naturalness"? But in the morass of these nonrelations, where, exactly, is the political, the political that is at some necessary level about relation in the broadest and most particular sense? Perhaps at this point we ought to question the applications of Lacanian theory to the political sphere. Perhaps the sociopolitical demands first of all the illusion of relations, a theater within which relation itself can at least be imagined and theorized.

And what does the lack of theater theory in American history index? The renitent history of American anti-intellectuality itself, a history that both desires and repudiates the theatrical, the enfant terrible, but will not locate its theatrical body in any body of theory as such nor within the theatrical frame as such, but, rather, in Other locations: novels and short stories, perhaps, or the cruel forms of minstrel theater. The desire for presence, for oracular speech[20] sounding beneath and against the graven word, or the presence of "real folk" behind the song and shuffle, is theater's moment: penetrating both word and presence, concealing and revealing the sightlines, the "gaze," the eye itself, the seeing that constitutes theater, the seeing that formulates theater's unconscious, concealed, as seeing always is, within the contours of the seen. Nowhere in American philosophy or art are these issues articulated with such power and profundity as in the works of Herman Melville.

Scrivening: Melville's Theater of Cruelty

In *Call Me Ishmael*, his idiosyncratic work on Melville's *Moby-Dick*, the poet Charles Olson wrote that "Melville prepared the way for *Moby-Dick* by ridiculing, in 1850, the idea that the literary genius in America would be, like Shakespeare, 'a writer of dramas.'"[21] And yet, as Olson later points out, and as Melville must certainly have seen, *Moby-Dick* is, at its hot heart, more theater than novel. In structure, which rises and falls like Elizabethan tragedy, as well as in action, stage direction, use of properties and voice, Melville's novel aligns itself, not with other contemporary novels, nor with drama, but with theater—not through mere textual allusions to Shakespeare, of which there are many, but through the impulse to action and seeming presence. The whale hunt, the heathen ravings in the storm, the frenzied performance on the quarterdeck, the physical appearance of the text itself, all point, Olson suggests, not to mere romance, but to Melville's rejection of, and corollary deep attachment to, the theaters of American consciousness.

Conceiving of Melville's book as theater, a theater opposed to "writing" or text, seems especially odd in a novel so self-consciously written. Every surface or plication in these pages is filled with inscription, carving, tattoo, signage, or writing. Indeed, this scripted excess becomes the very proposition of the book as book, which is nothing but inscription, endless and aboriginal writing that indicates in its profusion the unsignifiability of the enigma it recovers—Moby Dick, both whale and novel.[22]

The question of the book's conception, of where the work begins, moreover, is the question of language itself. For where, precisely are we to locate the novel's loomings? In its opening line? Indeed, the provisional enunciation "Call me Ishmael" (God hears)—the usual line chosen as the novel's beginning—begs the very self-interrogation that the writing pursues, for nowhere in the novel are we given sure evidence that Ishmael is indeed the narrator's "real" name. Or are we perhaps to go back further, to the line's etymology before the first entry in "Extracts" on whales, "supplied by a sub-sub-librarian"? Or perhaps back further, in "Etymology" itself and the multilingual forms of the word *whale* that emerge epiphanic on the page as the whale might breach from an indecipherable and enigmatic sea into apprehension, Artaud's "hairs standing on end." Or in the structure of the Grammar that frames it, the epiphany of a ghostly Kantian a priori, supplied "by a late consumptive usher to a grammar school"? Or perhaps even before this, in the drawn maps and sea-charts, or in the table of contents, itself an enigmatic manifest bubbling up from the try-pots of the unconscious, or the dedication to Hawthorne, that homoerotic pitfall, or the titling of the work itself?

Uncertain conception, fragmented parentage, narration by the "floating signification" of the self-designated Ishmaelite—we are left to question, finally, the enigmatic presence of the book as book, an enigma that aligns itself asymptotically with that graven, inscrutable body within the book, Moby Dick, a phallic linkage suggested by the copular hyphen in the book's title, a hyphen that appears nowhere else in the novel.[23] We see the ever-present writing in Queequeg's tattooed, cross-word-puzzled face, "stuck over with large, blackish looking squares," a face that is reinscribed later in the coffin/sea-chest/lifebuoy that saves Ishmael after "the drama's done"; we see the inscribed, paper-white brow and body of the whale, furrowed, and marked like Ahab's own whitened, wrinkled forehead; we see the lines disappearing on the surface of the sea in the *Pequod's* wandering wake, reinscribed on the charts and maps that spill over Ahab's table; we read it in Ahab's own body, struck and engraved from top to bottom by the lightning bolt; we note it in the strange tattooed skin of Tashtego, the other harpooneer, who reinscribes other blooded images into the flesh of his prey. There are signs and letters, Bibles and news stories. There is the likening of the whale to the Heidelburg Tun, that huge wine cask covered with centuries of graffiti and engravings. There is Queequeg's mark and the "hollow" of that mark,[24] there is the dark, indecipherable painting in the Spouter Inn. There is the Spanish ounce of gold, circled round with exotic markings, punctuated by a single nail to the quarterdeck mast and serving as a kind of Rorschach image that draws out the phantasms of seamen—the dream's navel—the image doubled in the nail's penetration of both ship and novel, into which all interpretation ends in false plenitude and exhaustion, the omphalos that operates, in Ernesto Laclau's words, as the "particular content [that] overflows its own particularity and becomes the incarnation of the absent fullness of society," the precise definition, Laclau tells us of the hegemonic relation, a relation that "presupposes the logic of the spectre," the domain of ghostings and illusion, placing hegemony squarely within the illusory frame of theater.[25] There are finally, and perhaps most emblematically, the engraved tablets of stone in the Whalemen's Chapel, a space of reflection where a "muffled silence" reigns, "only broken . . . by the shrieks of the storm,"[26] a theater whose multiple stages are the black-bordered tablets engraved with the "bitter blanks" that commemorate the drowned, tablets that represent, each inscription, an absent body gone beneath the surface of an indifferent sea,[27] absent bodies still voicing and voiced in the shrieking wind: engravings marking the passing of voice through the dying body.

And it is thus that the "writtenness" of the book at each turn is circumscribed by the spoken—what Olson calls "wild and whirling words." And this push toward the incantatory word, the wild ejaculation, the agonized cries and animalistic sobs, begins, as it does in any actor's Lear, with the near silent exhalation of breath. Here is Herbert Blau describing the voice of the actor in the theater:

> What is the voice? All we know is that something comes up through the nervous system which is incommunicable and disjunct, bereft of flesh once out of the body, silencing the body as it goes—all the more as it goes into language, which is the history from which it came. Even when not voiced, words inciting breath, breath becoming words in a remembrance of breath, voice giving voice, voicing.[28]

And so also in "Extracts," a textual premonition of this voicing from the travel writings of Richard Hakluyt becomes immediately overcast with the aspirations of the spoken voice:

> While you take in hand to school others, and to teach them by what name a whale-fish is to be called in our tongue, leaving out, through ignorance, the letter H, which alone maketh up the signification of the word, you deliver that which is not true. (1)

The implication, that the essential meaning of the word (and the thing it represents) resides in the pure audibility of the breath that speaks it— the aspiration of "the letter H"—appeals to a presence preceding the obdurately written word. The suggestion that such a missing letter/sound might "damage" the text and render it untrue suggests a truly performative moment, arising in the gap between word and enunciation, the space in which the truth of the play hangs by a phonological, epistemological thread.[29]

It is in that theatrical lapse that the writing of Melville's novel, the writing that points to its own inscription over and over again, is split.

The indicative desire of the book is not the desire for the body's sign, but for the Real body itself pulsing beneath the writing, the force of voice before language, the actor pivoting before us like Ahab on the boards, propelled by a Lacanian *jouissance*, the push of consciousness pursuing itself. The static "writtenness" of the book covers over this oracular theatricality that appears and dissolves through the pages like the wake from the *Pequod*'s prow, and functions, indeed, as the unconscious "text" in all of Melville's work. This concealment and activation of the performative by the written becomes a secondary inflection of the theatrical. The ruse or "play" of writing masks the theater in/of the novel's desire: the power and force of *Moby-Dick*'s most well known and arresting moments attesting to its desire for enactment, performance, or theater. So alongside, within, or prior to the "prisonhouse" of the written word is another insistence, another kind of tension—the human voice, seeking its substance, its body and origin, the disappearing voice that lifts itself, again and again, from the textual authoritarianism of the Book, and echoes across the water, "Hast seen it? Hast seen the White Whale?"

Hakluyt's insistence on aspiration in the word "whale," the injunction to breath and breath into language, suggests, within and without the registers of the unconscious, the absolute necessity for the spoken word in the apprehension of the enigma: "'What do ye do when ye see a whale, men?'" cries Ahab on the quarterdeck. "'Sing out for him!' was the impulsive rejoinder from a score of clubbed voices" (141). He who sings out receives the boon. The singing and the calling and the agonized wails resound throughout the book: "It was Moby Dick that dismasted me; Moby Dick that brought me to this dead stump I stand on now," moans Ahab, and then cries out in "a terrific, loud, animal sob" (143). The enigma that is the whale is the enigma of a vanishing presence, of speech, and the dispossessed power of the voice.

Indeed, as Ahab stands on the quarterdeck, preparing for the great performance that is to come (a performance, in fact, introduced by a stage direction, "Enter Ahab: Then, all"), the narrator notes his appearance, reading in his "ribbed and dented brow" the turmoil that is to come:

> But on the occasion in question, those dents looked deeper, even as his nervous step that morning left a deeper mark. And, so full of his thought was Ahab, that at every turn that he made . . . you

> could almost see that thought turn in him as he turned, and pace in
> him as he paced; so completely possessing him, indeed, that it all
> but seemed the inward mould of every outward movement. (141)

What is this but the most acute observation and desire of the actor? He
that has "that within which passes show," but must show it anyway in
the passing. This is the moment of conversion, externalizing, showing,
enacting—the whale breaching and breaking surface and thus apprehended in the circle of the eye, seen and then vanishing in the seeing,
the enigma that is death in life.

And this is but a warm-up exercise, for it is after that Ahab
launches into his pulsing, ritualistic, and hieratic performance, welding
the crew together in the shared communion of blood and gold, screw-
ing desire and courage to the iconic doubloon nailed to the om-phalic
mast, pegging the text to the crosstree like the stage managers of the
Renaissance theaters. The harpooneers cross lances, invoking the pro-
tocols of chiasmas, pledge their lives, and drink in the demonic theater
of Ahab's desire, the theater of death: death to the whale, death to
enigma, death to story and its theater, death to the unconscious and
desire itself. Ahab is, in this scene, the very image of the nineteenth-
century American actor, Edwin Forrest, perhaps, full of sound and
fury, "sawing the air" with his hands, raising his fist like Adam Trueman, "to strike through the mask" of mere appearance. He is, as Olson
puts it, echoing Artaud, "like a man cut away from the stake,"[30] reach-
ing through the flames for the lineaments of the knowable beyond the
strictures of reason: "how," Ahab asks, "can the prisoner reach outside
except by thrusting through the wall?" He seeks that which gives form
to thought and desire, "some unknown but still reasoning thing [that]
puts forth the mouldings of its features from behind the unreasoning
mask" (144). Something very like the unconscious itself. Or theater.

And then, as if to ratify the ontological entry into the logic of
appearances that we might call theater, we move from the stage of the
quarterdeck into a manifestly dramatic form. "Sunset" begins with a
another stage direction—"The cabin; by the stern windows; Ahab sitting alone, and gazing out" (146)—that introduces a long dramatic
monologue by Ahab. Ishmael, the seemingly original narrator, and
thus narrative impulse itself, is excluded by theatrical form and the
actor's voice. Ahab speaks, and the text does not mark off his speech
with quotation marks, or even a narrative introduction. We are hearing
Ahab's soliloquy spoken from the promptbook, the only interruption

the single stage direction that is recounted in the present tense (as stage directions generally are) midway through his speech: "waving his hand, he moves from the window." Then there is a scene change, and, in "Midnight, Forecastle," we find ourselves in the play-text, or the text as play. Dialogue is set in dramatic form. Stage directions are ubiquitous, as are songs, calls, and vernacular speech. Here the book is a virtual compendium of Brechtian gests, or nexus of voices clamoring in oracular song. It is in this scene that we hear from an entire constellation of characters that have been silent up to this point, voices from the interior, voices that will remain silent hereafter: an "Old Manx Sailor," a "St. Jago's Sailor," a "Sicilian Sailor," the presentation of a heteroglossic, multicultural, and ghostly crew, echoing the heteroglossic opening history in "Extracts," drawn from "the long vaticans and street stalls of the earth"—the history of the whale, human aspiration, in voice and song.

Following this dramatic scene, we are led to another monologue, this time by Ishmael, that picks up directly from the quarterdeck scene. We are listening to Ishmael speaking, again, without benefit of the novelistic convention of quotation marks or third-person reportage—and both voices, Ishmael's and Ahab's, seem, in different ways, to insist themselves as spoken speech, as "living" vital speech seemingly uninfected by the intrusion of narrative convention. Both monologues frame and contextualize the dramatic section of the book.

And yet this framed sounding is once again subverted by the chapter that follows: an ode to the fearful whiteness of the whale, an extension of Ishmael's voice, but a speech that becomes, once again, more like a sermon in tone and style, a warning about the emptiness of whiteness, the white rage of *The Octoroon*, the "colorless all-color" that encodes white culture's fear of its insubstance, and in that fear the terror of "the historically unstable constructs of gender and sexuality" as well.[31] Here, again, whiteness is constituted by what it is not in the same way that theater is constituted by what it is not (and here we include representation and its writings—and the seeing of writing— but more primarily and precisely the writing of seeing). In this way, then, theater is writing, subtends writing. It is, in a word, the writing of itself as text—novel as theater, but also theater as book.

And yet, despite the sheer theatrical power of the sermon on whiteness, the prior dramatic interlude recedes back into novelistic narrative, as if the drama were mere aberration from/within the narrative, a novelistic "slip of the tongue," or the appearance of some phantasm of presence within the literary work, like the *unheimlich* of dream. And then, a coda, something like a return of the repressed; the voice appears again as hallucinatory presence—the chapter "Hark!" in which the crew members hear the stowaway harpooneers, or think they do, and respond with the theatrical inquiry once again: "Hist! Did you hear that noise Cabaco?" (Did you hear? Have you seen?) while Ahab, like a demonic Dante seeing Christ reflected in the eye of Beatrice, sees the sun-god seeing the phantasm, Moby Dick: "Where is Moby Dick? This instant thou must be eyeing him. These eyes of mine look into the very eye that is even now equally beholding him; aye, and into the eye that is even now equally beholding the objects on the unknown, thither side of thee, thou sun!" (411–12). So he speaks peering through the keyhole of his quadrant, his words a psychotic inversion of Thomas Shepard's own rhetorical excess: Ahab, who earlier describes the ocean itself as a great green eye, gazing upward at the sky, seeing itself seeing in the very eye of God reflected in the sun's circle.

And here, finally, is the crucial turn: for aside from the sign of the whale itself, the book is circumscribed, circle within circle, hoop within hoop, by the recurring sign of the eye, which seemingly opens, like the writing and inscription that encodes it, on page after page, appearing and disappearing, closing finally, in the last image of the swirling whirlpool, sucking all down with it, the buttonlike black bubble at its center the eye's pupil, delivering to Ishmael from the vast formlessness of the sea beneath him the hollow vessel of his salvation: Queequeg's vacant, inscribed coffin, popping to the surface like an indecipherable letter from the interior.

Here and throughout, *Moby-Dick,* like the aura of an unnamable trauma, tempts to endless interpretation: eye and I, skyhawk and hammer, whale and sea, spar and harpoon, tattoo and scar, the milky sperm and its treacherous ooze, float before the reader's eye, each encircled therein, within the hoop of seeming sight. For all of its theatrical imagery—the compulsion to presence in the spoken word, the Dionysian frenzy on the quarterdeck, the Shakespearean asides and references, the uses of stage direction, and the promptbook form itself at the book's navel—it is the central presence of the eye, and the eye eyeing, that most profoundly circumscribes the book-as-theater, the eye the eye of the Other, in whose gaze "you meet not a seeing eye, but a blind one."[32]

And in the pupil of that eye, at the center of that hoop, holding and shaking his hooped tambourine, contained in and containing the circumference of the seen, dances the little minstrel Pip. Pip, little seed, Ahab's black seed, holder of the ring, cast adrift in the ocean, where his own eyelike "ringed horizon began to expand about him miserably" into madness. Pip, whose utter isolation in the pupil of God's eye (*pupil:* from *pupilla* fem., "orphan child, a child without a mother") brings him finally to "man's insanity" that is "heaven's sense":

> The sea had jeeringly kept his finite body up, but drowned the infinite of his soul. Not drowned entirely, though. Rather carried down alive to wondrous depths, where strange shapes of the unwarped primal world glided to and fro before his passive eyes, and the misermerman, Wisdom, revealed his hoarded heaps; and among the joyous, heartless, ever-juvenile eternities, Pip saw the multitudinous, God-omnipresent, coral insects, that out of the firmament of waters heaved the colossal orbs. He saw God's foot upon the treadle of the loom, and spoke it; and therefore his shipmates called him mad. (347)

And indeed, his madness echoes a passage from Hegel, quoted by Slavoj Žižek, in which Hegel invokes the night of the human mind, the other side of reason, and suggests that it is this night that best describes human consciousness:

> The human being is this night, this empty nothing, that contains everything in its simplicity—an unending wealth of many representations, images, of which none belong to him—or which are not present. This night, the inner of nature, that exists here—pure self—in phantasmagorical representations, is night all around it, in which here shoots a bloody head—there another white ghastly apparition, suddenly here before it, and just so disappears. One catches sight of this night when one looks human beings in the eye—into a night that becomes awful.[33]

Žižek explicates this night as "the point of utter madness in which phantasmic apparitions of 'partial objects' err around,"[34] in which, looking in the other's eye, we come to understand that the props of sanity are indeed the phantasms of madness. And so, in the other's eye we seem to disappear. We see this disappearance in Pip's incantation, and return a second time to this particular grammatical invocation of the theatrical:

"This way comes Pip—poor boy! would he had died, or I; he's half horrible to me. He too has been watching all of these inter-preters—myself included—and look now, he comes to read, with that unearthly idiot face. Stand away again and hear him. Hark!"

"I look, you look, he looks; we look, ye look, they look."

"Upon my soul, he's been studying Murray's Grammar!" (362)

But Pip's invocation to the seeing arises within the darkness of his own disappearance to himself. Here he speaks to the Manxman:

Pip? whom call ye Pip? Pip jumped from the whaleboat. Pip's miss-ing. Let's see now if ye haven't fished him up here, fisherman. It drags hard: I guess he's holding on. Jerk him, Tahiti! Jerk him off; we haul in no cowards here. Ho! there's his arm just breaking water. A hatchet! A hatchet! cut it off—we haul in no cowards here. Captain Ahab! sir, sir! here's Pip, trying to get on board again. (427)

Pip is a ghost, a part-object, Ahab's puppet and other, both detached and connected, an articulation. "[T]hou art tied to me by cords woven of my heart-strings," Ahab tells poor disappeared Pip, who, had he felt such love earlier (and the attendant demand that marks personhood), would "perhaps . . . ne'er been lost" (428). But now his image has been torn from him. In the terms of the Lacanian lamentation, he has become the hole in consciousness we call *Verwerfung* or foreclusion, psychosis or the "blackness of darkness." Pip, born of madness, becomes, in his rebirth as absence, like *Fashion*'s Gertrude or Herne's bastard child, yet another incarnation of the enfante terrible.

In his terror-stricken aspect, and his articulation against the *non du Pere*, Ahab, he also becomes Ahab's inversion: Ahab who, in his own self-absorbed blindness is all I devoid of eye, becomes Pip, who in his psychosis is all eye devoid of I, black as blackness itself, "standing in" as prop, covering the space of Ahab's lost leg, his displaced member: "No, no, no! ye have not a whole body, sir; do ye but use poor me for your one lost leg; only tread upon me, sir; I ask no more, so I remain a part of ye" (436). Pip, in other words, becomes the phallus, and in par-ticular, dis/replaces Ahab's phallus. The small black "boy" becomes the locus, like the giant white Moby Dick himself,[35] both of Ahab's *jouissance* and his castration—and in the scission, the nativity of the ter-rible child.

Act III: Convulsions

The stage wall is stuffed unevenly

with heads, throats; cracked, oddly

broken melodies.

—Antonin Artaud

5

What Child Is This? O'Neill, Albee, Shepard, and the Body of the Repressed

Slavoj Žižek, commenting on the appearance (or misappearance) of "the sublime object of desire" in the films of Luis Buñuel, writes that "what the object is masking, dissimulating, by its massive, fascinating presence, is not some other positivity, but *its own place,* the void, the lack that it is filling in by its presence—the lack in the Other."[1] The "object of desire"—at once banal, but also the "cover" for the real "object" that is itself the now ubiquitous Lacanian "lack in the Other"— frames itself within a space of desire already in place to receive it. Indeed, earlier Žižek reminds us of the Lacanian logic of such an object, in which "the place logically precedes objects which occupy it." The space that precedes all objects, the frame that organizes materiality within the concealed authorial power of being/watched, is, of course, theater, but it is also the historical remembrance of the tragic.

But what, specifically, does the tragic represent here? Walter Benjamin, in *The Origin of German Tragic Drama,* discusses the tragic as a split in history between an older ideological tradition and a new one, not unlike the Foucauldian rupture, an epistemic split in whose gap stands the tragic hero, riven between the two worlds. The tragic, then, is the poststructural split or rupture in history and self with its repressed element of terror and pain restored.

Today, among the many and varied ideological categories split by the tragic and Imaginary modern/poststructural divide, arguably none is more central than the problem of subjectivity, in which the cogito— long seen within the traditions of the Enlightenment as the arbiter of the subject/self's unity and cohesion—is, in the poststructural mode, multiple, fragmentary, decentered, contingent, even illusory.[2] This subjective contingency is often presumed to be, out of Lacan, for example, the source of confusion and anxiety in the self, as well as the source of countless sociocultural forms of oppression; the mythic agency of subjectivity is what allows for the very possibility of domination and submission. Given the present study's engagement with these same or similar categories—*aphanisis*, the blank space of desire, absence, the lack in the Other—it ought to be obvious that I am not swimming counter to the poststructural trend that views the self/subject as generically deficient, wounded, or fragmented. I am, however, eager to recall this subject's other source of agony and fear: the obdurate real of the self. Indeed, especially in the present case, through all of the shiftings and decenterings and aphanises, we have to wonder, if, at the edges of cultural analysis, the site of contingency is the real scene at all. Perhaps the real scene might be something akin to the self as black hole—a seeming rip in the substance of culture-consciousness that acts like a lack—a zero-mass that is in fact the site of an infinite density—the hard kernel of the self's impenetrability that we can ascribe to "the lack in the Other," but that often feels less a lack than a burden.

This is the burden of *subjection*, of being subject to (guilt, pain, remorse), a term that invokes the older sense of subjectivity: not mere individuality, but "appendagehood," being subject to the monarch, for example, or to the laws of the church. This older sense of the word suggests the *cost* of subjectivity, the sacrifice of one's body, the endurance of pain and servitude that the earlier work of Foucault suggests, but does not, indeed cannot, dwell upon. The repression of subjectivity's "other side"—self as site of guilt, pain, and remorse, entails confusion about the phenomenological experience of selfhood, as well as confusion about the category of subjectivity itself. Ute Guzzoni, pondering the state of "deconstructive subjectivity," states her desire *for* a decentered, insubstantial self, a desire that seemingly springs from the guilt of accumulated political sins:

> Do we still want to be subjects? In my view, no. As subjects Europeans discovered and colonized foreign continents, Christians converted other peoples, men disciplined their wives, and husbands and wives disciplined their children.[3]

But while the desire for subjectivity's end, couched within the call for responsible sociopolitical behavior, is clear enough, what is most interesting is that the examples of subjectivity's excesses are located not within the realm of the individual subject at all, but rather within the realm of *the collective:* the nation, the church, and the family. This confusion, representative of current concern with subjectivity cum collective, is revealing. It bespeaks a deconstructive cross-contamination in which the subject is "always already" defined by, disappears into, the culture within which she speaks, while that same culture in turn speaks with the seemingly unified voice of subjectivity. Culture seems to disappear within the voice of the individual. This is, of course, an ancient issue, going back at least to Plotinus. However, the current version of this problem is that while we acknowledge the material existence of history and culture as *force* (evanescent though it may be), we tend to dismiss subjectivity as vapid, nonexistent, mere "subject position."[4] But if we acknowledge the material existence of the cultural, political, and ideological forces that *construct* "subject positions," we must also acknowledge the material existence of subjectivity as something of its own unified force, as something more than mere contingency. On the other hand, if we discount the subject as multiple, fragmented, and decentered, we must, it seems to me, also acknowledge the collective as such: the collective—cultural, political, racial—as an ego-ideal prone to the same fictions and self-delusions as any other ego-ideal.

This "contingency of culture" has been acknowledged in the work of Bhabha, Butler, and Laclau and Mouffe, but, in my estimation, unconvincingly. The real center of gravity in much current theoretical discourse is weighted against the substance of subject and for the "truth" of culture. Thus while it remains possible for us to discuss the voices/attitudes/appearances of cultures *as-if* they were unified and whole, the individual is silenced through a self-enforced conformity.[5] Alain Finkielkraut writes:

> [S]upporters of a multicultural society demand the right of everybody to wear a uniform. . . . Then, in a singular feat of reasoning, they present as the ultimate achievement of individual freedom the absolute dominance of the collectivity: "To help the immigrants, we must first of all respect them as they are and as they want to be according to their national identity, their cultural specificity, their spiritual and religious heritage." But what if a culture teaches people to inflict corporal punishment on delinquents, to reject barren women, to kill adulterous women, to consider the testimony of one man the same as the testimony of two women. . . ?[6]

In other words, the infliction of political repression emerges not out of some center within a seemingly integrated, unified subject, but from the collective, from the very cultural groups and subgroups that are the defining force of "subject position." Within the confusions of identities, the potential for political repression in the name of multicultural liberation looms large:

> In a world deserted by transcendence, fanatics no longer evoke the name of God to justify barbaric customs; they call on identity politics instead. Unable to appeal to heaven, they defend their beliefs with history and difference. . . . It was at the expense of their culture that European individuals gained, one by one, all their rights. In the end it is the critique of tradition that constitutes the spiritual foundation of Europe, a fact the philosophy of decolonization has let us forget by persuading us that the individual is nothing more than a cultural phenomenon.[7]

The final result of such muddled and childish thinking, according to Finkielkraut (the inability to take on the somber weight of responsibility, the weight of ethical action contra the insubstance of self, the difficult business of negotiation and compliance or self-sacrifice), is the relinquishing of critical thought, the closing off of the Symbolic and the surrender to the Imaginary—the condition of perpetual childhood:

> [W]hat passes today for communication attests to the fact that the non-verbal hemisphere [of the brain] won out: music videos over conversation. Society has "finally become adolescent." The huge [rock] concerts may not have succeeded in getting relief to the victims of famine in Ethiopia, but they did establish an international hymn: "We are the world, we are the children."[8]

And although Lacan might cast a jaundiced eye at such calls for self-abnegation, there is in his work a corollary demand for the eradication of this same child: the child that represents the inability to act. This fixation with the paralyzed child-self, the decentered and contingent self as hidden object of desire, takes on a particular resonance on the stages of modern American theater. Emerging from the cradled "realism" of Herne's theatrical ideology, refracted through the psychotic vision of the child in Melville and the child-man of minstrel culture, the Imaginary child—the literal object of reproduction—operates as a fulcrum in the struggle for apprehension. This struggle ends, in each case, in the death/disappearance of the infant, as in O'Neill's *Desire under the Elms* and Edward Albee's *Who's Afraid of Virginia Woolf?* and with the grim resurrection of the repressed in Sam Shepard's *Buried Child*. The enfants terrible represent, in each case, a space of theatrical terror—the terror of contingencies, certainly, but also the terror of *huit clos*, no escape from the demands of selfhood into the safe confinement of a "subject position."

Oedipal *Spit and Image:* Mimesis *and* Excretio Seminis *Redux*

In the spiraling contexts of the current study, Eugene O'Neill's anachronistic *Desire under the Elms* plays Janus-faced. The dramatic text, shocking in its (more or less) sympathetic approach to incest and infanticide, is intractably modern, but it also looks back at itself as both theater and history, pulling from theater/history its own image of itself displaced. Set in New England in 1850, the play evokes both the time and the locale of Rip's village in Jefferson's *Rip Van Winkle*, Adam Trueman's farm in Ritchie's *Fashion*, and, indicating a lineage of time and locale stretching back to Federalist culture itself, the home of Jonathan and Manley in Tyler's *The Contrast*—the Appalachian valleys of the northeast United States, meager land concealing an unspoken history of political resistance and discord buried in its soil. From Shays's Rebellion in the late eighteenth century to the Anti-Renter movement some sixty years later and beyond, the history of this region has been intimately tied to the brutal working conditions of its tenant farms, and the blood of class warfare fought against the duplicities of landowners and politicians.

The play itself, in its form and disposition, seems also a re-etching of the concerns with duplicity and authenticity, coiled up within a kind of aphasia similar to what we find in *The Contrast*. But here the issues are not so funny. The play, which begins with a barely contained Oedipal animosity between brothers and father, moves inexorably toward both lurid desire and violence in the meeting of son Eben and newly arrived (step)mother, Abbey. Sibling rivalry quickly escalates to virtual political intrigue focused on the sexual economy of Abbie's body, the locus of the Real. Though the issues addressed in the play-text are not overtly political, the political is deflected into the registers of the psychic in the Oedipal struggle between sons and father, a struggle that takes on political timbres in the questions raised about both paternity and patriarchy flayed in the cross-cut between desire and repression. The play represents, at some level, the Oedipal struggle of the nation, trying to define its independence through *incorporation*.[9]

The medium of the play's repressive action is tied, as it is in other O'Neill plays, to speech-act—or more specifically, to dialect or enunciation—and image, or more exactly, reference *to* image. Accents, and idiomatic peculiarities, difficult at times to decipher, operate as a kind of cover-up. In the opening scene, for example, the two older brothers are discussing ways of getting their father's farm away from him. They wish him dead and then consider whether they might have him committed:

> PETER: Left us in the fields an evenin' like this. Hitched up an' druv off into the West. That's plum onnateral. He hain't never been off this farm 'ceptin t' the village in thirty year or more, not since he married Eben's maw. *(A pause. Shrewdly)* I calc'late we might git him declared crazy by the court.
> SIMEON: He skinned 'em too slick. He got the best o' all on 'em. They'd never b'lieve him crazy. *(a pause)* We got t' wait—till he's under ground.
> EBEN: *(with sardonic chuckle)* Honor thy father! *(They turned startled, and stare at him. He grins, then scowls)* I pray he's died. *(They stare at him. He continues matter of factly)* Supper's ready.
> SIMEON and PETER: *(together)* Ay-eh.[10]

The single response, "Ay-eh"—dialogue rendered as ejaculation—is used incantatorily throughout the play. Here it represents repressed insight and emotion, an assent to unrecognized desire. All of the murderous duplicity hidden from Ephraim, the father, lies concealed in that single, split and doubled, dialogic affirmative. Are they responding to supper being served, or to their shared desire for the father's death? The denial at the opening of the next scene ("Looky here! Ye'd oughtn't 't said that, Eben") merely underscores the ambiguity of the older brothers' feelings.

The dialect of the play operates repressively in a larger sense as well: employed by O'Neill to convey "local color" and thus the "American" quality of the characters, the text seems, rather, a fairly clumsy rendering of what was apparently an accent typical of northern Maine in O'Neill's own time—a dialogic weakness in some of O'Neill's other plays as well. O'Neill, then, reimagines a dialect from the 1850s that he has (or we have) no knowledge of; he reproduces an Imaginary dialect—a marginal or displaced *parole*—that conceals, by O'Neill's own admission, as much as it reveals. Some of the words are, at first sight, almost indecipherable ("A good step maw's scurse"? "he turned out a drunken spreer"?), while in one notable case O'Neill uses "eye dialect," a way of writing dialect that, while presenting the unique pronunciations of region or time, also rewrites words that are *not* pronounced in nonstandard ways, in order to produce the *effect* of dialect—"what air yew cacklin' about?" Eben says to Abbie, who is mocking his formal Sunday dress. "Yew!" Abbie replies. The presentation of the word *yew* for *you* is an example of eye dialect—the two words are pronounced the same way, but spelled differently in order to create the impression that "you/yew" is spoken in dialect. What is interesting in this particular instance of eye dialect is that it is virtually the *only* instance. *Yew/you* is virtually the only word that undergoes this type of subterfuge throughout the play,[11] and it is the word used to project the objective self, the "you" masked, as it were, concealed beneath the image of the rough-hewn American farmer, himself the epitome of what we might call "I dialect"—the theatrical formulation of identity through cultural repetition. "Eye dialect," then, or "I dialect" is the linguistic equivalent of Trueman's rustic costume, which serves both to present the "image" of the true American and to conceal, in its objectifying, displacing function, the reality of American nonexistence. "Yew" is not a translation or stand-in for *you*, but rather the space of the self's disappearance. It is the linguistic equivalent of the stage upon which the self is both reproduced and disappears, the stage upon which the unreality of the American is repressed beneath the seeming authenticity of the dialect that creates his image. The shifting stages of the pronomial here supplant the Oedipal/political struggle.

At other times in the play, however, the repressed takes on almost literal concrete form. From the first scene, for example, with its evocative image of Ephraim and his sons toiling on the farm, "making walls—stone atop o' stone—making walls till yer hearts' a stone ye heft up out o' the way o' growth onto a stone wall t' wall in yer heart," the play is a relentless portrayal of such hardened, screwed-down emotions: bottled-up lusts, contempt, greed, and barely restrained rage.

The forms of the Oedipal emerge through the actions of the sons, and more specifically the youngest son, Eben, who desires the death of the father in order to assume his place as owner and head of the farm.

Eben takes Ephraim's wife—his stepmother—as his lover and begets a child with her in an apparently unconscious stratagem to dethrone his father and insure his own inheritance. Ephraim thinks the child his own and decides to bequeath the farm to him, thus actually bequeathing it indirectly to Eben, through Eben's son. Meanwhile, the anima compelling Eben's actions, his dead mother, moves through the textures of the play as specter—that state of (non)being which Derrida identifies as the liminal space of Capital—a specter that, in some sense demands incorporation. Thus in the body of the infant and in the ghost of Eben's mother, we glimpse the movement toward the embodiment of an incestuous desire that produces, in the end, the mere specter of that incorporation—the presence, in mere appearance itself, of death. The actual movement toward incorporation, though, occurs, as it does in the realms of Capital, through the mechanisms of repression—itself an in-corporation of (denied) desire as symptom. O'Neill himself states the thematic of repression as the leitmotif of the play, the "inhibited life lust" of New England (read Puritan) culture. Ephraim senses the repressed in almost visible form: "Even the music can't drive it out— somethin'. Ye kin feel it droppin' off the elums, climbin' up the roof, sneakin' down the chimney, pokin' in the corners!" (3.2). Of course, the "somethin'" that Ephraim senses is embodied in the child that sleeps silently in the upstairs bedroom. The child represents nothing less than the incarnation of the repressed, the reproduced body of desire hidden from sight. The corollary to this body in Capital would be something like the cultural, unsignifiable desires of hegemony, certainly, but beyond this, the in-corporation of death-as-object.

What is of particular interest here, then, is the placement of the child within the Oedipal net. Like *Margaret Fleming* before, and Albee's *Who's Afraid of Virginia Woolf?* and Shepard's *Buried Child* after, the ontological status of the child becomes a central issue in the play. Whereas in *Margaret Fleming* social responsibility determines the shifting status of the adopted son, the issue is not so clear in the more recent plays. Indeed, the issue of uncertain paternity, a more properly psychosexual and existential anxiety, is often overlooked in *Desire*. Certainly Ephraim would have some reason to believe the child his; despite his literal and Oedipal blindness, he does not seem a man so prone to self-delusion that he would think his wife could conceive without having sex. She presumably has had intercourse with him, in which case the paternity of the nameless child is radically uncertain. The child in O'Neill's play is thus doomed to certain illegitimacy, is doomed, in fact, to a kind of inescapable false existence. If incestuously conceived, it is falsely Ephraim's. If not, if it is in fact Ephraim's son, it is still the child of deceit and subterfuge, and Abbie and Eben will still believe it to be theirs.

This Oedipal blindness of Ephraim ("Them eyes o' your'n can't see that fur") marks the edge of a *critical* misapprehension, a thoughtlessness aptly represented by Ephraim's continual threats to blow Eben's brains up into the elms. But while we quickly catch on to the many references to Ephraim's poor eyesight and cast him in the Oedipal role, it is easy to overlook (our Oedipal blindness) the fact that it is Eben who is more properly cast in the role of the father from the very beginning of the play when he buys his brother's share of the farm and becomes— in another uncertain patristic relationship—the sole owner of the farm that Eben claims was his mother's. Moreover, he and Abbie, like many viewers, readers, and critics of the play, seem to forget the real possibility that the child is not theirs, but belongs instead to Ephraim and Abbie's union. Ephraim's recognition of Abbey's duplicity late in the play ("ye lied—holding' herself from me—sayin' ye'd already conceived"), with its shifting pronoun and elliptical meaning, only confuses the issue more. When Abbie murders the child at the end of the play, we are not certain whom she has murdered—Eben's son or brother, Ephraim's son or grandson, her own son or grandson.[12] The namelessness of the child thus comes to represent or *reproduce* its own nonexistence, a nonexistence that is underscored by the literal absence in the play of the baby-as-sign, the baby who is never seen, even as a bundled prop, and never heard, however hard we may listen. And the listening is the crucial stance. As Serge Leclaire, in *A Child Is Being Murdered*, has it:

> Analytical listening implies bringing into play the spot of silence that is the place of transference. What is given there is the space for a real act of intelligence in terms of the logic of exclusion, a passage beyond the web of representatives, a way of passing through the mirror.[13]

This opening of the analytic space, the space that I have called theater, demands of the theorist "a knowledge of *what speaking means*, what decisive shadows words can hide."[14] This is crucial to understanding the image of the murdered child, because "[w]ords are prey to the universal work of repression in which every family unit, group, or social 'order,' takes part, and they never stop reverting to muteness."[15] This process of listening to muteness, of seeing in speech or silence what is being spoken, hinges on the very image of a silent child, the *in-fans:*

> Here another side of the killing-the-child phantasy: by naming the child *in-fans,* the discourse of repression pounces on the fact that he does not use words, so it can make of him, unfairly, the one who does not speak. It is true that it would be convenient for princes, parents, and teachers of all sorts if each "subject" were only to repeat faithfully what he is told and if the child did not disturb the order of repression by speaking the truth. . . . The little interloper must be made to behave, to look, precisely like the picture of good behavior.[16]

This is the "first killing" that signals the subject's unending struggle to possess herself by breaking through the silencing function of the collective, to become a subject within her own subject position, to reject the position of the *infans.* Here, again, we see a redirection away from the purely sociopolitical Lacanian discourse of the subject. In Leclaire, at least, the need to reconstitute and resituate the subject becomes the first, and, ironically, the primary political concern; the subject, in fact, becomes the primal political reality: a subject who, in the registers of "subject position" has been silenced and continues in its infantilization.

In O'Neill's play, this *infans,* absence of speech/speech-as-absence, is represented by a body that is not there. There is no baby, and the reproduction the baby represents is not reproduced in the play. The infant itself thus comes to represent some level or formation of symbolic self-cancellation, an aphasia, both in the play and in the play's history. The representation of the infant as an embodiment of failed responsibility—Eben's responsibility both to his father and Abbey, Abbey's failed responsibility as wife and mother to Eben—remains cradled in silence, as does the representation of the infant as production itself. The baby, the linchpin of Ephraim's plan to redistribute his wealth as he pleases, and the linchpin also of Eben's plan to thwart his father's desire while satisfying his own—this fulcrum for the machinations of a desire driven purely by Capital is silenced. The repressed content of capitalism remains unspoken, a tragic deficiency delivered to death by a psychotic mother.

In an inversion and foreshadowing of the death of the child by its mother, the suggestion of the unending chain of the production-of-death, Eben speaks of his own mother's death from overwork at the hand of his father:

> PETER: *(after a pause—judicially)* She was good even t' him.
> EBEN: *(fiercely)* An' fur thanks he killed her!
> SIMEON: *(after a pause)* No one never kills nobody. It's allus some-
> thin'. That's the murderer. (1.2)

The *somethin'* that murders Eben's mother, the *somethin'* represented by the silent, absent body of the murdered infant, the *somethin'* that is "pokin' about in the dark," represents the insubstantial substance of the repressed. A rage at the heart of things moves beyond the linea-ments of the social entirely—outside gender, outside race, outside sex-uality, outside history, the very "outside" that cancels the possibility of human relation. A rage threatens, in fact, to erase the social, a rage born of unspeakable desire: the psychosis of mourning, perhaps, sensed in the ghosted presence of Eben's Maw.

Here we might begin to sense the more powerful lineations of that absent figure of Maw who is maw, a silent and cavernous hungering belly at play's center, the consuming other of Capital's re-production. Eben is, after all, his Maw's "spittin' image," her double—a labor pro-duction that Derrida equates with trauma and its mourning:

> Mourning always follows a trauma. I have tried to show elsewhere that the work of mourning is not one kind of work among others. It is work itself, work in general, the trait by means of which one ought perhaps to reconsider the very concept of production.[17]

Whatever traumatic significance the absent mother may have had for O'Neill himself, the maw in *Desire under the Elms* crosses back and forth over the Imaginary boundary between Oedipal desire and the desires of Capital. These desires are unleashed by the hungering maw, the maternal phallus that overruns the failed *Nom du Père* in the play, Ephraim, who as "Paw" (the bestial hand gesturing the ineffectual paternal "No"? The morpheme separated from the Maw by the silent difference between the phonemes \p\ and \m\, voiced and unvoiced, labial-plosive and labial-fricative?) cannot break the bond between Eben and his dead mother, even after he kills her. Here, as in Lacan, the breakdown of the paternal function, so sought after in the theoretical landscapes of poststructural thought, the erasure of enforced patriarchal distance between child and Imaginary mother, also represents the breakdown of critical function, a closing off of the symbolic. This closure represents both Eben's and Abbey's inability to control desire, both libidinal and murderous, through the structuring principles of the symbolic order. The failure of the Oedipal relation, far from undermining the systems of Capital, produces the myriad psychotic orders of production themselves—the "child-who-is-being-beaten" and murdered, the reproduction of the Unholy Family, the reestablishment, at play's end, of the fetishized farm as commodity. "It's a jim-dandy farm, no denyin'," says the sheriff. "Wished I owned it myself."

It is interesting, finally, that in the Derridean terrain of spectrality, which I mentioned above, it is spectrality itself—here the spectral presence of Eben's dead mother, but also the spectral presence of desire— that links itself to the *jouissance*[18] of O'Neill's text, the "something" that does the murder, that lurks in the corners of perception, just out of reach, in the darkness. The "something" of desire that analysis calls the "little o other" *(petit objet a)*, desire's object, mutates through the plays of this period into an Other monstrous desire, the desire for enormity.

Spitting Nails

The "psychotic anxiety" embodied in the absent-present *infans* is also the anxiety that Walter Davis identifies as the driving force of another American play constructed upon the absent body of a theatrical infant, Albee's *Who's Afraid of Virginia Woolf?*[19]

In many ways, Albee's play is a dismal recapitulation and inversion of the earlier comedy of manners, a kind of tragedy of bad manners sustained through lacerating jokes and sadistically witty repartee. George, a history professor, and his wife, Martha (who is also the daughter of the university president—another Oedipal standoff) entertain a new faculty member and his wife, Nick and Honey, in their home after a late-night party has ended. The play is virtually plotless. The "story" that is told through the action is actually many stories, and the stories themselves are subsumed within the "play" of sarcasm, derision, and insult. The drama, then, very much like the play in the comedies of manners, is the play of language, wit, and visual subterfuge: the re-play of theater itself. In this sense *Who's Afraid of Virginia Woolf?* quickly moves outside the circumscription of any single critical approach and forces us to confront the violence of theater itself as the driving "meaning" of the play.

Indeed, Davis, who has written the definitive psychoanalytic reading of this play, tries quite specifically in his analysis to move beyond the commonplaces of current critical theory in order to demonstrate that the play points to a rupture and violence far deeper than the mere *ressentiment* of political ideology—a terror rooted within the marrow of the bones, a genetic terror that in fact threatens to obliterate history. George, a historian by profession, names this terror: it is the terror of the historical-materialist in the face of the genetic inevitability of death. George cryptically and elliptically refers to it as "Historical Inevitability": "he's quite terrifying, with his chromosomes, and all,"[20] he says of Nick the biologist, punning both on the genetic virility Nick seemingly displays and the ominous world of genetic, cloned inevitability that his profession represents. Nick represents a world in which biological stability and predictability threaten to eradicate all difference, what we might, ironically, call life itself.

The threat against difference, the threat against disruption, rupture, transgression itself is, in the context of the play, a threat against the lives of George and Martha themselves—lives that are defined precisely through a seemingly endless succession of disruptions, instabilities, and unpredictabilities. George's attacks on Nick throughout the play thus "stand in" once again for a lack, the want in George and Martha's life that constitutes it: the thing missing in their marriage that makes their marriage the unique thing that it is, the thing missing that keeps their "psychotic anxiety" at bay, the terror of nothingness. This missing thing is, and is represented by, the Imaginary child that George and Martha procreate, the anointed illusion that holds not only their relationship, but their sanity, in place.

Even though this is "merely" an illusory child, it is a child troubled and troubling nonetheless. Late in the play, George and Martha describe their illusory progeny in minute and heartbreaking detail:

GEORGE: . . . nightmares . . .
MARTHA: . . . *sleep.* . . He was a restless child . . .
GEORGE: . . . *(Soft chuckle, head-shaking of disbelief)* . . . Oh Lord . . .
MARTHA: . . . sleep . . . and a croup tent . . . a pale green croup
    tent, and the shining kettle hissing in the one light of the room
    that time he was sick . . . those four days . . . and animal crackers, and the bow and arrow he kept under his bed . . .
GEORGE: . . . the arrows with rubber cups at their tip . . .
MARTHA: . . . at their tip, which he kept beneath his bed . . .

GEORGE: Why? Why, Martha?
MARTHA: . . . for fear . . . for fear of . . .
GEORGE: For fear. Just that: for fear. (219)

Indeed, the ground of their aggression in the play centers most profoundly and distressingly on their varying perceptions of parental relationship to the absent child: George attacks Martha for an incestuous
desire and portrays her as the proverbial smothering mother whose
concern for her son is driven by sexual predation. Martha, on the other
hand, locates the Imaginary child's terror in disgust and rage at his
weak, ineffectual father, in his Oedipal desire to murder that father.
The thematics of desire in O'Neill's play have returned; once again the
Oedipal relation has been seemingly overturned with disastrous
results, but here we begin to sniff out the more profound terror: it is not
merely the reversal of the Oedipal relation that invites catastrophe, but
any relation, any *human* relation, because all human relation continuously threatens to reveal itself as nonexistence.

Nick and Honey, the "guests" who bear witness to the excoria-
tions of George and Martha, also undergo their own Passion play
when George, using the information Nick has given him while chat-
ting during Honey's first absence, reveals that their relationship is
also built upon a nonexistent child, a false pregnancy. George, retali-
ating for his own humiliation at the hands of Martha, relates Honey
and Nick's story in fairy-tale form: "The Mouse got all puffed up one
day, and she went over to Blondie's house, and she stuck out her
puff, and she said . . . look at me!" Honey uses the false pregnancy to
coerce Nick into marriage, after which the "the puff went away . . .
like *magic* . . . pouf!" Nick and Honey's nonexistent child, like the
unseen, unnamed child in O'Neill's play, occupies "real" Imaginary
space. Honey's belly enlarges, Nick tells us, then deflates ("She blew
up, and then she went down" [94]). Like Eben, Abbie, and Ephraim,
who each and alone gazes into the womblike cradle at the absent
child, the characters in Albee's play also encircle a fascinated and
repressed primal scene—not the dimmed vision of copulating parents, though, but the dazzling, psychotic space of theater. The ontological status of the child in both plays is aligned with Žižek's discussion of the space of the Other: "[I]f we subtract from the illusion the
illusion itself (its positive content) what remains is not simply nothing, but a determinate nothing, the void in the structure which
opened the space for the 'illusion.' "[21]

The scene during which George and Martha's child is both born and dies is, in fact, rife with the epistemologies of this illusory space, this theater. Albee sets up the final unmaskings (if you can call them that) in a brief exchange between George and Nick that bristles with the suggestion of a Lacanian psychotic state:

> NICK: I'll play the charades like you've got 'em set up . . . I'll play in your language . . . I'll be what you say I am.
> GEORGE: You are already . . . you just don't know it. (150)

From this point on the illusions and delusions are seemingly exposed and rejected: "You're deluded . . . Martha, you're deluded," says George, after Martha insists it is George's desire that she humiliate him, not hers: "I thought you were at least on to yourself" (153). This is, of course, ironic, inasmuch as Martha is in nearly every theatrical sense of the word "on," in every sense, that is, but the crucial sense—she is not "on" to her self, to her "subject position." Correspondingly, she objects, "I'm on to myself" and in the splitting between I and me sets in motion the shift into misappearances that characterizes the final scene. Before the final anagnoresis occurs, however, Nick, who at this point displaces the audience/reader as the victim of the theatrical play between Martha and George, expresses disbelief when Martha claims George as the one true love of her life. Martha responds:

> MARTHA: You don't believe it.
> NICK: *(mocking)* Why, of course I do.
> MARTHA: You always deal in appearances? (190)

Nick, the scientist, the empiricist, is duped because he believes what he sees. The game seems real, and so it must be. But he never asks himself the question that would confound the empiricist in the world of appearances: what would a "real" game be? How would a "real" game appear to be different from a false one? Moreover, Martha's insight into "mere appearances" is not as simple as it may at first seem. Martha is not claiming that the aggression she and George direct toward one another is merely make-believe, but that what *is* occurring is far more complex and inexplicable than Nick knows *because* it seems so real. When she "unmasks the illusion" for him, she is in no way claiming that the aggression is "fake," or that her disgust for George is unreal. Again, Žižek on illusion:

To "unmask" the illusion does not mean that "there is nothing to see behind it": what we must be able to see is precisely this *nothing as such*—beyond the phenomena, there is nothing *but this nothing itself, "nothing" which is the subject*. To conceive the appearance as "mere appearance" the subject effectively has to go beyond it, to "pass over" it, but what he finds there is his own act of passage.[22]

Hence when Martha tells George that he is "nothing," and that she "can't come together with nothing," when she tells him, "I watched you, and *you* weren't *there!*" (158), she is not merely expressing her disgust at his "worthlessness," but at his state of radical nonbeing, which eventually threatens *her* very being, inasmuch as she has her self only in him, in her attacks on him. As Walter Davis suggests, this is the inverse of what we think of as "true love" born of devotion. It is also, reading Martha's lines through the words of Žižek, an acknowledgment, once again, of the failure of symbolic thought, a failure to account for the nothing brooding behind the materiality of theory, theater.

George, however, has a bit more understanding of the workings of disappearance and illusion. He understands their intractability when the final exchange between him and Martha occurs, set up, once again, by Nick, functioning as surrogate audience:

> NICK: Hell, I don't know when you people are lying, or what.
> MARTHA: You're damned right!
> GEORGE: You're not supposed to.
> MARTHA: Right. (200)

This, among other possible interpretations is the explicit pronouncement of the theatrical "hauntology": the appearance of the lie masquerading as truth, truth told in the costume of illusion, the inability *outside the theater* to know truth from illusion, a distinction itself born in and through the theaters of consciousness. Both Martha and George understand the "game," the constant elusion, the fantasy that turns madness into life, the tragic state of mind that stands impotent before the quandary.

Yet though she sees the "game" and its contours, Martha herself does not understand the violence of the illusion, the violence of the *theater* as George does. "Truth and illusion. Who knows the difference, eh, toots? Eh?" he says to her. Martha responds, "You were never in the Mediterranean . . . truth or illusion . . . either way." At this point the truth/illusion binary becomes nearly incantatory: "Truth and illusion, George; you don't know the difference." "No; but we must carry on as though we did." And again, "Truth or illusion, George. Doesn't it matter to you . . . at all?" George responds with word and action, "SNAP! *(Silence)* You got your answer, baby?" (201–4).

And the answer *is*, in some sense, "baby." The description of George and Martha's "child," a child born within the very space of truth/illusion and the limen of that space, now takes center stage. The child is born of illusion (George and Martha's fantasy), born within an illusion (the play itself), and so embodies the Real of illusion itself, but illusion repressed, disappeared by proclamation. What is repressed within the body of the imaginary infant again is the space of theater—the singular illusion that proclaims itself to be nothing more *than* illusion.

Here we can shift registers and resituate this repressed in a different, if somewhat more obvious frame: the play's references to American culture and history. The parents of this imaginary child are named George and Martha, after all, the father and mother of our country seen large through the lens of history-as-narrative, the narrative of greatness, national unity born of a patriotic, prototypic, and Imaginary nuclear family. George is also a historian, a man "preoccupied with history," and an academic, indeed a putative historicist in today's disposition, locked, unlike many contemporary historicists, in mortal combat with illusion, or with the inability to tell, both personally and historically, truth from illusion, suggesting in the final scenes of the play that the distinction is, in the "solutions" of pragmatism, only and merely academic. Thus once again, at the heart of the play lay the corpse of the repressed, the stillborn space of theater misrecognized, infant illusion done in by an alcoholic historian.

The structure and through-line of the play are, in many respects, archival. The action and development move through a series of dredging operations of memory and confabulation, and a revisitation of the ubiquitous American amnesia, beginning with Martha trying to remember a movie title ("What a dump. Hey, what's that from? 'What a dump!'" [3–4]), George and Martha referencing previous games ("Just don't start on the bit, that's all" [18]), Nick recounting the conditions of his courtship and marriage to Honey, all overlaid with George's pronounced "preoccupation with history" and the unseen presence of the *Nom du Père*, Martha's father, who is himself possessed of a "sense of history . . . of . . . continuation" (79).

But what are we to make of this history whose substance is illusion, whose figuration *in* the play is mere repetition (the play, after all, ends with a suggestion of future performances before other guests, other audiences)? We should, perhaps, at this point reexamine my original suggestion that the substance of George and Martha's life together is predicated on a sort of Foucauldian rupture. This, it seems to me, is false: their life is predicated on the *illusion* of rupture and discontinuity. The rupturing agon is mere repetition, the return of the Same. In the acting, and the acting *as if* they were merely acting, both George and Martha embody the murderous aspect of Joseph Jefferson's memory theater: the Same of the reproduced appearing as if it had never appeared before.

What George and Martha seem to be searching for and avoiding at the same time is the agon of selfhood—the pain of the tragic that grounds subjectivity. As a commentary on current historical/political theory—the shifting registers of gender/class/culture/race, the emergence of "hybridities" that structure the *perception* of ego—it remains ineluctably true that one's self is the provenance of pain, or terror, and that pain and terror wait to remind us of the inescapable condition of being selves alone.

In Albee's play, we engage in the dance of a certain theory, a revisitation of theory's dance in *Fashion* that represents at the psychic level the disarticulation of self through the revelation of the self's delusions. Here those delusions are psychosexual, but they could just as easily be political, class-related, historical, cultural. This dance seemingly leaves Nick and Honey bereft at play's end, lost within their estranged selves, submerged in the agony of mutually isolated subjectivities. But is this really true of George and Martha? Is theirs a confrontation with the agon of the real, or a theoretical dance around it, an experiment, an empirical testing, or deconstructive play around, or analytic resistance to, that agon? Playing at being hurt, playing at hurting, attacking, counterattacking, their theory/performance *enacts* an agon that allows them to leave the real pain of the self untouched. George and Martha undertake a mutual deconstruction of selves, by which, through which, they absolve themselves of the responsibility for the deconstructive violence they create. But at play's end, we are given to see that the obdurate self that has been seemingly deconstructed has remained unscathed. George and Martha are really performance theorists par excellence, trying to find in the representations and performances of life, life itself—even if only vicariously experienced as pain and terror in the other(s). And this could not happen—this theoretical examination of the predicament of performance theory—in any other venue but the play. The play reminds us of irreducible interdependence—the interplay—between theater, its performances, and its theories. The play serves to point out, in other words, that every performance, every theory, every performative is *first of all* theater. The hopeless realization that we are "only" watching a play when we see *Who's Afraid of Virginia Woolf?* is precisely the point of the play as play: we always dwell within the futile realization that when we most want to escape theater, it is theater we are invoking: the confrontation with the Symbolic as pain. The theoretical dance of the theater here is, once again, the dance around an absent child.

Spitting Mad

In Sam Shepard's *Buried Child*, the cycles of family dysfunction play out yet again, but what appears as hysteria or neurosis in O'Neill and Albee—the hysteria of perceived impotence or omnipotence in the Other, the neurotic desire to fill the lack in the Other—emerges here as something approaching psychosis. This effect is created in part through the use of expressionistic textures overlaid with the timbres and accent of authentic "Americana" played out as farce, but a psychosis whose real substance resides more directly in the dissolution of the paternal function both *in* the play, and *of* the play itself. Whereas in the earlier plays, the paternal function is represented as an inversion, here the paternal function of the play as a *representation* begins to unravel. Hence the poststructural feel of the text, which not only resists easy interpretation, but, prefiguring the performance art of the 1970s and 1980s, moves in the direction of psychotic discourse itself. It is part story or allegory, to be sure, but also approaches the condition of language-as-object, the "scripted speech" of the mother Halie, the one who initiates the Lacanian primordial attachment to the mother, an attachment that effectively erases sexual difference in the play as a whole, but also the appearance, at the play's very center, of hallucination returning in the Real, both in the figure of the character Vince, and in the appearance of the play itself as the disinterred remains of (an) American history.

To be sure, *Buried Child* does not dissolve into the schizoid (that will emerge more fully in Shepard's later work, like *Tongues* and *Savage/Love*). It begins by recovering something like an inverted fertility myth. Early on, while Dodge is having a dissociative dialogue with an unseen Halie, Tilden, the oldest son, enters carrying corn that he has picked "Right out back" where, according to his father and mother, no corn has grown "since about nineteen thirty-five."[23] But this fertility myth—which, like similar myths, requires blood sacrifice to replenish the earth—coincides with distinctly American images. Set on a farm in the heartland, the entire visual dispensation is, at first glance at least, quintessentially American: "It's like a Norman Rockwell cover or something," Shelley says when she and Vince first arrive (83). But bucolic appearances quickly give way to something infinitely cruel and malignant: although much of the ambience is the same—snarling dialogue, alcohol abuse, infidelity, the arrival of "strangers" and their immersion in the dysfunction, the intimation early on of a mysterious child—we are far from the world of Albee. We are somewhere else entirely, a place both familiar and strange, an *unheimlich*. We move within something like the topology of the unconscious or the domain of the repressed and its inevitable return. We hear something akin to the seeming sense of psychotic speech—the surreal persecutory ravings of Judge Schreber or the toxic poems of Artaud le Momo. Indeed, the real demiurge of this play is the repressed madness of O'Neill played out on the landscapes of *Desire*.

Buried Child is also a homecoming play, a form that oftentimes reflects something like a return of the repressed. Here son Vince and his girlfriend, Shelley, come back to his ancestral home, a farm in Illinois, the heartland. They are on their way out west, to New Mexico (from New York?), but when they arrive, Vince finds that no one recognizes him: not his dying grandfather, Dodge, hair shorn and scalp cut in a ritual castration by his son, Bradley; nor Bradley, who is himself a one-legged figuration of castration (Ahab redux?), completely helpless without his prosthesis; nor Vince's father, the nearly autistic Tilden, who is "profoundly burned out and displaced" (69) and who, fetishizing Shelley's rabbit-fur jacket, dissociates and psychotically feminizes himself; nor the seemingly proper but licentious Halie, the family's mother and grandmother and very embodiment of the Lacanian maternal phallus, another Maw, who is having an affair with Father Dewis, and who has, the play suggests, years before given illegitimate birth to a baby by her son Tilden, a baby that Dodge drowns and buries "out back." Never having left, we return once again to Oedipal realms, and the play appears on the theatrical landscape in a doubled design: it is a play about the return of the repressed in the character Vince, who appears to be the very child that was murdered, emerging from the underground burrows of the unconscious. But it is also the return, thematically and psychosexually, of an obsession with the Oedipal, the struggle for power over an incestuous and proscribed desire demarcated in the absent infant's body, the infant who is the absolute cast of the repressed—without speech once again, aphasic, crying out its desire in an articulated silence. But here the struggle takes place within the erosion of meaning itself—the Oedipal has returned as farce, displaced by the maternal force of "excess of *jouissance,*" or the psychotic's static unity with and fullness within his own subjectivity. In the image of the castrated males, meaning itself seems to fail, as when, for example, Dodge at one point claims, counter to the other statements in the play, that the buried child is his. "[M]y flesh and blood's buried out in the backyard" (77), he cries, while Tilden, spiritually castrated, tells Shelley the opposite: "I had a son once but we buried him" (92).

Yet for all of its strangeness one discovers in reading the play analytically, through the layers of almost stereotypical American contours, something of a historical past. This is a play that directly addresses history and memory as deficiency, beginning almost immediately with a misremembrance by Halie, who recalls horse races on Sundays and New Year's in the past, a memory that Dodge tells her is plainly false:

> HALIE'S VOICE: They used to race on New Year's! I remember that.
> DODGE: They never raced on New Year's!
> HALIE'S VOICE: Sometimes they did.
> DODGE: They never did.
> HALIE'S VOICE: Before we were married they did! (65)

Halie in the beginning seems to represent something like a maternal superego, the prim and proper guardian of morals and standards ("Everyone was dressed to the nines. Not like today. Not like they dress today" [66]). But she is actually usurping Dodge's function as the author of his own history. She begins subtly changing his memories, until she begins to erase them entirely. "So what difference does it make," says Dodge. "Everybody knows, everybody's forgot" (77).

When Vince returns (Vince who *is* the Return), the issue of memory and recognition takes center stage:

> VINCE: I'm Vince! Your grandson!
> DODGE: Vince. My grandson.

VINCE: Tilden's son.
DODGE: Tilden's son, Vince.
VINCE: You haven't seen me for a long time.
DODGE: When was the last time?
VINCE: I don't remember.
DODGE: You don't remember?
VINCE: No.
DODGE: You don't remember. How am I supposed to remember if
      you don't remember? (89)

This exchange suggests the failure of analysis, an aborted attempt to recover the past within a narrative. But which way, precisely, is the analysis moving, and to what purpose? Vince is trying to find (construct) a past, while Dodge is trying to unload one. We cannot tell which attempt it is that fails because the analysis ends in the complete insolvency of memory in the other. Memory, then, is not presented here as an autonomous action by one character (as when Adam Trueman recounts the story of his life), an autonomous action that fails. Rather, memory is a process of exchange, a dialectic that would, if it worked, recover the past. Dodge's memory seemingly depends upon Vince's, Vince's on Dodge's. Vince's failure to remember allows Dodge to claim memory failure as well. This failure of shared memory is the failure of history. And history is for the other characters (excepting Vince and Shelley, who seemingly have no history) precisely what needs to fail. History is not merely dead, it *is* death:

> DODGE: What's to remember? Halie's the one with the photo
>   album. She's the one you should talk to. She'll set you straight
>   on the heritage if that's what you're interested in. She's traced it
>   all the way back to the grave.
> SHELLEY: What do you mean?
> DODGE: What do you think I mean? How far back can you go? A
>   long line of corpses! There's not a living soul behind me. Not a
>   one. Who's holding me in their memory? Who gives a damn
>   about bones in the ground? (112)

Like George, Dodge is both haunted by history and rejects it, or tries to. The problem for him lies in the Nietzschean history that cannot be forgotten or repressed, and so crushes him beneath its weight. Ironically, then, the secret to his misery does not lie in historical archive, but in the pain that is both present to him and not, like the body present but hidden, "buried out back." Shelley, referring to Halie's collection of photos on the upstairs bedroom wall, assumes the role of historicist to Dodge's metaphysician:

> SHELLEY: You never look at those pictures up there?
> DODGE: What pictures!
> SHELLEY: Your whole life's up there hanging on the wall. Somebody who looks just like you. Somebody who looks just like you used to look.
> DODGE: That isn't me! That was never me! This is me. Right here. This is it. The whole shootin' match, sitting right in front of you.
> SHELLEY: So the past never happened as far as you're concerned?
> DODGE: The past? Jesus Christ. The past. What do you know about the past?
> SHELLEY: Not much. I know there was a farm. (111)

Dodge seems to be intimating a rejection of something like historicism for history. The primary historical archive represented by Halie's photos has nothing to do with the history that he tries to elude, because that history, the real history, is killing him. The archive, Dodge intimates, has nothing to do with who he is, what his pain is now. While he can ignore the archive because it is the merest representation of something outside history, the pain of his own history can't so easily be ignored. However, when Vince, the embodiment of the crime and its attendant pain, returns, it is in the present cut away from the past ("When was the last time?" "I don't remember"). *He is a hallucination,* an excision/foreclusion that allows him to assume a kind of bland, cheerful approach to the violence of life and its banalities. Vince does not struggle to forget the past; the past simply does not exist for him (as it would not in his hallucinatory role as the returned Child), or exists only as future—that Americanism again. But while Vince is pure hallucination (and within the theatrical enterprise he is, like all actors, something like hallucination), he is the hallucination that is every American, cut from his past, the locus of a denied violence that has the effect of dissolving the real into the hallucinatory, and the hallucinatory into the real. He/we are mere actors, shriveling the space of the symbolic to almost nothing. The issue, then, is not that our nation/history/culture is some sort of mass hallucination, but that we seem to be the hallucinated remains of that very foreclosed history. Hallucinated remains, waiting, nonetheless, to be crushed beneath the outrage of our history of disappearances, our sole contact with reality glimpsed through the paranoia of conspiracy theory itself.[24]

In the play, not only is the past a mere reliquary of disappearances, the characters *in* the present are themselves disappearing before our eyes; Dodge is wasting away, a mere ghost of a man. Speaking of Bradley's concern with the appearance of Dodge's hair, Dodge says to Halie, "My appearance is out of his domain! It's even out of mine! In fact, it's disappeared! I'm an invisible man!" (68). Similarly, when describing the last time she saw her other dead son, Ansel, Halie (who disappears herself with Father Dewis through the middle portion of the play) tells Dodge, "I watched him leave. I watched him throw gardenias as he helped her into the limousine. I watched his face disappear behind the glass" (74). This description of Ansel's disappearance parallels Vince's own disappearance into a vision of memory and history-as-present reflected back to him in the windshield as he drives to the Iowa border at night in the rain. It also parallels Dodge's earlier proclamations about the dead lineages of history, but is here captured within the reflective circle of his eye:

> I could see myself in the windshield. My face. My eyes. I studied my face. Studied everything about it. As though I was looking at another man. As though I could see his whole race behind him. Like a mummy's face. I saw him dead and alive at the same time. In the same breath. In the windshield, I watched him breathe as though he were frozen in time. And every breath marked him. Marked him forever without him knowing. And then his face changed. His face became his father's face . . . and his father's face changed into his grandfather's face. And it went on like that. Clear on back to faces I'd never seen before but recognized. Still recognized the bones underneath . . . I followed my family clear into Iowa. Every last one. Straight into the Corn Belt and further. Straight back as far as they'd take me. Then it all dissolved. Everything dissolved. (130)

The image of the eye, looking all the way back to history's beginnings in America, looking back to the very eye of Thomas Shepard himself, dominates the sequences of history, both in culture and in the family itself. The "heroic" and absent Ansel, the Other dead son, meets his demise because he, like Trueman's daughter, "was blind with love. Blind." Halie, by contrast, foresees his death in the face of his new wife: "I saw it in her eyes . . . she told me with her eyes that she'd murder him in his bed" (74). Later, Dodge, falling like Rip into a drugged dream, misremembers a home run by Stan Musial[25] and re-creates the memory through invocation to sight: "I marked it. I marked it with my eyes." Finally, Shelley, at play's end, remarks on the failure of her own vision in the re-creation of Vince's past:

> He made all of you sound familiar to me. Every one of you. For every name I had an image. Every time he'd tell me a name, I'd see the person. In fact, each of you was so clear in my mind that I actually believed it was you. I really believed when I walked through that door that the people who lived here would turn out to be the same people in my imagination. But I don't recognize any of you. Not one. Not even the slightest resemblance.
> DEWIS: Well you can hardly blame others for not fulfilling your hallucination. (121)

Shelley's construction of Vince's past doesn't just miss the mark. It displaces Vince's history with hallucination, equating the insubstantiality of Vince as subject with the insubstantiality of the history that produces him. The suggestion is, of course, that if the historical subject is multiple, fragmentary, and hollow, so is the history that produces him. Dodge's, Shelley's, and Vince's understandings of history, then, align themselves with the three different renderings of Nietzschean history: history as paralysis, history as forgetting, and history as hallucination. Seeing the lineage from which he, as cipher, emerges, Vince forgets, just as Dodge, claiming forgetfulness, cannot. Vince embodies a historical forgetting that allows him to act, however pedestrian that action might be: in a closing scene that borders on the expressionistic, Dodge dies unnoticed, Vince inherits the farm, and Tilden enters with the muddy, desiccated, disinterred corpse of a buried child. Vince presumably will go on to live in blissful ignorance, while Dodge now will be the one buried beneath the mud of memory and history "out back." Shelley, on the other hand, is bereft when the history she constructs fails, as constructed histories must beneath the tidal force of History itself. Here history is simply a remembered grief. Nothing, finally, has been discovered, and nothing learned. The play recirculates emptiness. Nothing to be done.

And at the center of it all, the buried child itself: "Little tiny baby just disappeared. It's not hard. It's so small. Almost invisible" (104): like the blue shadow in the fingernail, the glint in the eye, the difference between the real and its theater, Pip and his double, a difference, an irruption or abruption so small as to be nearly, or in fact, nonexistent. This difference constructs history and language, almost invisible, the castrating effect of the abolition of the law of castration: the spectral other once again, a nothing of seeming substance, or a substance so ephemeral it, like a black hole, approaches nothingness but is still the locus of a desire so weighty and painful, it could only be desire itself resisting its own erasure.

6

Splitting the Difference: Performance and Its Double in American Culture

Gender, suggests Judith Butler, is not so much a permanent state, or the "congealing" of a specific sexual identity, as it is a performed moment, in which sexual identity "becomes" through the moment of enactment in the body: "[O]ne is not simply a [gendered] body, but, in some very key sense, one does one's body."[1] This performativity is not a performance, however. Performance as a more or less consciously elucidated act or series of acts can never be performative in Butler's terms, because performance is too a priori, too conscious of itself and its biases and internal, social forces. Performance is more a showing than a becoming. The forces at work in performativity are more insidious, hidden, concealed, and self-concealing.

Missing from Butler's early performative theory is any elaborated notion of theater and its mode of showing, mise-en-scène. Theater, we surmise, would be at an even further remove from performance, steeped as it is in historical convention, architectures, texts, and received meanings. Theater, even more than performance, stinks of the visible, the obvious and obviously seen. Whether Butler might agree with this assessment of theater or not, such assumptions do guide much of performance theory today, which investigates nearly every performative mode imaginable, seeing the sociocultural inflections in each, elevating performance and performativity to the more all-inclusive category, relegating theater to a rather minor form or subcategory of performance or the performative, not realizing, as did Artaud, that theater is the very site in which performance and performativity arises and is problematized, that theater is the site of the hidden, but is also the locus of the obvious, of repetition or "the scripted." Said another way: theater, the "seeing place," is the site of distancing, of what we might call, emerging from consciousness, Brechtian alienation or critical thought. Theater, then, as I am using the term,[2] often seemingly subtends theory, apprehends it—sometimes proleptically, like Artaud's "hairs standing on end"—and sees both itself and its theory through the illusions of thought, or thoughts of illusion.

And yet theory, as in Butler's work, often assumes itself subtending or demystifying theater when, in fact, in assuming such an illusory, "transcendent" position outside mise-en-scène, it is frequently apprehended *by* theater, especially when it fails to take theater into account. When this happens, the distance closes, as Brecht understood, and we can no longer see theater. It vanishes into itself, though it is still there, peering through the veil. As theater seemingly disappears, we lose focus—we lose, in a sense, our critical faculties. Theater, as the site of both representation and transformation, has always, somewhere, seen this. Theory often has not.

And yet ironically Butler's dismissal of theater is also a repetition of theater's own trepidations about its motives. From *The Contrast* through *Who's Afraid of Virginia Woolf?* and *The America Play*, theater has also been the site in which the forms of the performative have been enacted under suspicion, for beneath the play of the obvious, theater always complicates and is complicated by performance and performativity—what Herbert Blau might call ghosting. Contrary to what Butler suggests, "the theatrical model," as she calls it, does not necessarily "take the gendered self to be prior to its acts,"[3] and when it does, it often does so with a distinctly perjur'd eye. The issue of the gendering of bodies onstage, in fact, is the central focus in much of the Western theatrical tradition. Each period, in its own historically unique way, indicates, shows, attemps to make manifest its own concealings, its own hiddenness across many seemingly natural but problematic social categories—gender, certainly, but also race and class, not to mention the most troublesome of all, the self-as-I. Perhaps the most notable exception to this hyperconsciousness in theatrical traditions is the American tradition, which, as I have been suggesting all along, is, despite its location within the most hypertheatricalized of cultures, most typically blind or resistant to such insight and tension. It is interesting to note that Butler, writing theory in America, would fall prey to a similar, prototypically American blindness.

The persistent (and naive) idea among some performance theorists that performance (and by genetic extraction, performativity) somehow eludes or gets by the problem of representation in theater because it (performance/performativity) is not "scripted," because it does not mask the "self," is brought into question by the appearance, from the 1970s through the 1990s, of a figuration of the performative that challenges these more socioculturally driven modes of performance theory: multiple personality syndrome and the site of its emergent history, recovered (and now, into the new millennium, steeply discounted) memories.[4] MPD victims seemingly enact tightly scripted but apparently unconscious performances, all the while acting in order to attain a "self-revelation" that is, or might be, one more illusion, one more subterfuge.[5] Keeping both American theater and its double within the sight lines, I would like to look at MPD as a pathology in which both performativity and social performance are outstripped by a mise-en-scène that veers past the merely performative and dangerously close to theater itself, threatening to erase the differences in its very misappearance. This mode of mise-en-scène, not precisely theater or even theater's true erasure, represents, moreover, its own repression at the sociocultural level as well. MPD, in other words, when it appears, when it recovers its own memories of itself, marks, as does much of performance theory, the symptom, the space of repression within the sociocultural fabric of American society in which theater as theory remains concealed.

Moreover, during the 1980s and 1990s in American culture the pathology of multiplicity was itself mirrored in the sociocritical scene by theories of multiplicity as psychically and politically curative. The work of Deleuze and Guattari comes most readily to mind, of course, but also the work of Foucault, with its ruptures and doublings, the aporias and multiplicities of Lacanian psychoanalysis, and the multiple production of meaning emerging from critical theory as a whole. The canonization of multiplicity in more current critical approaches like multiculturalism and Queer theory, with its multivalent forms of sexual performance and display, suggests an apotheosis of multiplicity within theory. MPD stands, within popular culture, as a mirrored image of these multiple meanings, as do other phenomena in the world of realpolitik. The breakup of the Soviet Union, the atomization of Yugoslavia, the increasingly unstable boundaries among the African countries, and now the strategies of radically alienated and anonymous violence deployed by the militia movements and terrorist cells also seem to stand in harrowing challenge to the assumption that multiplicity and instability, in and of themselves, are inherently liberatory.

Within these theoretical assumptions, we see in the phenomenon of MPD the problematic issues: a deconstructed self that is very often not an empowered self, disconnected from the false bondage of a persistent sense of gendered identity, but a self whose very individual power is lost in its own dissolving gender. We often see, moreover, a self reconstructed in the image of others—racial and gendered—that does not even begin to escape from the stereotypes of gender, race, or even class: a destabilization of identity that more easily leads to victimization by power than to subversion of (patriarchal) power. And while one might argue that such a self-subject has no other options but to reenact the social roles given, this begs an obvious question: what other roles or strategies are available, especially to the rank-and-file, nonacademic oppressed?

While this chapter does not specifically answer these charges, it contrasts MPD differentially to certain modes of performance and performance art and theory in order to raise questions about the "situatedness" of theories of identity in American culture, and, once again, the relation of identity to memory and history. It also seeks to underscore the price culture pays when it represses its own theater and theatrical ontology[6] in its pursuit of identity as destabilization, as disappearance.[7]

Traum

In 1985, Beatrice Roth presented *The Father* in the Performing Garage in New York City.[8] The piece, which explores the spiritual upheaval in her father's life, is filled with very particular images from her past. The descriptions are at once suggestive and particular. The powerful, almost mythic image of her father in prayer, "his totality wrapped in stripe and fringe / his forehead strapped in leather ribbon," is poised against the delicacy of remembered detail: "[H]e fed the pet canary while he dovened [prayed]."[9] What is perhaps most captivating overall is the indeterminacy of the most important remembered moments.

> he bends
> and with practiced certainty
> cups and kisses
> drinking drowning flooding every bone and hollow

natural so natural
the shock is thunderous.
In the corner
in the shadows
in her dark and watchful cornea
lightning strikes splitting vision[10]

There is in this passage, as in others, a powerful, even violent image out of memory—a suggestion of violation, an intimation that one is viewing something forbidden—death, perhaps, or something equally obscene. Vision is split, doubled, and something, possibly some crime, is hidden even more deeply, the father, "burying with her / in the ground / their secret."[11] But whatever the event, its readable contours are hidden in the metaphorical play. This is memory as poetry, history as emotion. The recovery of trauma *as* history.

The recollection of her father is not an unusual convention in performance art from the period of the 1980s and early 1990s, which often used memories of parents, childhood events, the breakup of marriages, suicides, or other traumatic life events as points of departure. What perhaps distinguishes Roth from other performance artists of this period is the kind of traditional ambiguity she creates. While other women artists were creating overtly autobiographical works that moved inexorably in the direction of parody and stand-up comedy (Holly Hughes, Laurie Anderson), the images of her father are allusive and powerful. Specific details suggest clear recollection. But we aren't sure, finally, what the nature of the trauma is that has in essence created the piece. Conversely, the artist herself seemingly remains who she is, taking in other voices, perhaps, singing, praying, but still occupying, if enigmatically, the site of her own identity.

I invoke Roth's piece here, however, to contrast it with the work of another performance artist who emerged during this same period, Karen Finley. She too, uses images from her past but uses them quite differently. The differences are not merely questions of performative style but suggest very different ontological approaches to the interconnected issues of identity, memory, and subjectivity. The differences, as I suggested earlier, point to broader cultural crises of identity, memory, and history, crises that are reformulated in different ways in our society, perhaps none more intriguingly than in the contours of multipersonality syndrome. Articulated through the primal trauma of childhood abuse, MPD enacts a fracture, the performance of rhizomatic thought, the curtain rising in the theater of multiplicities—a theater of the subject reconstructed, redefined against the perceived abuses of patriarchal horror.[12] The synchronicity and synergy between this American pathology and the work of theorists and performance artists delineates not merely an idiosyncratic American trait, but a reordering of individual memory, history, and identity that has implications beyond American history and culture.

When commentary on Finley's work first began to appear in the pages of scholarly journals in the late 1980s and early 1990s, the concerns were similar to those expressed within her performances. What do we make, politically and artistically, of the raging obscenity at the center of this work? What does it mean when a woman artist and self-proclaimed feminist inhabits the space of the obscene in which she both assaults and desexualizes her body through language and the mythologies of fecal decay? Even to theorists who avoided the more obvious issues and imageries, the problem of power and identity raised in Finley's work was still propped against the implicit "marginality" (read obscenity) of her work. Most reaction to her work, right wing or left, centered on the coprophilic and scatological qualities of her performances and the relationship of those qualities to issues of power and censorship. Consequently, even though critics like Lynda Hart suggested that the impact of Finley's work lay in its ability to "abandon the unity of the humanist 'I,' to shift around, between, among subject and object positions, to confound spectators who desire to locate an identity behind the construction of subjectivity," such suggestions were still powerfully entwined in the outrage and profanity of her work, its demonic quality, a fact that Hart seemingly deflects when she refers to the content of Finley's performance as "food loathing as a trope for motherhood," choosing to ignore the obvious trope of food as excrement.[13] Here the power of obscenity resides in the very avoidance of the potentially obscene meaning of the work. We are, it seems, back within the Puritan context. In Finley the body is both ecstatic and filthy, covered in a figurative *excretio seminis*, dissemination appearing as the literal substance of the work, food smeared like jism, like vomit or excrement over the crawling skin, but sublimated in Hart's criticism, which is encoded, like Wigglesworth's coy Latinate evasions, within the safe metalanguages of an ideology that chooses, instead, to concentrate on spiritual decenteredness in order to avoid stepping in shit.

The power of Finley's work, in fact, depends not on its chaotic, decentering form, but on its marginalizing content, even if it is repressed. So important was that content to Finley's performance that her more recent work, following the Puritan inclinations of Hart, perhaps, and lacking the extremity of these obscene referents (though still often shocking), seems more to bewilder critics than to offend them. To be sure, the sense of dislocation and disarticulation is still there in her newer pieces, like *The American Chestnut* (1995): pain, terror, and dissociation. They are not immersed in the Sadean extremes of earlier material like *Constant State of Desire*, but they are overlooked by critics who now see in Finley an emergent political vision previously lacking. Consequently, within the current concerns with the ideologies of performance, moving out of an ethos of difference, deferral, and multiplicity, the very appearance of multiplicity of voices and viewpoints in Finley's art is displaced—a multiplicity that was earlier equated with the political import of her work, but now concealed within the continuities, the sameness of late and early work. I would like, briefly, to reappraise Finley's earlier work, specifically *Constant State of Desire*,[14] through the perspective of this concern with multiplicity and memory, underscoring what remains, and remains unresolved, in Finley: her possession by the multiple voices of cultural tyranny, and the assumption that it is this multiplicity that is central to the meaning of her work. In this sense, at least, Finley's work hasn't changed.

Karen Finley began *The Constant State of Desire*, which was first performed in 1986 at the Kitchen, within the allusions and language of childhood sexual abuse:

> Like when my father finally told me he loved me after forty years then went into the bathroom, locked the door, put up pictures of children from the Sears catalog, arranged mirrors, black stockings and garters to look at while he masturbated as he hung himself from the shower stall. . . . And the reason why my father committed suicide is that he no longer found me attractive.[15]

Here, as in Roth's work, the images are concrete, if somewhat tawdry, but the traumatic moment is described in a direct yet removed style— the monologue opens with Finley speaking in the third person, "She dreams. She dreams of strangling birds."[16] The story about "her" and "her dreams" eventually circles down to "I," when she reveals what seem to be powerful memories of her own father. The transition from the "she" to the "I" and then finally back to "you" suggests memories that are perpetually dislocated, disembodied. We don't know who is talking: Finley, a persona she has invented, or some fragment of each. The question here finally is not what happened, but to whom it happened, for in performance, Karen Finley most decidedly does not occupy the site of her own identity. She is demon and exorcist, raw id and migrating ego, pushing remembrance and so history into seemingly pure presence and the purely present of performance. Lenora Champagne, in her collection of texts by women performance artists, describes her this way: "She . . . characteristically closes her eyes when she shifts from a casual, seemingly improvised chat with the audience into the words of one of her characters, whose voice seems to come from deep within, as though some lost soul is speaking through her."[17] Similarly, Finley tells *Village Voice* writer C. Carr that when she watches videotapes of herself, "I have to close my eyes. I don't know who that person is." "She performs in a trance," Carr tells us, "and has never rehearsed a piece."[18]

> Finley's characters have no boundaries. They flow into each other over the course of a monologue as it moves from one emotional peak to the next, the dislocated genders and narratives held together by a feverish, dream-like logic. The very boundaries of the body collapse.[19]

During this piece Finley inhabits or is inhabited by any number of personae and speaks in other voices—her own, as well as the voices of psychopaths, pedophiles, child-murderers, frenzied macho-men, and nearly catatonic women. The total effect is certainly akin to something like possession, as voice after voice emerges and demands attention, voice after voice pouring out of a soul that might be merely voice, empty and emptied as the dream ends and speech silences itself. At one point in the opening monologue the speaker (who?) dreams she hangs from a fifth-story ledge, her mouth open to scream, but

> the wind was in a mean mood and took her cries halfway round the world to a child's crib, so its mother could hear her own child's cries. . . . This dream was considered very important to the doctors. For in the past she had dreams of tortures, rapes and beatings, where no sounds would come out of her mouth at all. She'd open her mouth and move her lips but no sounds would come out at all.[20]

In her spoken dream the mute infants of O'Neill, Albee, and Shepard have been given voice, while she herself is bereft of utterance ("no sounds would come out at all") during the traumatic remembrance. The silenced voice of *traum* and trauma reappears in the images of ordeal—child rape and abuse—that lie buried in the dreamed seedbed of Finley's rage. When she leaves "the doctors" (therapists?) and finally shifts to something like "her" voice, speaking now of "I" instead of "she," she tells us she wants no more deaths on her conscience. "I already have an abortion on my conscience from when a member of my own family raped me. Don't worry, I won't mention your name. Don't worry, I won't mention your name." The use of repeated phrases, the split-brained perceptual doubling,[21] runs throughout the piece, but moves contra Roth, from doubling into the explicitly multiple.

The voices that emerge in *The Constant State of Desire* not only inhabit an abusive rage and trauma, but are inhabited by it. The voices seem always to point back to the something that happened—the rapes tortures beatings—but we never know for sure to whom they happened, to Finley, or some excrescence of dreamed memory and culture. At one point, in signature style of the period, Finley uses what seems to be an explicit image of child-abuse:

> And the first memory, memory I have, I have of my father, is he putting me into the refrigerator. He takes off all of my clothes and puts my five-year-old bare bottom onto the silver rack of the icebox. . . . then he opens up the vegetable bin and takes out the carrots, the celery, the zucchini, and cucumbers. Then he starts working on my little hole. Starts working my little hole. "Showing me what it's like to be a mama," he says. "Showing me what its like to be a woman. To be loved. That's a daddy's job," he tells me.[22]

She seems to be after something over the edge of trauma here, and we're not sure what to make of the substance of her description. The food descriptions, like her preoccupation with actual food in her performances, carries an edge of coprophilic absurdity that seems a secretion of culture itself. In fact, she herself describes a working style in which an amalgam of media enter her, possessing her, in some way: "She writes material out of what is floating in the cultural ether, stimulated by books and TV."[23] She pours food onto and into her body as words and images pour into and from her mouth, a true logorrhea.

Finley's language, in this early piece, often suggests case-studies of certain kinds of extreme child-abuse, like satanic ritual abuse, in which, according to some therapists, children talk of being placed in cages or closed boxes. "One described being in a chest freezer with her feet in ice cubes. Another spoke of being lowered into deep water from the end of a rope."[24] In either case, both patient and artist, the "she" and the "I," seem compelled to revisit the site of *that* primal terror, *that* moment of unspeakable fear. Carr suggests that in Finley's case, the rage that fills her performance is the result of her desire to "dive into the horror,"[25] to pursue the site of the actual trauma lying beneath the horrific descriptions of it. In fact, the more graphic and raging her tirades become, her use of "the tired old vocabulary of abuse"[26] merely serves to point up the inadequacy of memory and words in the face of real terror, the terror that is the primal fact, what psychoanalysis calls the It, spiraling, like Pip's madness, outside the circle of mere text or performance. At the same time, there was, in these earlier pieces, nothing "theatrical" about Finley's performance. She did not and does not take on the attributes or speak in the voices of her personae, as do other feminist performers like Lily Tomlin or Anna Deavere Smith. This "inability to act," a comment that crops up in audience reactions to her work, mirrors suspicions that follow descriptions of MPD performances—in the space of the purely performative, within the purview of theater, there is, it seems, nothing and all illusory about Finley's work. That, it seems to me, is its most salient point.

And yet, as I mentioned above, there has recently been a telling shift in Finley's performances. In *The American Chestnut,* she maintains some similar approaches to her material: she still inhabits other voices, shifts pronouns/identities, still hinges her work on incidents of sexual violence. There is a scene, based on an actual incident in her life, in which she describes being chased and raped by two men. The recollection is powerful and direct, yet maintains the same ambiguity as many of the scenes in *Constant State of Desire.* There is no way to tell, within recollection and remembering, what is real and what is misremembered, what might be Finley's voice and which the voice of an "alter." She still speaks in the languages of dislocation. One recent interviewer comments,

[A]s I hear the voice in your performance, I think, "Who is speaking?" . . . essentially I feel you are pulling from different parts of your personality . . . shifting from being the oppressor to being a victim, from being a leper to being someone calling someone a leper.[27]

She remains, in this piece, the "medium" that she described herself to be in the 1980s, but now, to gloss McLuhan, the medium has become mediation, the codification of a political viewpoint that is more focused, and by some accounts, de-energized. She now "breaks character" when she addresses audience members who laugh at inappropriate times. She reads portions of her performance, and in doing so effectively distances herself and the audience from them. She has become, apparently, closer to Brecht than Artaud in her approach to performance. Finley's earlier personae, those eruptions from the psychic seedbed, have been tamed through their entry into political discourse. The terror of her earlier work has perhaps slipped into the coercions of ideology; it has become, to quote Brecht, "theatered down."

Trauma

Although the terror has become more codified over time, terror still seems to be the principle behind Finley's Dionysian performative,[28] trying to cut through the tissue of thought, ritual, and theater. Theater itself is in part born of the need to inhabit this terror and is nurtured through the tragic belief that habitation will tame it by encoding what was hitherto uncoded. But in exploring the unseeable roots of the human fear of death, pain, and madness through performance, performance enunciates those fears, and in doing so codifies or represses them through a kind of Adornian desublimation. Brecht understood this problem, as did Artaud. Moreover, these enunciative codes mold cultural thought and perception through that social mediation we call theater or performance. In this schema, theater is at once that cultural formulation involving script and stage and actor, and, as I said at the outset, the very condition of consciousness split against itself. Theater is formed in that very split, finding its being and its voice in the betweenness, threatening at each moment to enfold all within the sulci of mind—consciousness as theater, theater born of the *mise en abîme*, the labyrinthine scene of the Other.

The traditions of Euro-American theater that contextualize questions of performance today are deeply embedded in this aesthetic of pain and fear, an aesthetic that has recently been eclipsed by the an-aesthetic of some forms of poststructural theory. This is an an-aesthetic that has preserved the forms of pain while eliminating its felt content, extolling fragmentation, multiplicities, and decenteredness while ignoring the cost in human misery brought about by the more Dionysian extremes of these poststructural categories. Recently, political critic James Glass has questioned theorists like Jean François Lyotard, Gilles Deleuze, and others because, he says, their models of cultural potential and growth ignore the misery of those who actually live out those models. All the talk of multiplicities, of the body without organs, of fragmentation and decenteredness ignores the real distress and terror of those who actually experience the world this way—the schizophrenics and brain-damaged patients living in asylums, or muttering over steam grates on city streets, the victims of domestic and street crime whose lives fragment in ways that can hardly be called productive or liberatory. In many important ways critical theory never bothered to confront the reality of what its theories sometimes suggested, never adequately spoke to the terror induced by the Other that they invoked—the terror that has always haunted the theaters of consciousness, a terror that, as in Finley's *Constant State of Desire,* is tied deeply to the threat and actuality of trauma. Indeed, Glass writes, it is "in trauma" that "otherness is born of the experience of terror." It is terror, he says, not the usual Lacanian "language," that "structures the unconscious." This terror-stricken formation that is consciousness—the text of terror, its "language"—exists in a "notoriously bad faith. Elaborate deceptions, complicated emotional patterns . . . linguistic masks represent neither what is real or authentic, either in the person or in language." These "linguistic masks" are "falsehoods constructed through dissociative mechanisms that protect consciousness from complete annihilation"—what we might call the mise-en-scène of consciousness existing as theater, forced to mask and deception as a way of confronting that which might otherwise prove too painful to confront: the Other in the guise of death, fear, or abandonment.[29]

But Glass is not discussing theater theory or performance, but rather multiple personality syndrome, a distinctly American invention, in which an individual (usually a woman) develops several distinct "personalities" differing in age, gender, and even species.[30] These personalities or "alters" develop, according to some therapists, as a result of repeated early childhood trauma—usually sexual abuse—that often remains "unremembered" or "repressed." During the original traumatic episodes, the child learns to dissociate herself from her tormentor by becoming, in essence, "someone else." In Glass's words, the person suffering the trauma is no longer the person she was, but becomes "a number of different alters that [have] been created over the years *to screen the terror*" (emphasis added). It is through these alters "and their abreactive experience" that the individual recovers the memories of abuse and arrives at a knowledge of a violent past.[31] This *abreaction*—a psychoanalytic term meaning, in essence, a catharsis—is invoked over and over again in Glass's book as the technique by which the individual exteriorizes her painful memories by giving them different personae and letting them "perform" for the analyst, who then begins a long process of "introducing" the alters to each other. Soon an ensemble of voices and clashing personalities emerges, a theater of *therapeutike*, which reenacts the events of the trauma. The individual, in other words, now disindividuated, now more collective than unitary, acts in a microtheater of cruelty within which she both reenacts and prevents the enacting of the trauma that gave her theater its birth.

Taken together, this is what is popularly known as multiple personality syndrome, or multiple personality disorder, now called DID—dissociative identity disorder, the name change ironically recapitulating the shifting content of the dissociative thing itself. This disorder has a rather short history, and one that is worth recounting briefly here, if for no other reason than to point out that multiplicity, too, has its history, and a history with a peculiarly American slant.[32]

Up until the late twentieth century, the number of documented cases of DID were very few. Initially, in fact, there were no instances of *multiple* personality, only cases in which a patient exhibited a doubled or "split" personality. Often this doubling involved contrasting or even opposite personalities—one passive and meek, the other aggressive, even violent. Such cases of *dedoublement* gave rise to popular stories like *The Strange Case of Dr. Jekyll and Mr. Hyde*, written by Robert Louis Stevenson in 1886, but were presaged by "possession" plays such as Heinrich von Kleist's *Penthisilea*.

It wasn't until the work of Charcot and Jules Voison in 1885 that an instance of *multiple* personality emerges. Although Voison at first used the earlier terminology of "first and second states" that had been applied to doubled personalities, he and Charcot soon realized that in the person of one Louis Vivet, a florid hysteric, such terms were inadequate. Within a year the term *multiple personality* appears in the literature in direct reference to Vivet. What is perhaps most interesting about his case is that as more and more therapists investigated Vivet, he seemed to develop more and more symptoms, more and more "personalities"—the multiplicity was, in some sense, not within his own personality(ies), but lay instead in the multiple personalities invading him with therapies from without.

And so it more or less remained, the occasional "hysteric" manifesting two, and later three or sometimes four "states." And the condition was unusual. As recently as 1972 fewer than fifty cases were known to have been documented. Even though there was debate as to how many of these cases were authentic, it was generally agreed that the condition was quite rare. Ten to fifteen years later, through the mid-1970s and 1980s, almost exclusively in the United States, there were suddenly thousands of cases reported. There was an "epidemic" of DID. Between the appearance of the movie *The Three Faces of Eve,* in 1957, which starred Joanne Woodward as the troubled multiple Eve, and the movie *Sybil,* in 1976, in which Woodward played the therapist, the image of the *multiple* was permanently inscribed in the American psyche. A new level and kind of duality/multiplicity developed: the multiple now appeared as a screen image, and DID could, as a cultural moment, watch itself, and in the mirroring, watch itself watch. The multiple, in other words, could now not only construct selves through the screen image, but could reconstruct itself constructing. The extent to which film may or may not have contributed, or even given birth, to the explosive phenomenon is an intriguing question, as is the appearance of the television remote control and the concomitant practice of channel surfing during this same period of time—an experience that has been likened to watching a multiple switching among her personalities.[33]

So what had begun in the literature as rare "doubled" personalities, in the period of a decade and a half developed into fairly common "multiple personalities." Moreover the number of personalities exhibited also increased—from three or four to ten or twenty to fifty or one hundred or more. What led to this explosive increase in the number of reported cases is a matter of some dispute. Supporters and innovators of DID therapies claim the increase is due to the widespread exposure of hitherto hidden cases of childhood sexual assault. It wasn't until the 1970s and 1980s, many therapists say, that people in the United States became aware of the extent to which children were being raped and assaulted in the home. As more and more people became aware, more and more came to realize that they, too, were the victims of early childhood sexual trauma. And because one of the major symptoms of DID is a state of amnesia when the victim shifts into one of her alters, many instances of DID went unnoticed. Sufferers simply didn't remember anything unusual following the apparent blackouts, what therapists called "lost time," not unlike the lost time of Rip's historical disloca-tions. Skeptics, on the other hand, attribute the increase in the number and severity of cases to the actions of therapists, many of them untrained or poorly trained, who have in essence "manufactured" the disorder in their patients. Similarly, at the cultural level, the ubiquity of actors on television and in movies, plus the plethora of entertainment industry "personalities," provided an overwhelming number of identi-ties to choose from, as identity became absolutely conflated with per-sonality, and the cult of celebrity picked up and discarded hot new faces at warp speed.

Here, then, is the first of the two major controversies regarding DID—is it "real" or is it merely an artifact of certain kinds of therapies mixed with the cultural currency of multiplicity? While defenders have pointed out the need to believe and support those traumatized uncon-ditionally, the skeptics have pointed to the myriad number of therapist-oriented books on the subject, each of which has its own list of "signs" that a patient has been abused. These lists, the critics suggest, might lead most people to believe that they have been victims of sexual abuse. Fear of the dark, gastrointestinal problems, alienation from the body, wearing baggy clothes, even dislike of tapioca pudding—these and myriad other rather common experiences were and are listed as poten-tial signs of childhood sexual abuse.

But perhaps more interesting than the many lists of "signs" that one may have been abused is the fact that the therapist and patients must seek signs at all. They must seek signs because the patients are, as I have said, often not aware that they were abused. They have "forgotten it" and must find ways to bring it once again to the surface. They do this through various therapies that allow them to "recover" memories.[34]

Once memories are recovered through the narratives and words of the various alters, the patient can be reintegrated. Therein lies the sec-ond of the great controversies of DID and recovered memory—how does one know, barring outside confirmation, that one's memories are in fact "true"? Does the import of one's memories depend on their external confirmation by others, or on the subjective impact they have in forming identity? Further, doesn't conflating memory and identity in this way obscure the deeper and more difficult problem of subjectiv-ity? Isn't the multiplication of identity, and the ability to switch iden-tity, merely a multiplication and obfuscation of the original problem? If identity—gendered, racial, classed—is decentered and unstable, how does mere multiplication or the ability to switch race or gender change the fundamental problem of identity and subjectivity? How precisely, is this—as many "new Wave" DID sufferers claim—liberatory, or even evolutionarily superior? And finally, even though the pathologies of DID are clearly not what gender theorists have in mind when they question cultural assumption about the stability of identity, what does DID itself suggest about such assumptions? Might the positing of some hegemonic idea of identity-stability be a straw-man argument? The prevalence of DID might suggest so, as might the currency of multiplicity in movies and TV. In this case both the appearance of DID and theories of decentered identity might, as I have suggested, be symptoms of an American society that has perhaps never had such "stable" and unchallenged experiences of subjectivity. American history in general, and in particular (to name a single instance) the history of American theater and the Hollywood movie, might suggest so. In this case, the problem, both philosophically and pragmatically, might not be the need to demonstrate the decentered and provisional quality of subjectivity, but rather the need to affirm identity in the midst of such fluid change—a need that, in the theater at least, must be *tragically* denied. This denial finds its contours, in terms of DID, at least, in the perceived unbelievability of the performance itself.

What, in fact, makes DID unbelievable, or at least arguable, to many observers is its failure—like Finley's performance—*as theater.* While on the one hand many object to the substantive claims of DID because its seems like so much bad acting, many suspicions seem to center on DID's very insistence on its own nontheatricality, on its "reality." Thus while the poststructural world continues to present us with theories of the insubstantiality of self, DID is trying, like some gender theory itself, to convince us of the self's (multiple) reality. Indeed, outside gender theory, experts in consciousness and identity like Daniel Dennett see multiplicity-as-identity as inevitable, a healthy and predictable response to modern fragmentation. But modern fragmentation and the painful decenteredness of identity has little to do with the indeterminacy of genders or races—*it has to do with the suspicion that I might be no one at all.* We are not talking about the fear of shifting identity, ultimately, but the fear of nonbeing, of death.

Corollary to this, what are we to make of the resistance among many in the DID community to reintegration? Many refuse to see themselves as anything other than normal, but still wish to insist on the mutual nonresponsibility among alters for any one alter's actions—if my alter "Bill," for example, exposes himself to a woman in a hotel room, should my other alters be held responsible for it? It depends, of course, on who is asking the question, one's therapist, or the special prosecutor.[35]

Apart from the obvious convenience of such mutual nonresponsibility, this dual desire—to remain distinct but in communication (to be articulate, in other words) is redolent of theater history's most enduring mythos—the eternal return of the myth of Osiris, and the Dionysian myths of dismemberment and resurrection. One of the earliest collections of DID case studies is, in fact, called *The Osiris Complex*. The issue here seems deeply embedded in the ontologies of theater, and not mere performance. DID appears as mise-en-scène, each persona emerging from an unending succession of mirrored images, each persona appearing from within an Other, and disappearing into otherness, no self set outside the self-seeing eye of the Dionysian circular gaze.

Of course the somewhat aged Dionysian theory of the origins of theater in the actual trauma of violence, human sacrifice, and cannibalism, evocative though it is, has been discounted as spurious or worse. Although the narratives are inhabited by real remembrance of trauma, beyond the limen of history, the recovered memories here are false, the wishful thinking of a still savage race. What is notable is the currency of the idea's reemergence. Such currency suggests a kind of resonance, a desire for the Dionysian mask that has reemerged in the mechanisms of DID and certain modes of performance art—the eventual disintegration of the unitary voice (Dionysus/chorus) into many, competing voices or alters (the dismembered body/actors) who narrate early, oftentimes the earliest events in one's life, or previous lives (myth/history and memory). The process of disintegration is oriented toward a hoped-for reintegration at a higher level, in which one will, through the empathy of the audience or therapist, understand the origins of ontologic or psychologic trauma by revisiting the terror. The pity and terror generate an "abreaction" (catharsis) that allows the patient to heal. But in order for this to happen, the patient (chorus/actors) must perform the narrative (play or performance) before an audience (the therapist). She who was dismembered in every sense of the word, is now remembered. She, perhaps for the first time, revisits the site of the trauma. What this suggests, however, is that in an important sense DID and its therapeutic exorcism is not the result of trauma, but, as in Finley's art, is the originator of it.[36] Thus the first question we raised—is DID "real" or an artifact of therapy—is answered, albeit not as satisfactorily as some might wish: DID is as real as theater is. And here we are back at the continuing problem plaguing American theatricalized conscious-ness: the problem of the authentic, and the threat of violence that inhab-its it. Indeed, in cases of what is called satanic ritual abuse, which I will discuss below, the seeming abusive events leading to DID are of the most horrific and excessive kind—body mutilations, human sacrifice, coprophagia, and cannibalism. The laundry lists of outrages, in fact, while rejecting the "merely" theatrical, echo Antonin Artaud's dictum in *The Theater and Its Double:*

> The theater will never find itself again—i.e., constitute a means of true illusion—except by furnishing the spectator with the truthful precipitate of dreams, in which his taste for crime, his erotic obses-sions, his savagery, his chimeras, his utopian sense of life and mat-ter, even his cannibalism, pours out, on a level not counterfeit and illusory, but interior.[37]

Satanic ritual abuse, then, whether it "really exists" or is instead a "true illusion," presenting the watcher with the "truthful precipitate of dreams," is, in Artaud's theater just that, a theater that remains hidden to itself, a theater whose substance lies not in the recoverable certainty of memory, but in the imprint of trauma—whatever its source—on the nerve ends of brain and body.

Indeed, *body memories*—the ability of the body to hold memory's traumatic imprint—is common to both Stanislavskian approaches to acting and to DID therapies. In a passage recalling both Stanislavski and Finley's unheard screams, as well as the reappearance of the *infans* of the murdered child, Ellen Bass and Laura Davis, two experts of the recovered-memory movement, tell us,

> It is also possible to remember only feelings. Memories are stored in our bodies, and it is possible to physically reexperience the ter-ror of abuse. Your body may clutch tight, or you may feel the screams you could not scream as a child. Or you may feel you are suffocating and cannot breathe.[38]

Bass and Davis then quote one of their patients directly:

> I would get body memories that would have no pictures to them at all. I would just start screaming and feel that something was com-

ing out of my body that I had no control over. . . . When my passion was aroused in some way, I would remember in my body, although I wouldn't have a conscious picture, just the screaming coming out of me.[39]

The irony here is that the truth of memory in DID, is, according to its proponents, objectively and empirically real[40] but finds its objectivity in a decidedly nonempirical, non-Kantian space—the space of body sensation and emotion.

But although body memories are a common point of departure for both DID and theater training, the difference between the two is not to be found in the difference between truth and "acting," but rather in the difference between truth and *meaning*. While the actor never forgets that reenacted memory is in some sense constructed or "purified" in Stanislavski's terms, Stanislavski himself chastises his students against mere acting: "Instead of drawing from your memory of life, you [take] your material from the theatrical archives of your mind." At the same time, the "life" that Stanislavski invokes is not the same as empirical truth, for in remembering, we must also remember that *"Time is a splendid filter for our remembered feeling—besides it is a great artist. It not only purifies, it also transmutes even painful realistic memories into poetry."*[41] There is, as Adorno would have understood, something undeniably appalling in this sentiment. The idea, nonetheless, serves to distinguish between the notion of the objective truth in memory— which Stanislavski thinks is unlikely if not impossible—and the meaning that resides in memory, a different, nonobjective kind of truth.

In DID, however, the memory is, according to early therapists like Bass and Davis at least, supposedly real and recoverable. And once the memory is "recovered," the self is "transformed"—once again, the secular American conversion experience. In fact, what is often overlooked in both recovered-memory and DID therapy, and in performance and performance theory, is the rather obvious intersection between certain modes of American religious practice, performance, and pathology. As I mentioned in the opening chapters of this book, the traditions of charismatic religion, what was once called Enthusiasm, have saturated virtually every corner of American life and have profoundly affected American history and culture. From the first Great Awakenings in the 1730s, through the spectacles of Cane Ridge, the performance of religion in America has been in some sense embodied through the spectacles of enthusiasm.

The most visible recent incarnation of this tradition is perhaps American Pentecostalism and its variants, born in Los Angeles in 1906 through the Enthusiastic glossolalia of one William Seymour, an African American preacher. Eventually, in 1914, Pentecostalism was institutionalized within the Assemblies of God, a church that tradition- ally attracted those who felt, like Finley, dispossessed and marginal- ized in American society. Harold Bloom has suggested that speaking in tongues and possession by the Spirit in Pentecostalism, and, within cer- tain Appalachian sects and cults, the more extreme, ecstatic practices of snake-handling and strychnine drinking, are examples of religions of inversion, displacing the vices of earthly life—intoxication, gambling, lying, cheating—with the intoxications of the Spirit, "gambling" one's life on the spirit, speaking in tongues, and confessing one's sins to God.[42] They are a kind of tantric fundamentalism. Within the purview of this "symbolism of inversion," Finley's work, both early and recent, represents a dispossession by the voices of patriarchy. The gospel of consumerism is preached as scatology, memory and history are fore- grounded as an unknowable but eternal present, and the self is perpet- ually lost to itself. Similarly, for victims of supposed satanic ritual abuse, the myth of American individualism, founded on religious faith and self-actualization, is displaced by the countermyth of American collectivism—the cult—born of profanity and victimhood.

More recently, the spectacle of Enthusiastic performance has appeared on a mass scale in such phenomena as the Promise Keepers and Million Man Marches, which have demonstrated a similar kind of mediated inversion—the notion of renewed promises predicated, of course, on the presumption of promises broken—held together through the charismatic celebrations of the Spirit. Meanwhile, at the political level, Ralph Reed, Pat Robertson, and the Christian Coalition have shown us the political efficacy of Enthusiastic show coupled with political hardball. The codification of religious ecstasy into political ide- ology is, perhaps, not so different from what we see in Finley's shift into more clearly articulated political positions out of her earlier Orphic spectacles. From the traditions of Enthusiastic religion in America, in fact, we see performers like Finley borrowing *from* conservative reli- gion traditions more than the reverse. Lynda Hart's assertion—an assertion that is still one of the theoretical assumptions of the Left—that conservative ideology absorbs leftist political theory to its own ends, is only half true. Leftist ideology must also see and acknowledge what it has taken from conservative traditions, in this case the peculiar attractions of charismatic performance.[43] Some scholars, in fact, believe charismatic or Enthusiastic performance to be the quintessential characteristic of American religion, indeed, of American identity itself. One could easily conclude that DID and the kind of performance art that Finley creates really have their roots in these Enthusiastic traditions of American spirituality (a point that Donna Haraway makes in typically blithe manner, and then leaves unexplored).[44] While various Christian groups may have their versions of spirit possession taking place in their revival tents, the post/humanist enclaves have theirs as well. Therapy groups have their DID, while the art and performance crowd has the vicarious thrill of Enthusiastic possession in their artists-on-the-edge. Theorists have their "visions of excess" in writers like Haraway. And we should not necessarily be put off by the seemingly radical ideological differences between Finley's brand of feminism and some of the Evangelical churches. Even within the traditions of American religions themselves, the various faiths are often radically different in underlying dogma, yet share common experiential characteristics; during divine possession, eyes close, the body rocks, new voices emerge and speak in tongues, often rising to the fevered pitch of prophecy. Visions are seen, and voices heard. The faithful may slip in and out of these states with great rapidity, as Karen Finley does during her performances, and as DID patients do during their fugues. Possession by the spirit (of?) seems integral to the American experience.

But sometimes, like the inversions of Enthusiastic experience itself, the spirit possession that emerges in DID and recovered memories is of a decidedly different type. Perhaps predictably, if not ironically, many of the most dramatic instances of recovered memories are memories of the above-mentioned satanic ritual abuse—a type of abuse that characteristically leads to DID—and arise within the charismatic Christian churches as a direct result of presumed demonic possession.[45] Although many such cases exist, perhaps none has been more carefully documented than the case of Paul Ingram, a sheriff in Olympia, Washington, and a devout fundamentalist Christian. In many ways, the Ingram incident remains the archetype for these cases. In 1988 Ingram was accused by his two daughters of sexual abuse.[46] The two young women had recently attended a Christian "youth camp" and been exposed to a Christian psychic who "saw" them being abused. At first they said they could remember nothing, but under the tutelage of the psychic-therapist, the memories came. Ingram initially denied the charges, but as the daughters "remembered" more and increasingly more bizarre instances of incest, he became convinced he had done ter-rible things even though he could not remember them. His daughters wouldn't lie, he said, so he must have abused them. He became con-vinced by his minister and the police that Satan had possessed him and blocked out his memories of abusing his daughters, and that he must somehow reconstruct them if he was to be cured and saved.

Soon after the initial allegations, in scenarios that could have been lifted from David Lynch's *Twin Peaks*[47] or the Grand Guignol, the daughters began remembering instances of abuse that had Satanist overtones. Robed figures had repeatedly raped them. Then there were figures standing in circles, chanting. Then full-blown Satanism, "barn-yard rituals, blood oaths, and high priests and priestesses."[48] Finally came bestiality and multiple infant murders.[49] The minister and police confronted Ingram with the new accusations and suggested that his soul was on the line—he had to admit to the charges or lose his soul to Satan. He assented. Later, when the children were given physical examinations by an investigating doctor, no signs were found of the many cuts, bloodlettings, and violent rapes that the daughters had reported.

Although Sandy Ingram, Paul's wife, also began under similar duress to recover memories of her participation in the cult abuse, no charges were filed against her, because no evidence could be found. Paul Ingram, however, based on his earlier confession, was sentenced to twenty years in prison after admitting to six counts of third-degree rape. Although he retracted his confession before his sentencing and now believes the memories he conjured were false, he is still serving out his term in a Washington State prison.

Apart from the bizarre nature of the story and its lurid attempts to portray a typical middle-class family as a nest of devil-worshipers, what is most germane to the present discussion is the way in which the "recovered" memories were retrieved. Like Karen Finley, like those filled with the Holy Spirit, Paul Ingram would rock back and forth, close his eyes, and fall into a trancelike state and speak "as though some lost soul" were speaking through him. His accounts, also like Fin-ley's, were in the present tense—unlike the usual confessional mode of past tense—and began with a quiet calm that eventually worked itself into a frenzy of "praying, sobbing, crying out in anguish, closing his eyes and rocking back and forth."[50] At one point he confabulates an incident in which he rapes his children and "may have told the children that they needed to learn the sex-acts and how to do them right,"[51] a phrase strongly reminiscent of Finley's daddy-figure, "showing me what it's like to be a woman. To be loved. That's a daddy's job." At the same time, there is in Paul Ingram's recountings a kind of detachment or dispossession. When he would fall into a trance state and describe various scenes of sexual abuse, he did so oddly, initially talking about what "he 'would have' done with little or no emotion, as if he were a detached observer *rather than the central character in the drama.*"[52] Like Finley, moving from "she" to "I," so Paul Ingram moved from the "I would" to the "I DID."

Although the Ingram family's story seemingly does not directly involve DID, it does indicate the central issue of DID and its therapies: where, precisely is the differentiation, the slippage into a new personality, occurring? In a passage describing a patient slipping into alterity, Glass notes that in certain cases of DID, the shift between identities is almost invisible:

> Nora's subtlety in personality shift was extraordinary. Although I found little evidence of discrete, isolated personalities, shifts appeared in tone and inflection, the movement of eyebrows, voice pitch, *imperceptible gestures.*[53]

How, Brecht might wonder, can a gesture be imperceptible? Although the therapist assures him that Nora has multiple identities, Glass himself is unable to see significant differences between supposed alters. He, like Paul Ingram, accepts the diagnosis, however, even though "Nora's personalities were difficult to see."[54] What this and the Ingram story seem to suggest—echoing DID's first appearance in Vivet—is that multiplicity is emerging not in the patient, but in the observer, not in the accused, but in the accuser. It is not Paul Ingram's daughters that are divided, nor is it Paul Ingram himself, but the investigators, the ministers, and detectives who literally create the split, who generate the multiple identity of Paul Ingram as police chief, loving father, and satanic monster: the split vision of the primal social triad that accuses him—the critical faculties of church, law, and family.[55]

Here, it seems to me, is the crux of this complex issue: from Vivet, through Finley, and Paul Ingram, observed multiplicity lives, apparently, as much in the eye of the seer as in the mind of the seen. The strong suggestion that multiplicity and decenteredness is itself *created through* the unified eye of power, through the notes of a master observer, seems to deeply problematize theories that posit multiplicity and decenteredness as a priori states. This is not to suggest that we are, in fact, unified and self-identical. Nor is it to suggest that identity and gender are stable, congealed states. It is to suggest that the theorist— like the DID patient, like Finley, like the actor, like Paul Ingram, the accused—inhabits a space absolutely infected by theater. It is to suggest that the perception of the insubstantial, the decentered, the provisional, is as much a product of theater and its illusions as is the perceptual illusion of a stable unified identity.

Remembrance

"Freud's theory," writes psychoanalyst Jean Laplanche, "is a theory of memory . . . best apprehended through pathological avatars: illusions or errors of memory, *fausse reconnaissance*, screen memories, etc."[56] This theory of memory, through which memories are reinterpreted and repositioned, hinges, Laplanche suggests, on the dynamic of translation and retranslation, which itself props itself against a state of human trauma akin to grief. Memory, like grief, exists in a kind of doubled reality. We grieve not merely because the person longed for is gone, but also because she is very much present. It is the duality of the condition of loss that brings about the pain. If the issue were merely loss, loss and forgetfulness, we would not suffer, but because we cannot rid ourselves of the presence of the person who is not there, we mourn.

The same seems generally true of memory. The problem in determining the substance of memory is not that a memory is present, causing us grief, or that it is absent, causing us frustration and anxiety. The difficulty is that memory precisely denotes in its very presence what is not there. Every memory therefore forbids us access to that memory's "real" content. The cure in each case—either to memory's doubled state, or grief's presence/absence—is to translate what is absent into what is present. But this is not the same as bringing something from "back there" to "up here." Memory is memory, after all, because there is nothing "back there" to bring up. We are in some sense always creating memory from scratch, just as memory is always creating us out of seeming nothingness. The same is true, of course, in theater. The apparently self-evident idea that theater repeats itself is false. The assumption that some "reality" lies behind theater is also false, for theater's reality, as Artaud understood, as Joseph Jefferson knew, is in its refusal of the re-presentation. Hence the issue both in theater and in memory is far more complicated than merely "recovering" memory or repeating performance. Memory as it attaches itself to unresolved trauma, for example, is intolerable not because it has been "repressed," but rather because it will not be translated. "The inability to recover the past," writes Cathy Caruth,

> is . . . closely and paradoxically tied up, in trauma, with the inability to have access to it. And this suggests that what returns in flashback is not simply an overwhelming experience that has been obstructed by a later repression or amnesia, but an event that is itself constituted, in part, by its lack of integration into consciousness.[57]

Certainly, the memory of trauma, then, like theater, *like the inception of the artwork itself*—in the theater, the appearance of mise-en-scène—operates as a kind of Lacanian foreclusion, as a reality that *"escapes* full consciousness as it occurs."[58] The return of the event as flashback or dream is a return akin to Lacan's understanding of hallucination, as something that is phantasmagorical to the observer, but real to the one who experiences it. The hallucinatory quality of the return is due, in part, to the fact that the event and its return are not and cannot be *integrated* into a narrative, into consciousness itself. As such, Caruth claims, one cannot have voluntary access to such an event and its memory traces. The truth of such an event, she says, lies in its incomprehensibility: she refers to "both *the truth of an event* and *the truth of its incomprehensibility*,"[59] what the filmmaker Claude Lanzmann, in reference to his films on the Holocaust, calls "blindness," or "the vital condition of creation."[60] This is also reminiscent of the process that Lacan describes as moving from reality to truth in the analytic session. The point of analysis, according to Lacan, is not to resuscitate the trauma itself—either as memory or "lived experience," but is rather to recover the truth of the trauma, its deepest meaning and significance.

The movement from incomprehensibility to the comprehensible involves a process of transmuting the trauma through narrative memory, which allows the story to be told and thus incorporated into a generalized knowledge of the past or history. When this happens, though, the narrative that allows incorporation forces the trauma to lose both its "precision and force."[61] We can mark the location of trauma, in other words, not by re-creating or recovering it, but by noticing where it begins to fade in its force and precision, where, in effect, it is translated

to a new site and becomes a "mere" representation or object, a reproduction that, as Nietzsche reminds us, must always find the correct tension between illusion, forgetting, and (correctly) remembering. History, like theater as mise-en-scène, thus becomes an amalgam of reality,
fiction, and desire, but an amalgam whose constituent parts can never
be isolated one from another. The "truth" of this art object (inasmuch as
such an object marks the edge of the traumatic) is thus contained in its
very rejection of the causal in favor of the reasonable, and the reasonable, while reasonable, is nonetheless always arguable. The same might
be said of history, of course, and in extricating the causal from our
understanding of history, we wrest history from the causally driven
theories of materialism. This wrested space, within which history
appears, is the space of consciousness—and consciousness of consciousness and the theatricalities that inhabit it—that I have described
as theater. This space is not the Symbolic per se, but the possibility of
thought and desire apprehending themselves in all of their angularities
and disreputable inclinations. This is the space within which we might
explore the vicissitudes of history, or gender, or race, remembering, at
the same time, that *the theater which gives these birth* will always have the
last say.

# Act IV: Abdication

I see two suns,

I see two cities of Thebes,

I see two seven gated cities . . .

—Pentheus, in *The Bacchae*

7

Nothing Doing

In Tony Kushner's *Angels in America*, out of the infinite abyss of priority, a "supplement at the origin" of his existence, Prior Walter's ancestors—the prior Priors, so to speak—situate their spectered substance within the etiologies of the plague, the myriad diseases of historical epochs past—the Black Death, cholera, "the pestilence." "I am . . . the scion of an ancient line," says the current Prior, the scion (sign) of history as contagion.[1] This and similar lines are usually read by Kushner's critics within the context of his concerns about AIDS. In this view, Prior's history, and so all priority, all history is "always already" about AIDS, about intolerance, hate, and exclusion, not unlike Maurice Blanchot's idea of history as disaster. But we might just as well reverse the particularity, and say that AIDS is always already about the plague, and that it is the plague that is the seeming apparition of history.

How are we to read Kushner's celestial/historical witness to this catastrophe, however? Shoshana Felman cautions against interpreting the manifest content of the plague in literature as its real/unconscious meaning. The "meaning" of illness, she writes

> is always fundamentally, in one way or another, the scandal of an illness, of a metaphorical or literal disease; and that the imperative of bearing witness, which here proceeds from the contagion of the plague—from the eruption of an evil that is radically incurable—is itself somehow a philosophical and ethical correlative of a situation *with no cure*, and of a radical human condition of exposure and vulnerability.[2]

No cure and no answer: "Am I going to die?" Prior asks his apparitions. The previous Prior responds, "We aren't allowed to discuss . . ."[3]

The horrible toll of the AIDS epidemic notwithstanding, then, the "meaning" of this plague within American culture needs deeper palpation beneath the skin of a too-quickly diagnosed homophobia, just as in Other "plagues of fantasy," symptoms need palpation within the pleural cavity of the political body, beneath the surface of racism, sexism, or classism. The unconscious content of this plague, these plagues, might be more directly apprehended in the parapraxes and symptomatologies of a fundamental American sickness articulated in its most horrific acts, that is, children murdering children—diseases with no perceivable etiology but the lack of etiology itself, no origin and thus no cure.

Alongside the AIDS-as-plague motif, however, Kushner also situates his play within another often mentioned, yet undertheorized, context. In the ecstatic claims of Prior's ancestors to his status as "Prophet, Seer, and Revelator," in Joe's and Harper's struggles with their marriage and identities, in the entire cosmology of angels and the revelations of the steel-paged books, Tony Kushner's deeper anima (animosity?) is the Church of Jesus Christ of Latter-Day Saints, or, using the popular term the members eschew: the Mormons. It is the presence of Mormonism within Kushner's play cycle more than any other single factor that gives these works their oddly powerful and conflicted voice—the bizarre celebration of cosmological ecstasy in the embrace of "homosexual disease" that is antithetical to Mormonism. For in Mormonism, homosexuality *is,* quite literally, the plague.

What then are we to find in this confluence between plague—cultured within the hysterical performative serum of American history—and the revelatory, prophetic, Gnostic cosmologies of Mormonism? According to Antonin Artaud, it is in precisely this confluence that the theater is born:

> If the essential theater is like the plague, it is not because it is contagious, but because like the plague it is the revelation, the bringing forth, the exteriorization of a depth of latent cruelty by means of which all the perverse possibilities of the mind, whether of an individual or a people, are localized.[4]

And indeed, from its roots in the revivals of the second Great Awakening, its early involvement with alchemy and Masonic ritual, in its revelatory and prophetic zeal, Mormonism, more than any other American religion *or* theater, enacts the theatrical-as-truth in disturbingly transgressive ways and stands as a kind of inverted western American image of eastern American Puritanism. Puritanism seemingly stripped away all modes of the performative in religion, relying instead on the authenticity of the interior scene of faith, and saw that "inside-outside" dichotomy undergo conversion through the "hystory" plays of religious Enthusiasm à la Cane Ridge, and then eventually move into the Baptist and Evangelical Christian churches. Mormonism transposed this Puritan "inside-outside" into a quite literal "hidden scene" of faith, the mystery-play/alchemical scenarios of the secret/sacred Endowment Ceremonies performed within the concealed celestial theaters of the Mormon temples. These scenarios, heavily influenced by the Masonic ritual/plays of secrecy and salvation of the early 1800s, and more pointedly, by the European rituals of alchemy and cabala, are carefully scripted and acted out. Members play the parts of God, Elohim, Adam, Peter, and Lucifer in surprisingly homely, if, like Kushner, didactic, renderings of scene and dialogue:

> PETER: Good morning.
> LUCIFER: Good morning gentlemen.
> PETER: What are you doing here?
> LUCIFER: Observing the teachings of these people.
> PETER: What is being taught?
> LUCIFER: The Philosophies of men, mingled with scripture.
> PETER: How is this teaching received?
> LUCIFER: Very well! Except this man does not seem to believe what is being taught.
> *(Peter approaches Adam and shakes his hand.)*
> PETER: Good morning. What do you think of this teaching?[5]

These segments of the endowment ceremony, one of the most sacred in Mormonism, read like skits or film improvs, and have, like the drama of mainstream America, been replaced in part by videotaped versions. Participants are still required to enact the homely dialogues, nonetheless, and are ritually costumed. They literally, at ceremony's end, pass through the veil that hangs from ceiling to floor—separating the acolytes from the celestial drama on stage—into knowledge, the reenactment of the story of creation and salvation, restoring, in Artaud's words, dormant conflicts and their powers, and giv[ing] these powers names we hail as symbols: and behold! before our eyes is fought a battle of symbols, one charging against another in an impossible melee; for there can be theater only from the moment when the impossible really begins and when the poetry which occurs on the stage sustains and superheats the realized symbols.[6]

"In the theater, as in the plague, there is something both victorious and vengeful," Artaud continues. And indeed, what is perhaps most interesting in this mystery play of cruelty near the beginning of the twenty-first century is what is no longer there. In the temple revision of 1990, several portions of the scenario were removed, lest they scandalize younger, and somewhat more progressive, Mormons. Among the parts excised were those that made reference to blacks as "the cursed race of Cain,"[7] and thus unworthy to become priests (i.e., Mormons). Indeed, in a phrase reminiscent of Zoe in *The Octoroon*, a comment by a Mormon leader in the mid-1960s pretty much encapsulated Mormon racial beliefs up until the late 1970s: "[I]f there is one drop of Negro blood in my children, as I have read to you, they receive the curse."[8] The 1990 revisions also removed strong references to women as subservient to men "as to God." But perhaps the most interesting change was the removal of the gruesome, symbolic oaths and gestures: "[W]e agree that our throats be cut ear to ear . . . our tongues torn out by their roots . . . our hearts and vitals torn from our bodies and given to the birds of the air and the beasts of the field . . . our bodies be cut asunder in the midst and all our bowels gush out"—all accompanied by gests that embodied these threats: throat slicing motions, the heart torn out, the belly slit open, each enacting the punishment that would be visited upon those who would reveal the temple secrets.[9]

The most important aspect of the endowment ceremony did remain after the 1990 revisions, however: the neo-Gnostic belief in the eternal separation of the genders. This belief, coupled with the haunted "theater of cruelty" that is Mormonism's past and present (and indeed, I must add here, the past and present of probably every religion), evokes a theater in which, like both the plague and alchemical theaters of Artaud, "the image of . . . carnage and . . . essential separation . . . releases conflict, disengages powers, liberates possibilities, and if these possibilities and these powers are dark, it is the fault not of the plague or of the theater, but of life." What is crucial here is that the faithful Mormon, like Artaud's "actor gesturing through the flames," does not see the endowment ceremony as theater at all, but as a kind of earthly transport, "a believable reality which gives the heart and the senses that kind of concrete bite which all true sensation requires,"[10] an other Enthusiasm in which what is most real is precisely *the theater* of faith, an inversion of the belief in the reality of the virtual as virtual, in the reality of theater as theater. This, of course, is not unusual in ritual and religious ceremony—the Roman Catholic Mass presents similar conundrums, as I have argued at length elsewhere.[11] What *is* unusual is the appearance of this theater of faith within a religious epistemology that is itself defined by a theatricality to which it remains blinded: cover-ups, counterfeits, discrepancies, contradictions, re-visions, and multiplicities in Mormonism's religious texts remain its ongoing scandal. More than any other religion in modern times (except perhaps Stalinism or Maoism), Mormonism has used its considerable wealth and power to eradicate or conceal the contradictions within its own multiple and at times radically different sacred documents.[12] Instead of trying to allow for multiplicities and contradictions in its sacred texts—as for example, the four quite different Gospel stories of the Christian faiths—Mormonism simply ignores or denies them and at times has gone through elaborate and expensive measures to repress them. Indeed, Artaud's description of theater in the time of cholera, born of the utter breakdown of faith, evokes the practice of Mormon elders of "lying for the Lord": saying whatever needs to be said in this time of depravity to protect the faith—another permutation of the Mormon theater of cruelty.

Kushner takes up this interpretive scandal—the many variations in Joseph Smith's own story of the divine revelation of the sacred golden plates and the discovery of the "sacred implements," the Urim and Thummin—in the speech of the Angel:

> And, lo, the Prophet was led by his nightly dreams to the hiding place of the Sacred Implements, and . . . Revision in the text: The Angel did help him to unearth them, for he was weak of body though not of will.[13]

The "revision in the text," like the pragmatic "mis-remembering" of the central sacred events in the story of Mormonism, is simply glossed over.

Kushner's angels in fact incarnate this discrepant chiasmas. They are at once multigendered—each not only having both vagina and penis, but severally (eight vaginas and "Hermaphroditically Equipped with a Bouquet of Phalli")—and multivocal ("I I I I"),[14] and thus of multiple identities. But though multiple and presumably "shifty," the angels at the same time represent stasis, Sameness, and the singularity of ideological calcification ("STOP MOVING! . . . HOBBLE YOURSELVES")[15] consonant with the extraordinary conservatism of Mormonism. Similarly, although they are prone to a prophetic excess that exhibits itself as Enthusiastic sexual license—"HOLY Estrus! HOLY Orifice! Ecstasis in Excelsis!"[16] the Angel cries in a celestial coming—they are also quite ordinary, mere organizers of events. "[T]hey're basically incredibly powerful bureaucrats," says Prior, but "they have no imagination . . . they're sort of fabulous and dull at the same time."[17] The angels are, in fact, an *emanation* of Prior (not merely imagined by him), the ordinary dying man who is himself prone to fits of prophetic excess, and who represents in his very name a kind of static divine lineage, an enduring primordial presence.

The scenes between Prior and the Angel, of course, are Kushner's revisitation of the "counterfeiter" Joseph Smith's encounters with the angel Moroni, and the subsequent finding of the golden tablets on which was written the Book of Mormon, one of the founding texts of Mormonism. Smith, the founder of Mormonism, evokes more than a little of the spirit of the counterfeiter Stephen Burroughs, both religious geniuses and consummate con-men (Smith, like Burroughs, was an occultist, diviner, and money-finder whose powers of divination eventually became quite literally divine).

One also sees in Kushner's polysexual Angel the suggestion of Mormonism's somewhat later embrace of polygamy—a strategy to insure maximum fecundity among Mormon women and bring as many "new souls" into the world as possible, and, more pragmatically, to alleviate the high proportion of female to male Mormons in their exodus west. Even Prior's stone spectacles, which of course invoke the problem of the opacity of the specular itself, are counterparts to the Urim and Thummin of Smith's encounter with Moroni, the oxymoronic "seeing stones" that allowed for the interpretation of the sacred texts and the establishment of Mormon cosmology. This cosmology is at once at the very heart of the American "western movement"—thus of America itself—and completely unknown to American culture at large.

The particulars of this cosmology are unique. Most non-Mormon "gentiles" think of Mormonism as a fairly straightforward, albeit conservative brand of patriarchal Christianity. But while Mormons profess belief in Jesus Christ (hence the proper name for the church: The Church of Jesus Christ of Latter-Day Saints), their belief system is, according to Harold Bloom's rather disingenuous endorsement at least, far closer to Jewish cabala or early Gnostic religion than it is to mainstream Christianity. The Mormons, for example, believe in multiple, even infinite gods (hence Kushner's angelic "I I I I") each inhabiting his own universe, with each loyal and faithful Mormon male destined to become, after death, his own god, presiding and having authority, like "our" God, over his own, private celestial fiefdom. We revisit again an infinite nesting of critical stances: each Mormon god overseeing a cosmos of mortals who might each eventually become Mormon gods overseeing a cosmos of mortals, ad infinitum—the cosmic theater as *mise en abîme*.

The notion, then, of authority is internally split in Mormon cosmology: the strict authoritarian adherence to doctrine in this life assures the Mormon man that he will enter the celestial kingdom as servant to no other god but himself, an authority unto no other but himself. This adumbrates the attraction of American poststructuralism (represented by Kushner's texts) to a similar kind of split within authority, and the move in recent decades to name the reader herself (as a "subject position" of course) as ultimate authority of a text's meaning. This is corollary to the impulse in Mormonism that also rejects eternal subservience to "higher authority" and seeks, in eternity, to become the absolute site of interpretive authority within oneself as god. Thus the Angel's instruction to Prior, "Open me Prophet. I I I I am the Book," and the subsequent *translation* of the book into Prior's own identity through the Angel's assertion that Prior has himself become "Vessel of the BOOK," in whose blood the future is written as "STASIS."[18] In a universe of infinite gods, like the academic universe of multiple contingencies, each contingent truth becomes absolute; inasmuch as I am able, within myself, to "rewrite" or change my perception of truth, and become a kind of authorial god, a prophet who has become "blind as prophets do," deciding moment by moment what constitutes truth, contingency becomes, ironically, a kind of guarantee of contingent truth's eternal verity. Similarly, Mormonism's understanding of eternity, which is not merely static, as it is for Kushner's angels, but *historical* (i.e., constantly changing, undergoing a continuous [re]organization by God), rejects the usual Christian notion of the afterlife as the Same and introjects *difference* into the eternal. This is a kind of historicist or constructivist approach that sees divine presence not as creative, but as *organizational*—the word Mormonism uses to connote God's interaction with his universe. Indeed, in defending the discrepancies of its own history, one Mormon apologist writes,

> Perhaps the main barrier to understanding the development of Mormon theology is an underlying assumption . . . that there is a cumulative unity of doctrine. . . . As a result, older revelations are interpreted by referring to current doctrinal positions. Thus, most members would suppose that a scripture or statement at any point in time has resulted from such orderly change. While this type of exegesis or interpretation may produce systematic theology and while it may satisfy those trying to understand and internalize current doctrine, *it is bad history since it leaves an unwarranted impression of continuity and consistency.*[19]

These Foucauldian cross-reflections—in which the history of Mormon thought is cast as a power relation that is discontinuous and ruptured—are not to say that Mormonism is "just like" poststructural forms of thought. It is to suggest that what sometimes seem the most radical departures of poststructuralism represent (as I have suggested throughout this book) what is most obdurately American in our systems of thought. Multiplicity, historicization (re: historicism), and oracular assertion, though in some sense "triggered" by poststructural/French theory, have found fertile ground here because they are in some fundamental way quintessentially American.

Again, by way of example, there is no more ubiquitous formulation in poststructural theory than "the return to": Lacan's return to Freud, of course, and the numerous "returns to Marx" in the Frankfurt school and beyond, and now, in the work of Žižek and others, the "return to Lacan." The epistemologies of "the return" echo the double inscription of Mormonism's own attitudes toward its textual discrepancies. While, on the one hand, both Mormonism and poststructuralism attempt to elucidate the founding texts by finessing or sometimes ignoring what the texts actually say—thus relying on what is said outside the text as the substance of the text—both still wish to maintain the authority of that text by assuring us that interpretative variations (discrepancies) in no way weaken the truth of the texts themselves. By recognizing discrepancy, and then trying to erase or sublimate its significance, both Mormonism and poststructural theories of interpretation

seek to erase the "law of castration"—the unitary voice of the text—
through the imposition of the law of castration: in Mormonism, by literally concealing or disavowing recognized difference, and in the case
of poststructuralism, by claiming final authority for the claim that there
is no final authority, that "the author is dead," and thus that multiplicity of interpretation—contingency—is the true, eternal state of things.[20]
Here is the double-bound issue presented as prologue by Aleksii Ante-
dilluvianovich Prelapsarianov:

> Change? Yes, we must have change, only show me the Theory, and
> I will be at the barricades, show me the book of the next Beautiful
> Theory, and I promise you these blind eyes will see again, just to
> read it, to devour that text. Show me the words that will reorder
> the world, or else keep silent.[21]

Change, the "World's Oldest Living Bolshevik" seems to suggest, is,
must be, grounded in a text, a Theory (note the caps) that *determines* historical change. Even though Prelapsarianov asks whether "the Past"
will "release us," it is the past (as preexistent Theory giving rise to
Praxis) that determines change. Change is thus predetermined, is, in
fact, already past, is, in a word, self-contradicting—impossible.

Indeed, Kushner is not immune to these seeming contradictions
and elisions; as Belize says when told of the Angel's miraculous
appearance to Prior: "The sexual politics of this are *very* confusing."
And by naming the character Prior as "Prophet, Seer, and Revelator,"
Kushner places him within the highest orders of the Mormon Church,
suggesting, at some level, that the plague-stricken of the ages—the victims of the Black Death and cholera, and now the victims of AIDS—are
themselves the high prophets of a New American Religion, a religion of
Ecstatic excess and static Sameness.

But while Kushner's queer Mormon prophet Prior nicely represents this American contradiction, the *Angels* cycle fails in its larger
vision because it will not recognize theater's plague. "All true freedom
is dark," says Artaud,

> and infallibly identified with sexual freedom which is also dark,
> although we do not know precisely why. . . . And that is why all
> the great Myths are dark, so that one cannot imagine, save in an
> atmosphere of carnage, torture, and bloodshed, all the magnificent

> Fables which recount to the multitudes the first sexual division and the first carnage of essence that appeared in creation.[22]

Theater's plague is that it creates and enforces separation, not only mere difference. This separation, like the mythic, theatrical impulses of Mormonism, determines an endless alienation between and *within* gender(s). But theater, unlike religion and unlike theory, demands the agon of that separation—its pain and its depravity. *Angels,* in legitimating Queerness, in normalizing same-sexuality, excises both "pere-versions" and depravity from the play cycle. Kushner's animosity toward Mormonism—a Mormonism that is, like Artaud's theater, a theater of Gnosis—represents his own inability *in* the theater to approach theater's place in American identity (or lack thereof). This lack underscores the melodramatic impulse in the plays—not only in the emotional and populist timbres of dialogue and situation, or even in the presentation of illness as empathic metaphor, but also in the fantastical appearance of the angels themselves—a reappearance of the melodramatic "sensation scenes," the counterpart to melodrama's endless train wrecks, explosions, and avalanches onstage, which still, as in the plays of Andrew Lloyd Webber, form the nucleus of popular American drama. Once again, the real theater of cruelty, the secretive, homophobic excesses of Mormon prophecy, or the daily, plague-scourged events of American society, exceed the theater that stands in failed witness to them. Even the character of Roy Cohn, whose failure is, ironically, that he denies depravity within himself, closes off the space within which the true darkness of human evil can be glimpsed, the depravity that is us, Queer or not, the dark, harrowing sin we find in Strindberg, or even Shakespeare. No gender, male, female, or Other, is spared the black heart that is the Real riddle of human history.

Suzan-Lori Parks's *The America Play,* perhaps more than any other text, demarcates the unconscious space of this study. The puzzled theatrical fragments of American history are stuck in a holding pattern around an abyss, the endless political and domestic violence and the violence of critique: the assassination of Abraham Lincoln in Ford's Theater, to be sure, but also the latent, plague-infested theater of it all, going back to the beginning, from the Puritan land-fall into the "Great Hole of History," through the obsessive-compulsive and repetitive theatrics of Capital emerging "somewhere in past-land that is somewhere back there," to the Mormonesque "Some inaccuracies are good for business," to the dead enfant terrible grown large in the collective mind, the Foundling Father, the embodiment of Alain Finkielkraut's "society that has finally become adolescent."[23]

The America Play in fact completes the urgency of Sam Shepard's *Buried Child*. The exhumation of a deathly repressed at that play's heart, the impacted keloid of some historical trauma tripping toward psychotic revelation, finds its completion-as-disintegration in Parks's text. Here words in fact become things ("HAW HAW HAW"), elliptical syntax is the norm ("Full fringe. The way he appears on the money"), and new figurations of speech fall away in favor of repetition ("LINCOLN/ BOOTH/LINCOLN/BOOTH"). All meaning moves toward "the environs of the Hole," to quote Lacan, the foreclosed space of an Absent in consciousness, history's emptiness out of which emerges the Real of hallucination—that which reigns outside the purview of the Father's law, abolishing it, instituting, instead, a theory of pure utterance severed eternally from meaning. Parks's play moves boldly toward the Brave New World of nonpatriarchal discourse, in fact, and unwittingly asks if that antipatriarchal shattered discourse is really where we want to live.

The America Play, set in the black box/Great Hole of History, generates this endless set of returns through a prototypically American invention: a Disneyesque interactive virtual-history performance, in which (for a price) one may sneak into a virtual Ford's Theater, into the virtual president's black box, and shoot a virtual Lincoln. The scenario is always (and never) the same, signaled by the virtual guffaws of the Great Man, played by a noncharacter called the Lesser Known, a black man in a series of fake beards who is himself the double of American history's blackface minstrel—originally a white man playing a black, and now, in the figure of the Lesser Known, a black man playing a white, Lincoln. In switching the race/role, and in the endless repetition of the moment of death, the play suggests that the singular historical moment of Lincoln's assassination conceals the numberless deaths of Others submerged beneath the national trauma of the presidential murder. At the same time, the repetition suggests the seeming unreality of national tragedy—the tendency of media, for example, to replay the crucial scenes—the Zapruder film, the shooting of Oswald by Ruby, James Brady twitching on the pavement, the Challenger explosion, the World Trade Center's towers collapsing—endlessly in the hope that repetition will somehow create some sense of shared reality. This reinscription of the traumatic (which, at the individual level, is diagnosed as post-traumatic stress disorder, or PTSD) as repetition, disconnected from "associative chains of meaning," moves in the direction of what Cathy Caruth, too easily discounting the Lacanian unconscious, suggests is the historical nature of PTSD:

> [T]raumatic experience . . . is not a pathology, that is, of falsehood or displacement of meaning, but of history itself. If PTSD must be understood as a pathological symptom, then it is not so much a symptom of the unconscious, as it is a symptom of history.[24]

Caruth goes on to explain that the issue in PTSD is not our recovery of memory, but memory's recovery of us. We cannot simply piece traumatic events together into "associative chains of meaning," but must come to understand instead that the hallucinatory qualities of experienced trauma are precisely what define trauma's reality.

> Central to the very immediacy of this experience . . . is a gap that carries the force of the event and does so precisely at the expense of simple knowledge and memory. The force of the experience would appear to arise precisely, in other words, in the collapse of its understanding.[25]

This is no mere invocation to recovered memory, however, no "simple amnesia," but rather the powerful recognition that the obsessive return of trauma—as dream, as memory, as history—necessitates its return as the fragmentary, that which specifically resists the very narrative unity that would give it "meaning." The insistent return of the fragmentary is, according to Caruth, the "truth" of trauma, opposed to its meaning: for the meaning of trauma is precisely that it can have no meaning to those who suffer its enormity. This return of the fragmentary as Real is thus perhaps at the farthest possible remove from the simply mimetic.

Parks's play, however, and the images of history in the play are little more than an overdetermination of mimesis, or rather mimetic images of mimesis, finding expression both in form and content:

> (Rest)
> A wink to Mr. Lincoln's pasteboard cutout.
> (Winks at Lincoln's pasteboard cutout)
> (Rest)[26]

Doubled images are themselves doubled, and doubled again: the repeated stage direction frames the actor speaking a line to a paste-board cutout, a double of Lincoln, hence of himself, which is doubled again in the stage direction giving action to the spoken line.

The mimetic history that is repeated, is repeated within the empty construct of the Great Hole, which is itself a double of the "real" Great Hole "in the middle of nowhere" (Illinois? an infant's Imaginary grave?), the hole that, in yet another doubling, "is an exact replica of the Great Hole of History" (159), a figuration of collective amnesia. This Great Hole is invoked over and over again in the play, functioning as a structural double (or multiple) of itself *as* text; the play at some level of angst is about nothing, the play is itself a Great Hole. This is suggested in the many permutations of "hole-ness": not only history and its lack, but at various times as vagina and womb, as grave, multiple graves, and multiplicity itself in the re-creation of history as kitsch: "[T]he hundreds of shallow holes he later digs the hundreds of shallow holes he'll use to bury his faux-historical knickknacks when he finally quits this business" (169).

The rage for mimesis is here aligned with a rage for artifact. Parks tries to invoke history in repetition, in the re-creation of the singular, nonrepeatable act of violence, the endlessly echoing endlessly repeated gunshots that appear/disappear throughout the play, drifting, like the play itself, like history, to silence. The terror that is history is thus emptied of content, becoming a cerebral Hole, a double of the hole in Lincoln's brain filled not with history as trauma, but rather with the disintegrated gray matter of historical detritus: a bust of Lincoln, a cherrywood jewel box, Washington's bones and his wooden teeth, glass trading beads, peace pacts, bills of trade, and so on, tracing American history back to its origins in Puritan culture and before, existing now not as historical narrative, but as midden, the compost heap of a New Historicism that, as the mimetic double of history, conceals in its archival fetishism history's deficiencies, historicism's own narrative insufficiency and its deadly clamors, in Parks's words, "the Hole and its Historicity," counterpart to the hole that *is* historicity, the history that hurts (162).

And who is the agent of this mimetic violence? The historian as gravedigger, the replication of Melville's consumptive usher, the Lesser Man as actor, the double who refashions again and again that fatal moment in history (as history?). The moment itself is the reinvention of history's rage at its own content, in this case the commonality between slavery and abolition, the complementary scripts of midcentury identity politics. The singular Lesser Man portrays Lincoln, the multiple paying guests portraying Booth, in the endless and oppressive Sameness and disruptive variation of the assassination scenario, a hysteria ending not in blindness now, but in deafness—the inability to reconstitute the diminished voices of history: "Little ringing in the ears. That's all. Slight deafness" (173). Brazil (echo of Belize), the historian gravedigger, is the double of this doubled Lesser Man, a laborer who is, as were his father, Stephen Burroughs, Joseph Smith, and Melville's confidence man, a mimic, a "pretender":

> Your Father was uh faker. Huh. One of thuh best. There wuduhnt nobody your Fathuh couldn't do. Did thuh living and thuh dead. Small-town and big-time. Made-up and historical. Fakin was your Daddys callin but diggin was his livelihood. (181)

Here the archivist/digger and actor become one in the character of Brazil. History, the great hole "and its historicity," is realigned with theater, "the passing of time, the crossing of space."

> BRAZIL: . . . At thuh original Great Hole . . . He and Her would sit on thuh lip and watch everybody who was ever anybody parade on by. Daily parades! Just like thuh Tee Vee. Mr. George Washington, for example, thuh Fathuh of our Country hisself. . . .
> LUCY: That Hole back East was a theme park, son. Keep your story to scale. (179–80)

Keeping your story to scale: this is Shakespeare's struggle in the history plays, American culture's struggle in its self-understanding. But in Parks, scale is precisely the issue. The enormity of American trauma has vanished beneath the overbearing demands of the forms she uses: the eternal return of the terror in the *sparagmos* of historical fragmentation becomes simple repetition. The revisitation of history that is fragmented, even in the Imaginary, is a revisitation that ought to carry with it the unbearable agony of Artaud's plague: the inassimilable carnage, millions dead and dying, rotting, bloating, and the force of thought that must confront the unthinkable. But this requires a history of thought, the edifice of cogito against which the fragments flow, an authoritative tradition threatened by the appearance of the fragmentary: here the *sparagmos* of history would be fearsome. But there is no historical/cultural sense of American identity. The lack that we experience, though very real, is not the same Lacanian lack posited against an obdurate, monolithic, cultural/political tradition as it was in Lacan's own France. In America there is no cogito to be dismantled, and there never has been; Parks's play, like Joseph Jefferson's *Rip*, plays out once again the American amnesis. Our history is, like all histories, easily given over to the theatrical. But our history, despising that theatrical, nonetheless allows a radically theatricalized culture/history to close off the Symbolic space within which we might understand that theater/culture. The problem for us is not so much the phallogocentrism of the cogito as it is our blindness, like Jonathan Ploughboy's blindness, to the very theater that constitutes us.

E pilogue

Reiterating the stylistics of Parks's own drama, I recapitulate: Good Friday, the feast of disappearances—the iconic figures of Christ draped with blue-black veils. The Lincolns go to the theater to forget the agony of national trauma. The presidential box hangs over the stage. Those seated in the box, hidden from the view of the audience, have a view of the stage and backstage areas. The president occupies this black-box theater masked with presidential bunting and flags, suspended within the theater, the space within which the real drama will occur. The Great Man arrives to the strains of "Hail to the Chief," steps from the shadows into the frame of the box, and gives brief audience. The play itself is given new lines in honor of Lincoln's presence.

Meanwhile, a famous actor in a family of great actors, Booth, haunts (Kafka's creature of the Burrow, the "hauntology" of history) the corridors and passageways beneath and behind the theater. He positions himself outside the box and then enters the concealed stage within. He chooses the opportune moment in the play, when Asa Trenchard, hero of *Our American Cousin* and the reapparition of Adam Trueman, refers to another character as a "sockdologizing old man-trap." *Sockdologer:* a deliverer of heavy blows, one who gives ideology as public berating, one who wears the sock or buskin. At the utterance, Booth pulls the trigger, shattering all into aphasic, amnesic noise. Utterance and gunshot become one. He leaps to the stage, "breaks a leg" (literally), turns, and delivers his last and most famous line: "Sic semper tyrannis." It is the theatrics of terrorism from Booth to McVeigh: "Thus always to tyrants." Death to liars and pretenders. Death to the politician, the alien, the immigrant. He disappears,[1] setting into motion the national production of grief and mourning, the theater of abjection with which we are now so familiar—the caisson bearing the casket, the riderless horse, boots backward in the stirrups, the little boy saluting, the arms pointing up from the balcony, the bloody hands holding the rosary, the body lying on the pavement, the quivering foot tapping out the tattoo of a ruptured brain, death-blossoms, the unthinkable collapse, and the volcanic cloud of dust, the hushed song, the firing of the volley, "Taps." The stage translating comedy to comedy, comedy to tragedy, tragedy to life, life back to the theaters of memory and grief.

And with the Lincoln assassination as melodramatic trope the translation of theater into political and now social violence in American history finds its most compelling and recent series of punctuations emerging in 1972. In that year Arthur Bremer, inspired by Lee Harvey Oswald's notoriety as assassin du jour, and taking as his role-model Alek, the violent psychopath in Stanley Kubrick's *Clockwork Orange*, tried to hunt down Richard Nixon in order to find some measure of recognition, some sense of real being, an authenticity that would be gained through a starring role on the evening news. When he couldn't get close enough to Nixon, Bremer turned his attention instead to Governor George Wallace, a presidential candidate, and shot him down in a parking lot on May 15, 1972, in Laurel, Maryland, paralyzing him for life. He recorded his hunt in a diary that was hidden and later discovered beneath a demolished bridge in Milwaukee, Wisconsin, published in *Harper's* magazine and used as the basis for a 1976 Martin Scorsese film, *Taxi Driver*, starring, among others, Robert De Niro as a deranged, sexually twisted would-be political assassin, and a young Jody Foster playing a teen-aged prostitute. In the audience at one of the countless showings of this film was one John Hinckley, who became obsessed with the celluloid Foster. On March 30, 1981, seeking recognition by Foster, some sense of real being and authenticity, an authenticity that would be gained through a starring role on the evening news, Hinckley made a dramatic assassination attempt on Ronald Reagan, Hollywood actor turned president. Tightening the epistemological circle was the 1992 production of Stephen Sondheim's musical *Assassins*, which presented portraits of the entire panoply of American assassins and assassin wannabees. And recently, closure and reopening appear most forcefully in Parks's rendition of American history with a "Great Hole" at its metaphorically ballistic center, its "Ground Zero." Waves of school shootings begin shortly after, capitalizing on the "fifteen minutes of fame" guarantee of the American mediation.

What is perhaps most interesting about this genealogy is that Travis Bickle—the prototypical marginalized assassin/killer represented by De Niro in *Taxi Driver*, a representation that is disturbingly aligned with the portrait that emerges in Bremer's diary—is, like most American killers, oddly disconnected from the culture of politics, film, music, and most certainly, theater. He knows almost nothing about movies, and his knowledge of politics is limited to a desire to rid New York of "the players," a character and sentiment not far from the attitude of Adam Trueman. Perhaps in such figures we see the contours of the shadowy "real" American, eschewing the shallowness of popular culture for the intensities of political violence, the fanatical vision of an "authentic patriot," substituting the militia-issued rifle-sight for the sight lines of stage or film, substituting reality for realism. In any case, the violence of a Bremer or Hinckley or a McVeigh, like the violence of a Harris or Klebold, seems less a product of filmic or virtual violence's influencing behavior than a cultural inability to read and critique, to see culture as culture, much like Jonathan Ploughboy's inability to see theater as theater, or the performance critic's inability to see the theatricality of critique itself, or even, we might surmise, Al Qaida's repudiation of the cultural forms of theater and critique—its militant puritanism the shadow of our own.

One result of this blindness is that the cause of this double bind—an American culture that seems arguably one of the most theatricalized, and the most hateful of any nuance of theatricality—will likely remain forever concealed. We are likely destined to remain a culture unable, even at sophisticated levels of analysis, to strike through the masks of its acting personae to the root causes of our culture's high theatricality and abhorrence of it. Certainly a truncated history, and so a history ignored, is of central import. A nation of immigrants and scattered indigenous peoples, a nation with no unifying traditions and no sense of enduring identity, also seems likely to produce the quick and ready role of the "true" American. And, in the face of such an identity lack, what would be more natural (and necessary) than "making it all up?" And in making it all up—in theatricalizing it—what more natural than an abhorrence of the theater, the very thing that would give the lie to an American identity constructed in/as absence? But in reading the diaries and researching the sources, how can we ever determine the root causes behind national self-deception, when self-deception is precisely deception without seeming cause or determination? We are once again in a hall of mirrors, for historical causality—like all arguments for causality—requires the presence, once again, of repeatability. Causality is thus bound to repetition, to rehearsal, to a species of theater.

The problem, then, is not merely a shallowness, a desire for the authentic beneath appearances: it is a profound lack in the intellectual heritage of American culture: the lack of thought, the stricturing of the Symbolic space, a critical dysfunction that seeks to reduce all intellectual activity to pragmatism. The need in the face of this lack is less the chronicling of American history or the naming of our -isms (sexism, racism, etc.) than the recognition that violence seems more connected to an inability and unwillingness to *speculate,* to philosophize about the relationships between violence and the desire for authenticity, for example, or the profound agon produced by the suppression of individual thought within the indices of identity politics.

Obviously, the sources of our heritage of political and mass murder are many and complex. But one begins to suspect that the theatrical plays a profound role in this self-replication: I would suggest that in American culture it is this theatricality, what we now call the virtual, coupled with a refusal or inability to see it, to speculate about it, to think through it, that leads to such deadly performance scenarios. James W. Clarke, in *American Assassins,* traces Bremer's violence to a mind in which contrasts, "distinctions—pleasure and pain, life and death, love and hate—became blurred."[2] And, we might surmise, the now illegible distinction between theater and life. The gradual reverberations of that gunshot, those gunshots, appear first on the stage as words, damaged and damaging words, violence born of a critical insularity, now reborn in the hands of children, grave and stainless, sights aligned with gaze and voice, black holes and lead projectiles, suction and expulsion. No Imaginary object here, but object as military surplus, the power to change history—personal and political—in a moment, to invoke the Real and cancel virtuality, beginning with the squeeze of a finger and ending with an ammonium-nitrate period at the end of an aphasic sentence. This, in the Lacanian scheme of things, is the theater of real utterance, the theater, in fact, of the Real.

NOTES

Introduction

1. All preceding quotes are from "The Columbine Tapes," by Nancy Gibbs and Timothy Roth, *Time*, December 20, 1999, 42–47. I won't even begin to describe the Enthusiastic theatrical scene following the killings: the ceremony of crosses, the cross-country evangelisms, the pious news stories . . .

2. The relation between the Lacanian Imaginary, Symbolic, and Real permeate this study: In Lacan, the Imaginary realm coincides with that part of human consciousness which understands itself and others through connections, associations, empathetic attachments to images, bodies, and objects. The Symbolic is the realm of thought that coincides with language, difference, detached consideration. The Real is whatever is real for the subject.

3. Slavoj Žižek, *The Ticklish Subject: The Absent Centre of Political Ontology* (New York: Verso, 1999), 249–50. Žižek dismisses the notion that there is any important element of American culture that can be called psychotic. He, in my estimation, grossly underestimates that psychopathology that is America.

4. The Name-of-the-Father, or *le Nom du Père*, is, in Lacanian thought, the site of authority and authorization, the place of the law, the location of significance and meaning. In translating the French into English, we lose Lacan's intended pun on the spoken phrase ("le Nom du Père") that sounds like both "the name-of-the-father," and the "the father's no," ("le non du Père") suggesting that it is the "no," the prohibition, that undergirds authority and meaning. Thus a text's meaning is produced as much by what it refuses to say, as what it presumably does. This has led to strange excesses in interpretation of texts. See my comments on "the return to" in chapter 7.

5. Slavoj Žižek, *Looking Awry: An Introduction to Jacques Lacan through Popular Culture* (Cambridge: MIT Press, 1997), 23.

6. See my discussion of Suzan-Lori Parks in the final chapter, in which the Lesser Known—a kind of child-man—is a key figure, guffawing his way through an endless procession of (virtual?) assassinations and death.

7. *Verwerfung* is the mechanism of refusal or repudiation in Freudian theory. This can operate either as repression or absolute refusal. Lacan takes up this latter, more radical notion of refusal in his own term *foreclusion*. Foreclu-

sion is the mechanism at the root of psychosis by which the Thing (trauma? the *Nom du Père* or process of signification?) is cast out of mind entirely, and reappears not as symptom in the body-mind, as it does in neurosis, but as psychotic hallucination in the Real, something that seems absolutely authentic to the psychotic.

8. By *episteme* I understand a period in history defined by certain modes and practices of knowledge. Episteme is the term popularized by Michel Foucault.

9. As Nasio states: "First, the unconscious is revealed in *an act* which surprises and exceeds the intention of the analysand [the "analysand," or subject of analysis, may, in the present study, be taken as the text and reader together] who speaks. The subject says more than he wants, and by saying, reveals its truth. . . . Rather than revealing a hidden unconscious that is already there, this act produces the unconscious and causes it to exist." Juan-David Nasio, *Five Lessons on the Psychoanalytic Theory of Jacques Lacan,* trans. David Pettigrew and Francois Raffoul (Albany: State University of New York Press, 1998), 46.

10. Nasio, *Five Lessons,* 23.

11. Nasio, *Five Lessons,* 32. See chapter 4 for the elucidation of this Melville reference.

12. The contingency theories of poststructural thought, most notably the work of Judith Butler, present truth as "always already" contingent. There is no continuity or stability to the truth; it changes moment to moment depending on contexts, historical forces, etc.

13. Here I am thinking of much Derridean thought, and also the work of Judith Butler.

14. Jacques Lacan, *Ecrits: A Selection,* trans. Alan Sheridan (New York: Norton, 1977), 50.

15. W. B. Worthen, "Drama, Performativity, and Performance," *PMLA* 113, no. 5 (1998): 1093.

16. Worthen, "Drama, Performativity, and Performance," 1094.

17. Worthen, "Drama, Performativity, and Performance," 1098.

18. See Yannis Stavrakakis, *Lacan and the Political* (New York: Routledge, 1999), esp. chap. 2, "The Lacanian Object: Dialectics of Social Impossibility."

19. *Hauntology* is the word coined by Ernesto Laclau in *Emancipation(s)* (New York: Verso, 1996), 67, in his discussion of Derrida's *Spectres of Marx: The State of the Debt, the Work of Mourning, and the New International,* trans. Peggy Kamuf (New York: Routledge, 1994). *Ghosting* is the term coined by Herbert Blau in the 1980s to describe much the same issue of disappearance contra specter in the acting process.

20. See, for example, Judith Butler's essay "Performative Acts and Gender Constitution," in *Performing Feminisms,* ed. Sue-Ellen Case (Baltimore: Johns Hopkins University Press, 1990). Although more than a decade old now, this essay articulates much of what remains the dominant discourse in gender politics and performance theory.

21. Judith Butler, *Bodies That Matter* (New York: Routledge, 1993).

22. Who, of course, worked relentlessly to rid his actors of exactly the type of stereotypic behaviors that performativity critics dismiss as "merely" theater.

23. McVeigh made no admissions of guilt, expressed no remorse, nor asked for mercy. He spoke only the following words: "If the court please, I wish to use the words of Justice Brandeis in *Olmstead* to speak for me. He wrote, 'Our government is the potent, the omnipresent teacher for good or for ill, it teaches the whole people by its example.' That's all I have." In the face of his sentencing, in other words, he read from a script.

24. Gilles Deleuze, *Difference and Repetition,* trans. Paul Patton (New York: Columbia University Press, 1968), 208.

25. Žižek, *Looking Awry,* 14.

26. Here, for example is Alexis de Tocqueville: "The Americans have no school of philosophy peculiar to themselves, and they pay very little attention to the rival European schools. Indeed, they hardly know their names," but follow a pragmatism that looks to "results without getting entangled in the means toward them." *Democracy in America,* trans. George Lawrence and ed. J. P. Mayer (New York: Harper and Row, 1966), 429. A more recent comment by an American philosopher on this country's historical lack of speculative philosophy:

> [Philosophy's] job was no longer to analyze experience into the real and unreal, the substantial and the insubstantial. Instead, it must be practical, critical, and reconstructive; it must aim at the successful transformation or amelioration of the experienced problems which call it forth and intrinsically situate it.

John J. Stuhr, ed., *Classical American Philosophy: Essential Readings and Interpretive Essays* (New York: Oxford University Press, 1987), 5–6.

27. Hillel Schwartz, *The Culture of the Copy: Striking Likenesses, Unreasonable Facsimiles* (New York: Zone Books, 1996), 290.

28. Such as the review, or the "dance of seductive reconciliation," to quote Jill Dolan, *Presence and Desire: Essays on Gender, Sexuality, Performance* (Ann Arbor: University of Michigan Press, 1993), 158.

29. Ernesto Laclau, in the introduction to Slavoj Žižek's *The Sublime Object of Ideology* (New York: Verso, 1989), xiv.

30. Žižek, *The Ticklish Subject,* 345–46.

31. Alain Finkielkraut, *The Defeat of the Mind,* ed. and trans. Judith Friedlander (New York: Columbia University Press, 1995), 23.

32. What Lacan calls *petit objet a,* the little "o" (or "a" from the French *autre*) other that becomes, in the interplay of multiple "othernesses," the (big "O") Other.

33. One of the young assassins, Kip Kinkel has, we are told, literal holes in his brain—holes that have, in the analysis of mediation, come to signify his murderous acts.

34. Joan Copjec, *Read My Desire: Lacan against the Historicists* (Cambridge: MIT Press, 1995), 27.

Chapter One

1. See for example, Jeremy Collier's attack on the English stage, "A Short View of the Immorality and Profaneness of the English Stage," written in 1689.

2. The more likely "theatrical" texts might be the sermons, and the accompanying performative milieu in which they were delivered. Indeed, along with the theatricality of the sermon was its function, especially in America, as a kind of collective repetition-compulsion ("What, has this thing appear'd again tonight?") that we might associate with the psychic life of theater. In a recent review of *Sermons*, a collection of American sermons edited by Michael Warner, Edmund S. Morgan writes that the

> experience [of sermons] of whatever kind in whatever church, carried an invitation to return for a repetition of it, for more sermons, more persuasion, not just in a pastoral visit but from the pulpit in the company of the whole congregation. In America the invitation was not encumbered by the compulsions or the limitations that surrounded sermons in the European world from which most Americans or their ancestors arrived. In that world, membership in the church was a corollary of citizenship in the state, and membership in a variety of other institutions was also determined more by birth than by choice. The absence of such established institutions has often been noted as a distinctive feature of American life, especially in the first two or three centuries after English settlement. While Americans were engaged in occupying the continent and ousting the native inhabitants, institutions could not keep up with the exponential growth of the population. Not only was there no established church, but there was no hereditary aristocracy, no standing army, no business monopolies, fewer of any of the institutions that elsewhere posed limits on what an individual could do, fewer even of the social customs and taboos that so often dictate human behavior, and necessarily fewer of the rites and ceremonies through which institutions identify themselves and their members. In this environment the persuasive power of sermons took the place of institutional compulsions and reduced the significance of ceremony, of feasts and fastings, sacraments and prayers, and every other liturgical rite.

New York Review of Books, September 23, 1999, 40–41. I am interested more, in this opening chapter, in the theatrical mind-set of the Puritans, however, and will, in large part, situate the issue of theatricality where it might not normally be sought: in the private, "hidden" realm of the diary.

3. *Blindsight* refers to a peculiar neuropathology in which the patient seems to be blind but will, for example, catch a ball thrown to him or her. Even though professing blindness, the patient seems to see, but seemingly wills not to.

4. And beyond this, echoes of a purely American Mormonism—but more on this in the final chapter.

5. I am not suggesting that America was the Puritans, or vice versa. I am suggesting, along similar lines as Sacvan Bercovitch and others, that the Puri-

tan sense of self became and remains the dominant "allegory" of the self in America. Thus although other groups, ideas, and forces challenged the supremacy of American Puritanism even within Puritanism (i.e., Roger Williams and Anne Hutchinson), such challenges and others were still defined by the allegory of Puritanism.

6. Antonin Artaud, *The Theater and Its Double*, trans. Mary Caroline Richards (New York: Grove Press, 1958), 51.

7. Artaud, *Theater and Its Double*, 122.

8. Jacques Derrida, *Writing and Difference*, trans. Alan Bass (Chicago: University of Chicago Press, 1978), 233.

9. Artaud, *Theater and Its Double*, 116.

10. Herman Melville, *Moby-Dick; or, The Whale*, vol. 6 of *The Writings of Herman Melville*, Northwestern-Newberry Edition, ed. Harrison Hayford, Hershel Parker, and G. Thomas Tanselle (Evanston: Northwestern University Press and Newberry Library, 1988).

11. Melville, *Moby-Dick*, 434.

12. John Winthrop, "A Modell of Christian Charity," in *An American Primer*, ed. Daniel Boorstin (New York: Penguin, 1966), 36.

13. Winthrop, "Modell of Christian Charity," 40.

14. Frederick Dolan, *Allegories of America: Narratives, Metaphysics, Politics* (Ithaca: Cornell University Press, 1994), 24.

15. Everett Emerson, *Puritanism in America: 1620–1750* (Boston: G. K. Hall, 1977), 123.

16. Winthrop, "Modell of Christian Charity," 40.

17. Much of the problematic "placement" of Wigglesworth's diaries in the literature of Puritanism was suggested to me by Edmund S. Morgan's introduction to *The Diary of Michael Wigglesworth*, ed. Edmund S. Morgan (New York: Harper and Row, 1946). Subsequent references to the diary are given in the text.

18. The parenthetical phrase, interestingly enough, was written in code, which I will discuss further below.

19. See Morgan's introduction to Wigglesworth's *Diary*.

20. Thomas Shepard, *God's Plot*, ed. Michael McGiffert (Amherst: University of Massachusetts Press, 1972, 1994), ix. Subsequent references are given in the text.

21. Shepard, *God's Plot*, "The Confessions."

22. Quoted in *Cane Ridge: America's Pentecost*, by Paul A. Conkin (Madison: University of Wisconsin Press, 1990), 93–94.

23. There is some question as to the status of these various awakenings in early American culture. Harold Bloom, a questionable scholar in this area, and others see the awakenings as retrospective effects: what occurred may have been rather uncentered and unfocused, and only in retrospect did the event gain its cultural and spiritual power. The "real" status of these events, however, is less important than the fact that historians continue to identify them as key events in American cultural history. The desire to locate these awakenings in such an important way demonstrates their power over the American historical imagination, if nothing else.

24. Conkin, *Cane Ridge*, 104.

25. Conkin, *Cane Ridge*, 106.

26. Juan-David Nasio, *Hysteria: The Splendid Child of Psychoanalysis*, trans. and ed. Susan Fairfield (Northvale: Jason Aronson, 1997), 6–7.

27. I hope the reader will forgive the neologism: I am trying to convey a state of mind containing a kind of pathological dissatisfaction.

28. While it is true that many of these movements and groups emerged in Europe prior to or alongside the American "experiment," most of them effectively died out or were translated to American soil, where they found fertile ground in which to grow and mutate.

29. Peggy Phelan, *Unmarked: The Politics of Performance* (New York: Routledge, 1993), 33.

Chapter Two

1. With apologies to Elaine Showalter.

2. Karen Halttunen, *Confidence Men and Painted Women: A Study of Middle-Class Culture in America, 1830–1970* (New Haven: Yale University Press, 1982).

3. See the preface to Halttunen's *Confidence Men* for a discussion of the broad strategy of her study.

4. Halttunen, *Confidence Men*, 109.

5. Halttunen, *Confidence Men*, 16. This specter arose again in the presidential election of 2000—both sides claiming a "stolen" election, both focusing on a fear of legerdemain in the counting of ballots.

6. Halttunen, *Confidence Men*, 17.

7. A split within the self that allows consciousness to come into being—the split that allows me to separate myself from what I am seeing, that allows me to speculate, but that also alienates me from myself.

8. Other critics have written about the importance of the confidence game in American culture as well: one of the earliest, but still relatively recent, books about the con man figure in American literature is Warwick Wadlington's *The Confidence Game in American Literature* (Princeton: Princeton University Press, 1975), a rather straightforward chronicle of the various types of con men represented in canonical American literature. Bruce McConachie, on the other hand, in *Melodramatic Formations: American Theater and Society, 1820–1870* (Iowa City: University of Iowa Press, 1992), approaches the issue politically and points out that the "middle-class theatrical hegemony" of nineteenth-century America tried to legitimate the view that one's social station is more or less determined at birth; one should not attempt to rise above one's inborn station. He fails to note, however, the double irony that theater should propagate the genuine, that it took a con game, the play, to communicate the political ideology of American culture that condemned the con. He correspondingly does not see himself in a similar situation: using analyses about theater and ideology within the academic con game to propagate his own notions of political propriety. See also McConachie's "Using the Concept of Cultural Hegemony to Write

Theater History," in *Interpreting the Theatrical Past*, ed. Thomas Postlewait and Bruce McConachie (Iowa City: University of Iowa Press, 1989).

Others see the con more clearly than McConachie. In *The Confidence Man in American Literature* (New York: Oxford Press, 1982), a book published in the same year as Halttunen's, Gary Lindberg explores the image of the confidence man specifically in American literature and suggests that he is a type of American hero, one who, in a rerendering of Franklinesque self-fashioning, uses the social uncertainties of American culture to his own best advantage. Lindberg, in fact, contra McConachie, implicates himself in the confidence game that is American capitalism in the final section of his book, wherein he names the very process of writing within the academy a part of the history of self-fashioning through the con, the con that he sees as America itself. This is also in part the theme of Walter Benn Michaels's *The Gold Standard and the Logic of Naturalism* (Berkeley and Los Angeles: University of California Press, 1987).

9. According to one interpretation, Lacan's famous "lack in the other" is generated when the infant, seeking mere relief from physical discomfort or pain (a need to relieve cold, hunger, etc.) receives unexpected "excess comfort," physical love from the caregiver. Thereafter, all human relations are characterized by the failure to provide this "unexpected" excess: what was received unexpectedly is now demanded, and human love is thus haunted by the lack (of the "unexpected" excess).

10. Alchemy was quite prevalent in early New England, arriving as it did ensconced within the more radical versions of Reformation Christianity, which was often quite taken with the sorceries and alchemy forbidden by the established Catholic and Protestant churches. See the final chapter's discussion of Joseph Smith and his involvement with "counterfeiting" and alchemy—an involvement made particularly ironic in recent decades following the scandalous Mormon forgeries of Mark Hofmann. See John L. Brooke, *The Refiner's Fire: The Making of Mormon Cosmology, 1644–1844* (Cambridge: Cambridge University Press, 1996).

11. For an interesting discussion of the relationship between money (and its illusory value), identity, and narrative (the substance of the scam is, after all, "false narrative," raising the issue of what true, or authentic, narrative might be) see Michaels, *Gold Standard*. See also Jean-Joseph Goux, *Symbolic Economies* (Ithaca: Cornell University Press, 1990), esp. chap. 3, "Monetary Economy and Idealist Philosophy."

12. *The Memoirs of Stephen Burroughs* (Boston: Northeastern University Press, 1988).

13. Here I disagree with Jeffrey Mason, who argues that the "myth of America" represented in the melodrama "does not offer a critique of culture." It most certainly does: a conservative critique to be sure, but critique nonetheless. Similarly, many contemporary cultural critics are also blind to the ways in which their work merely recapitulates a theoretical conservatism that wishes to reduce all experience to "the cultural." I can easily imagine a time when the work of current cultural criticism will be similarly dismissed as lacking in critical acumen. See *Melodrama and the Myth of America* (Bloomington: Indiana University Press, 1993), 194.

14. See my *Stages of Terror: Terrorism, Ideology, and Coercion as Theater History* (Bloomington: Indiana University Press, 1991), esp. the second half of chapter 4, "Gesturing through the Flames," in which I discuss the uses of wit as cruelty in English Restoration theater.

15. The Astor Place Riot in 1849, for example, was initiated by a rivalry between two actors, William Macready, an English actor held in high esteem in both Europe and America, and Edwin Forrest, a very popular American actor (but of arguable talents, at least according to Herman Melville), who, in an imagined rivalry with Macready, reopened the political wounds of Revolutionary America by accusing Macready of scheming to embarrass and humiliate him. The rivalry was quickly cast as a rivalry between English (and European in general) and American culture. The debate over which acting style— Macready's more cerebral and Forrest's tending to bombast—best suited the "American" temperament became the flash point for horrific violence. Twenty-two persons were killed and dozens injured when a rioting crowd protesting Macready's appearance at the Astor Place Opera House was fired upon by the militia. The irony that a particular theatrical style—theater at a second remove, if you will—should be the criteria for what constitutes the true American was apparently lost on those involved in the debate. Like the Lincoln assassination, which I will discuss a bit later on, the Astor Place riot represents the folding over of theater back into culture: the context and content of theater providing the coverage for the act of political terrorism. In the image of the Lincoln assassination, that violence, that staged moment of the Real became perhaps the single most important representational turning point of American culture.

16. I realize the problems created by this notion of a single American mind. There is, of course, no such thing. I am indicating here the myth or idea of "the American" born, in part, through the totalizing vision of American theater and politico-mythic life.

17. See David Grimsted, *Melodrama Unveiled* (Berkeley and Los Angeles: University of California Press, 1968), esp. chap. 8 on melodramatic structure.

18. *The Contrast,* in *Representative American Plays,* ed. Arthur Hobson Quinn (New York: Appleton-Century-Crofts, 1957), 51. I am not aware of any extant, significantly updated editions of this play. Subsequent references are given in the text.

19. For a more detailed discussion of the relation between fear and violence and theater, see my *Stages of Terror.*

20. Indeed, one of the more convincing arguments against the assumption that *The Contrast* was understood by audiences to be satirizing melodramatic sincerity is the more recent reception of *Forrest Gump,* in which the title character was portrayed as a hero, noble and genuine. Here the authentic is aligned with stupidity, even if "stupid is as stupid does," an odd reference to the role of the theatrical, once again, in the formation of identity.

21. Dolan, *Allegories of America,* 48.

22. This deep Puritanical suspicion of theater, based on its repugnant ability to deceive and present a view of life that seems natural and commonsensical but that is, in fact, only the deluded decadence of status quo social norms (not certainly Jonathan's words, but capturing, I think, his outrage at the the-

atrical) has reappeared in some forms of feminism that see in theatrical realism the evil of false consciousness.

23. I am of course chastened by the work of Barbara Herrnstein Smith, who, in noting the very slipperiness of such transformations (is it Letitia, Charlotte, or Maria who "reappears" as Seraphina Tiffany? Do we draw correspondence between Manley and Trueman, or between Manley and Colonel Howard?) discounts the very notion of thematic continuities, indeed of thematic criticism itself. See her "Narrative Versions, Narrative Theories," *Critical Inquiry* 7, no. 1 (1980): 219. Werner Sollers has I think very effectively challenged this rejection of thematic criticism in his work. See especially his essay "The Bluish Tinge in the Halfmoons; or, Fingernails as a Racial Sign: The Study of a Motif," in *Thematics: New Approaches,* ed. Bremond, Landy, and Pavel (Albany: State University of New York Press, 1995), which I will discuss more at length in the following chapter.

24. Lacan sees failure as causal—neurosis and psychosis are both precipitated by lack or failure. In Lacan, psychosis is caused by the failure, or lack, of the signifying order—words no longer signify, appearing as mere objects.

25. This but a single example of this sort of American theatrical tradition of violent nationalism. A bit later on, for example, we meet the aforementioned Mose the Fireboy, who travels the world picking fights with foreigners by way of enforcing respect for American ideals—the use of violence to compel belief apparently being one of them.

26. Anna Cora Mowatt Ritchie, *Fashion,* in Quinn, *Representative American Plays,* 238. Subsequent references are given in the text.

27. Jacques Lacan, *The Four Fundamental Concepts of Psychoanalysis,* ed. J.-A Miller, trans. Alan Sheridan (London: Penguin, 1986), 214.

28. Nasio, *Hysteria,* 106.

29. Nasio, *Hysteria,* 10.

30. Moreover, Trueman, a rich landowner in upstate New York, a father who refuses to let his daughter marry "the wrong man," fits rather well the description of the Rensselaerian land barons of Ritchie's time. These were men who, like Trueman, owned huge tracts of farmland in the Appalachian Valley and forced tenant farmers to pay exorbitant rents. They protected their investments by assuring marriage only within the circles of other landowners, and enforcing rent collection by means of legal force. The Rensselaerians incited large-scale resistance and rebellion among the tenant farmers. Even as a character in a play Trueman may very well not be what he seems: dressed in buckskin or not, living in the country or not, the land barons were, it seems, the very picture of refined foppishness that Trueman seemingly abhors in the city-dwellers. See Howard Zinn's *A People's History of the United States* (New York: HarperCollins, 1980, 1990). See esp. chap. 10, "The Other Civil War."

31. Indeed, in a nearly unthinkable coincidence, during the course of composing this book, I noted the extraordinary popularity of *The Truman Show,* a Hollywood film about a man whose life is, unsuspected by him, the subject of a global television show compiled through massive covert surveillance—a man who thinks himself real, but whose life, unbeknownst to him, is absolutely theatricalized. Theater and reality, Trueman and Conman, become the Same.

32. Zinn's *People's History*, 51.

33. Slavoj Žižek, *The Metastases of Enjoyment: Six Essays on Women and Causality* (New York: Verso, 1994), 76.

34. See Albert Furtwangler's *Assassin on Stage* (Urbana: University of Illinois Press, 1991) for a fuller discussion of the play.

35. Tom Taylor, *Our American Cousin* (n.p., 1869), 10, 19.

36. Taylor, *Our American Cousin*, 37.

37. Again, for a lengthy and fascinating description of this moment, and the entire interplay between the theater, and the assassination, between the Booth family as actors and the notoriety of John Wilkes, see Furtwangler, *Assassin on Stage*, 100–107.

Chapter Three

1. See the introduction to *Nation and Narration*, ed. Homi Bhabha (New York: Routledge, 1990), 3.

2. All references to Irving's work are from *The Complete Tales of Washington Irving*, ed. Charles Neider (New York: Da Capo Press, 1998), 15. Subsequent references are given in the text.

3. And note below the illusory half-moons in the Octoroon's fingernails, another ghostly apparition.

4. See Nietzsche, *On the Advantage and Disadvantage of History for Life*, trans. Peter Preuss (Indianapolis: Hackett, 1980), 10.

5. See *The Autobiography of Joseph Jefferson*, ed. Bernard Bailyn (Cambridge: Harvard University Press, 1964), esp. the chapter "Reflections on the Art of Acting."

6. Jefferson, *Autobiography*, 318.

7. Herbert Blau, *To All Appearances: Ideology and Performance* (New York: Routledge, 1992), 49.

8. Bhabha, *Nation and Narration*, 3.

9. *Rip Van Winkle* "as played by Joseph Jefferson," in Quinn, *Representative American Plays*, 413.

10. Jefferson, *Rip Van Winkle*, 419.

11. Jefferson, *Autobiography*, 335.

12. This equivalence, of course, is negated in the anxiety over the Immigrant: the Other at the perimeter that corresponds to the Other in the interior.

13. An interesting parallel is suggested in the appearance of the American tall tale, in this particular case the (true) story of Johnny Appleseed, traveling across the land, disseminating the Puritan ethic of work, and agricultural work at that, relandscaping the native American ecosystem as an English garden.

14. Reflecting, oddly, the status of the play's authorship itself: Irving's story, taken over by Jefferson, rewritten by Boucicault, taken over again by Jefferson, who became absolutely identified with the role.

15. Herbert Blau, "Ideology and Performance," *Theater Journal* 35 (December 1983): 460.

16. So, too, the historicist approach to the theater: the pronouncement of

one historicist that "[t]heatre historians who labor, collecting and fitting together fragments of both the creative process and the performed artwork, can get close to that *dynamic sensory presence*," i.e., the sensory experience of the performance itself, seems terribly self-deluding. Robert K. Sarlos, "Performance Reconstruction: The Vital Link between Past and Future," in *Interpreting the Theatrical Past: Essays in the Historiography of Performance*, edited by Thomas Postlewait and Bruce McConachie (Iowa City: University of Iowa Press, 198).

17. The most popular, of course, was the stage version of Harriet Beecher Stowe's *Uncle Tom's Cabin*, a novel/play that engages many of the same issues of perceptions and difference negotiated through color. The issue is more richly developed, I believe, in Boucicault's play, which is the reason I have chosen to discuss it.

18. The play also mirrors the bizarre ontology embedded in the phenomenon of blackface minstrelsy that was popular in the latter half of the century, in which white performers mimicked blacks, and later blacks mimicked themselves (i.e. wore blackface to make their blackness more "real"). Whites were not blacks, and blacks were not themselves. See discussion in chapter 5.

19. Dion Boucicault, *The Octoroon*, in Quinn, *Representative American Plays*, 383.

20. Sollers, "Bluish Tinge," 72.

21. Harley Erdman, "Caught in the 'Eye of the Eternal': Justice, Race, and the Camera, from *The Octoroon* to Rodney King," in *Theater Journal* 54 (October 1993): 333–48.

22. Boucicault, *The Octoroon*, 382. Subsequent references are given in the text.

23. Joseph Roach, "Slave Spectacles and Tragic Octoroons: A Cultural Genealogy of Antebellum Performance," in *Theater Survey* 33 (November 1992): 167–87.

24. Recently, however, the empirical "science" of fingerprint identification has been brought under suspicion. See "Smudged! The Blurry Science of Fingerprints," by Simon Cole in *Lingua Franca*, November 2000, 54–62.

25. Maurice Merleau-Ponty, *The Visible and the Invisible*, ed. Claude Lefort, trans. Alphonso Lingis (Evanston: Northwestern University Press, 1968), 132.

26. And of course at the level of the unconscious, the difference between the reds might very well be erased by sameness—her dress causes me to shudder because of an unconscious association of that red satin with blood.

27. Zoe, interestingly, responds to this suggestion by crying out, "Let me pass! O pray let me go!" articulating, of course both her desire to "pass" and her inability to allow herself to. George, after all, is willing to marry her, saying, "I can overcome the obstacle," to which Zoe responds "But *I* cannot."

28. One of Anthony Wilden's objections to Lacanian thought, expressed most fully in *System and Structure*, is that difference in Lacan was "always implicitly conceived of as ABSOLUTE difference, i.e. as (Imaginary) opposition." *System and Structure: Essays in Communication and Exchange*, 2d ed. (New York: Tavistock/Methuen, 1972), 472.

29. Homi K. Bhabha, "Of Mimicry and Man: The Ambivalence of Colonial Discourse," in *The Location of Culture* (New York: Routledge, 1994), 91.

30. Merleau-Ponty, *Visible and Invisible*, 134.

31. Bhabha, "Of Mimicry and Man," 89.

32. Bhabha, "Of Mimicry and Man," 89.

33. See Warner Berthoff, *The Ferment of Realism: American Literature, 1884–1919* (New York: Free Press, 1965); Michaels, *Gold Standard*; Michael Davitt Bell, *The Problem of American Realism* (Chicago: University of Chicago Press, 1993); and Brook Thomas, *American Literary Realism and the Failed Promise of Contract* (Berkeley and Los Angeles: University of California Press, 1997).

34. Berthoff, *The Ferment of Realism*, 3.

35. William Harmon, C. Hugh Holman, et al., *A Handbook to Literature*, 7th edition (New Jersey: Prentice Hall, 1996), 428.

36. Dolan's misperception of the ideological symmetry between her feminism and the realism she abhors suggests something of a "straw-man argument," or even more ironically in light of feminism's abhorrence of essentialism (a term much misused) an essentialization of realism itself. Whose version of realism is being discussed, after all, and what are its identifying characteristics? If she is using, as per her citations, Catherine Belsey's definition, she must realize there are many who reject it as confused and confusing. Belsey's claim that "realist narrative . . . turns on the creation of enigma through the precipitation of disorder which throws into disarray the conventional cultural and signifying systems," apart from being murky, describes an enormous range of work, much if not most decidedly nonrealist (avant-garde art, for example). And whether "classical" realist narrative "moves inevitably towards closure" is questionable, to say the least. How does Ambrose Bierce's story "Chickamauga," a story many would classify as "a classic realist narrative," move toward closure, exactly? Moreover, the invocation to verisimilitude as the hallmark of realism, the notion that a supposed isomorphism between life and art is realism's defining characteristic is, it seems to me, naive. Finally, in invoking Belsey as her authorial support, Dolan reveals a somewhat deficient understanding of the debates surrounding American realism (the intended object of her discussion of lesbian/feminist performance): Belsey is, after all, discussing European realism, which is much more strongly oriented toward questions of ontology and philosophical debate, a fact that Dolan either misses or dismisses as irrelevant. Not only is the distinction not irrelevant, it is perhaps the most salient facet of the argument surrounding American realism in performance studies.

For a somewhat more positive but still critical response to Dolan's article see J. Ellen Gainor's "The Provincetown Player's Experiments with Realism," in *Realism and the American Dramatic Tradition*, ed. William W. Demastes (Tuscaloosa: University of Alabama Press, 1996).

37. See, for example, Demastes, *American Dramatic Tradition*.

38. Berthoff, *The Ferment of Realism*, 2.

39. See Jonathan's Crary's *Techniques of the Observer* (Cambridge: MIT Press, 1992). Crary points out the serious discrepancy between the blithe assertions that the nineteenth century was dominated by realism, and the fascination with what we would today call "virtual worlds."

40. Copjec, *Read My Desire,* 37.

41. James Herne, *Margaret Fleming,* in Quinn, *Representative American Plays.*

42. Herne, *Margaret Fleming,* 543.

43. Nasio, *Hysteria,* 132.

44. Nasio, *Hysteria,* 4.

45. George Bataille, "The Eye," in *Visions of Excess: Selected Writings, 1927–1939* (Minneapolis: University of Minnesota Press, 1985), 17.

46. This is Hillary Putnam's argument in *Realism with a Human Face* (Cambridge: Harvard University Press, 1990). This is also the crux of the wide-ranging debate among philosophers and cognitive theorists, a diverse group including not only Putnam and John Searle, but Thomas Nagel, Colin McGinn, Patricia Churchland, Owen Flanagan, and many others, none of whom are cited within the confines of the feminist debate on realism.

47. Herne, *Margaret Fleming,* 544.

48. We see the issue more strongly in Ibsen's brand of realism. When Nora leaves in *A Doll's House,* we may very well feel the powerful sense of her liberation almost immediately eclipsed by a terrible lacuna—the terror of an unknown, of the unknowable, not only in what Nora may face in the world, but also in the obdurate (I would argue) inscrutability of her motives.

Chapter Four

1. Nathaniel Hawthorne, "The Minister's Black Veil," in *The Complete Novels and Selected Tales of Nathaniel Hawthorne* (New York: Modern Library, 1937, 1965). Subsequent references are given in the text.

2. To clarify: *aphanisis* refers, generally speaking, to the seeming self-disappearance that occurs when we try to apprehend identity, and can find it only in the images of others. *Vel* (cognate with the root of *velocity*) refers to the dynamic of the appearance and disappearance of the self to itself: my experience of identity as intolerably weighty (in my guilt), or as nonexistent (in my anxiety).

3. See Lacan, *Four Fundamental Concepts,* 210. I find the image of myself, my identity, in others, and finally in the Other (a kind of culmination of others), but the other is, after all, a construct of my own desires. I create the Other creating me. Thus the reciprocity of desire, the *vel.*

4. See Copjec, *Read My Desire,* esp. chap. 4.

5. Jacques Derrida, *Monolingualism of the Other; or, The Prosthesis of Origin* (Stanford: Stanford University Press, 1998), 72–73.

6. Copjec, *Read My Desire,* 35.

7. Most of the historical background here is taken from *Blacking Up: The Minstrel Show in Nineteenth-Century America,* by Robert C. Toll (New York: Oxford University Press, 1974), but is augmented by the work of Eric Lott's *Love and Theft: Blackface Minstrelsy and the American Working Class* (New York: Oxford University Press, 1993). See note 10 below.

8. Butler, "Performative Acts," 270.

9. See Dale Cockrell, *Demons of Disorder: Early Blackface Minstrels and Their World* (Cambridge: Cambridge University Press, 1997), which acknowledges the racially stereotypic nature of blackface, but emphasizes the enjoyment that audiences took in the songs and stories over any racist joy in ridicule white audiences might have felt, or any deeper anxieties the shows might have masked.

10. See Lott's excellent *Love and Theft*, in which he explores the economic linkages between blackface performance and American capitalism, but also, like Cockrell, emphasizes the enjoyment the working class (including urban blacks) took in the material presented in the minstrel shows. Again, even though Lott acknowledges the "theft" of African American cultural capital by white artists, he does not, even when discussing the "unconscious" of blackface as a cultural moment, dwell on the specifically psychoanalytic: his "unconscious" is largely the Jamesonian sociological unconscious.

11. Lott, *Love and Theft*, 39.

12. Lott, *Love and Theft*, 39.

13. Ellison is quoted by Lott, *Love and Theft*, 25.

14. Note that the Wooster Group caused a profound stir when it performed in blackface in 1981, in a piece entitled *Route 1 & 9* at the Performing Garage in New York City.

15. From F. Reynolds (n.p., 1809), quoted by Cockrell, *Demons of Disorder*, 13.

16. This story is related in Lott, *Love and Theft*, 18–19.

17. Lott, *Love and Theft*, 18–19.

18. Indeed, there is, it seems to me a certain irony in minstrelsy that remains with us today: here in Tampa, a recent NPR fund-raising special used a very popular previously aired program on doo-wop music as its vehicle. Many of the acts exhibited clear residues of the minstrel show ("The Duke of Earl"). The NPR audience is, of course, disproportionately white, highly educated, and decidedly liberal in its political views.

19. See Lott, *Love and Theft*, chap. 8, "Uncle Tomitudes."

20. This is the speech of the analyst, according to Bruce Fink. See *Lacanian Psychoanalysis: Theory and Technique* (Cambridge: Harvard University Press, 1997), chap. 4, "Interpretation: Opening Up the Space of Desire."

21. Charles Olson, *Call Me Ishmael* (San Francisco: City Lights Books, 1947), 16.

22. This approach is touched upon by Sharon Cameron in *The Corporeal Self: Allegories of the Body in Melville and Hawthorne* (Baltimore: Johns Hopkins University Press, 1981), in which she focuses on the many kinds of writing and inscription in the book as indicative of a world of bodily perception that is removed from reality, and that desires the reality it represents. While Cameron's book is quite interesting in many respects, it also neglects the deeper, philosophical problematics of writing and its "reality": a problematic that will be further highlighted, I believe, through the ensuing discussion of theater.

23. This oddity was pointed out to me by Hersh Zeifman. I have not been able to discover why, precisely, the name Moby-Dick is hyphenated in the title

and nowhere else. The enigma of Moby Dick is thus as much an enigma of name as it is novel.

24. Writing is the "hollow" of it's own mark, according to Michel Foucault in *The Archaeology of Knowledge and the Discourse on Language,* trans. A. M. Sheridan Smith (New York: Pantheon, 1972), because it represents the absence of what it represents. Queequeg's mark is the "hollow of its own mark" in the novel because the mark as it has been reproduced in the text apparently differs from the mark inscribed by Melville in the original manuscript—a change made by the typesetter, necessitated by the insufficiency of typefaces available.

25. Laclau, *Emancipation(s),* 72.

26. Herman Melville, *Moby-Dick,* ed. Harrison Hayford and Hershel Parker, Norton Critical Edition (New York: W. W. Norton, 1967), 39. Subsequent references are to this edition and are given in the text.

27. I should remind the reader that these blanks in fact actually exist in the small whaling chapel on Nantucket Island: a reminder that the longing for presence is experienced as actual grief.

28. Herbert Blau, *Take Up the Bodies: Theater at the Vanishing Point* (Urbana: University of Illinois Press, 1982), 164.

29. See Jacques Derrida, *Dissemination,* trans. Barbara Johnson (Chicago: University of Chicago Press, 1981), 98.

30. Olson, *Call Me Ishmael,* 84.

31. Blau, *Take Up the Bodies,* 146–47.

32. Copjec, *Read My Desire,* 36.

33. Slavoj Žižek, "The Cartesian Subject versus the Cartesian Theatre," in *Cogito and the Unconscious,* ed. Slavoj Žižek (Durham: Duke University Press, 1998), 258.

34. Žižek, "The Cartesian Subject," 259.

35. This type of juxtaposition between the very large and very small, black and white, male and female was the special province of P. T. Barnum's theatrical strategy—his exposition of two white beluga whales, one called Moby Dick, set against the earlier exposition of the small, shriveled Feejee "mermaid," or his famous photo showing the contrast between the giantess Anna Swan and the Lilliputian King that stood as signature images out of Barnum's grand theatricalizing of American life. Like Stephen Burroughs and Joseph Smith before him, and countless others after, Barnum was a consummate master of the "humbug"—the spectacle that was at once real and unreal, a paradox caught in his obsession with disparate pairing.

Chapter Five

1. Žižek, *Sublime Object of Ideology,* 195.

2. But see also Žižek's essay "Cartesian Subject," in which he points out that the multiple, decentered subject within the Enlightenment tradition goes back at least as far as German Idealism and Hölderlin, Schelling, and Novalis.

3. Ute Guzzoni, "Do We Still Want to Be Subjects?" in *Deconstructive Sub-*

jectivities, ed. Simon Critchley and Peter Dews (New York: SUNY Press, 1996), 215.

4. See Chantal Mouffe and Ernesto Laclau, *Hegemony and Socialist Strategy: Towards a Radical Democratic Politics* (New York: Verso, 1985), 114–15, in which the "problem of the discursive or prediscursive character of the category of subject" is dismissed as unimportant to the theory of "radical democracy." While this may be true within the contexts of Mouffe and Laclau's theory, which concentrates more on the relations between "subject positions," the "problem of the discursive or prediscursive character of the category of subject" has not been adequately theorized in terms of the self's agon, its ecstasies, or its terrors.

5. And indeed, while writers like Homi Bhabha acknowledge and celebrate the multiplicity and variegated nature of culture, there is, in the substrata of his work, an assumption that culture, for all of its multiplicities, does exist as a category of theory in a way that the subject does not.

6. Finkielkraut, *Defeat of the Mind*, 105, quoting Father M. Lelong.

7. Finkielkraut, *Defeat of the Mind*, 106.

8. Finkielkraut, *Defeat of the Mind*, 133.

9. I will be using this term throughout in its two distinct senses: making something corporeal, and the act of turning production into capital, as in the incorporation of a business.

10. Eugene O'Neill, *Desire under the Elms*, in *Complete Plays, 1920–1931* (New York: Library of America, 1988), 1.1. Citations refer to act and scene and are given in the text.

11. There are other minor examples, Abbie's use of the word "agen" in 1.4, for example. But the repeated use of "yew" for *you* is by far the most conspicuous example.

12. Of course, Abbie may well know the truth of the child's paternity—she is, after all, aware of her own menstrual cycle. However, this potential knowledge and power, located literally within her body, remains hidden, unspoken, and unacknowledged. She may know, but there is no way for us to—even the revelation of the child's paternity, given within the context of her other duplicities and desires, is suspect.

13. Serge Leclaire, *A Child Is Being Murdered*, trans. Marie-Claude Hays (Stanford: Stanford University Press, 1998), 58.

14. Leclaire, *Child Is Being Murdered*, 58.

15. Leclaire, *Child Is Being Murdered*, 59.

16. Leclaire, *Child Is Being Murdered*, 59.

17. Derrida, *Spectres of Marx*, 97.

18. *Jouissance* is the term used by Lacan and Lacanians to indicate something like the intensity of pleasure bordering on pain in the experience of desire. In this sense *jouissance* displaces the Freudian Id. By *jouissance*, here, I mean something like the pursuit of desire, not desire itself: the thing that drives desire to possess itself.

19. Walter A. Davis, *Get the Guests: Psychoanalysis, Modern American Drama, and the Audience* (Madison: University of Wisconsin Press, 1994). See esp. chap. 5, "The Academic Overture: *Who's Afraid of Virginia Woolf?*"

20. Edward Albee, *Who's Afraid of Virginia Woolf?* (New York: Atheneum Press, 1981), 62. Subsequent references are given in the text.

21. Žižek, *Sublime Object of Ideology,* 195.

22. Žižek, *Sublime Object of Ideology,* 195.

23. Sam Shepard, *Buried Child,* in *Seven Plays* (New York: Bantam Books, 1984), 69. Further citations are given in the text.

24. The century-long destabilization of history into "conceptual shards— ethno-history, psycho-history, social history, history of things and ideas and mentalities, cliometrics, micro-history," in the words of Hakim Bey, acts as a counterweight to the perception of history as conspiracy. Conspiracy history or theory, perhaps the most popular form of historical consciousness in contemporary American culture, runs counter to the postmodern notion of history as "small narrative." Here, great, shadowy, mysterious plans, laid by great, shadowy, mysterious men in secret places, determines the course of history—the Kennedy assassination plot, the secrets of Area 51, the moon-landing boondoggle, ad nauseum, suggest a concealed scaffolding upon which the mundane facts of history rest. The conspiracy mind-set, then, suggests a desire to see behind the scenes, beneath the surface, in order to get a glimpse of "real" history. Conspiracy theory, in other words, represents the other side of theatricalized America. The repression of American theatricality, the theatricality that *is* American life, returns as conspiracy—the real bodies buried beneath the false spectacle of American life. This is perhaps the real meaning of the Buried Child in the endless desire for exhumations: Kennedy's corpse, alien bodies, Elvis's empty grave.

The desire for conspiratorial knowledge, then, is a necessary and legitimate quest for historical specificity beneath the quest for history's theater. But in the theater, at theater's core, history like its conspiracies, is always given over to illusion. See Hakim Bey, http://www.t0.or.at/hakimbey/hakimbey.htm.

25. Note the contradictory "Bases loaded. Runners on first and third," but also the fact that Musial and Dodge would have been about the same age— Dodge would hardly have been "a kid."

Chapter Six

1. Butler, "Performative Acts," 272. For a brilliant discussion of this issue in Butler's work, see Elin Diamond's *Unmaking Mimesis: Essays on Feminism and Theater* (New York: Routledge, 1997), esp. chap. 6, "Performance and Temporality."

2. See section 3, Remembrance. Also see my *Stages of Terror,* esp. the introduction.

3. Butler, "Performative Acts," 271.

4. As this chapter was nearing completion, I happened upon Elaine Showalter's *Hystories* (New York: Columbia University Press, 1997), a study of the forms of hysteria in this century and the stories they tell. Showalter touches upon some of the same aspects of DID and recovered memories that I have, and even at one point discusses the performative qualities of hysteria. And

although she notes the relationship of DID and recovered memories to American life and culture, she does not see the deeper historical roots and ramifications of these forms of hysteria that speak to both the lack or dislocation of identity in American cultural history, and the closure of memory (history) in a nation that might be defined by those very characteristics: lack of historical identity, and lack of or repression of history itself. Moreover, the relationships between DID and recovered memory are not contextualized in any wider sense. Thus Showalter's discussion of hysteria and performance mentions playtexts that depict "hysteria," but not performances, like Finley's, that seemingly produce it. Similarly, she does not see the wide and deep penetration of the theatrical in American life, of which hysteria is merely one form.

5. See Jeanie Forte, "Women's Performance Art: Feminism and Postmodernism," in *Performing Feminisms*, 251–69. Forte promotes the notion that "women's performance is born of self-revelation as political motive" and insists that women's performances elude the ontology of appearances and representation because the performers "are not acting," forgetting, following Butler and others, that it is impossible not to act oneself, most especially on the stage.

6. I ought to make it clear at this point, however, that there is little debate over the reality and widespread existence of sexual abuse. There is also little doubt that many suffer profoundly because of it. The debate concerns the modality—in the case of DID, a performative modality—of its emergence and treatment. Elizabeth Loftus quotes James Hillman in *The Myth of Repressed Memory: False Memories and Allegations of Sexual Abuse* (New York: St. Martin's Press, 1994): "They are molested, they are abused, and in many cases it's absolutely devastating. But therapy makes it even more devastating by the way it thinks about it. It isn't just the trauma that does the damage, it's remembering traumatically." It's remembering in the Dionysian, we might say, remembering in the unrepentant *traum* of theater.

7. In fact, this is at the center of the debate among Judith Butler, Seyla Benhabib, Drucilla Cornell, and Nancy Fraser in *Feminist Contentions: A Philosophical Exchange*, ed. Linda Nicholson (New York: Routledge, 1995). The surgical removal of the theatrical from the performative robs the notion of the performative of its necessary sense of duplicity—which renders the notion of the performative rather less interesting, in my estimation.

8. Beatrice Roth, *The Father*, in *Out from Under: Texts by Women Performance Artists*, ed. Lenora Champagne (New York: Theater Communications Group, 1990), 37.

9. Roth, *The Father*, 37.

10. Roth, *The Father*, 38–39.

11. Roth, *The Father*, 39.

12. I should note here that one of the current debates regarding MPD is whether it is a pathology at all, or a "better" state of identity. A quick visit to web-sites and chat rooms quickly reveals the animosity MPD victims have toward the therapy community because MPD is, among victims, not seen as pathological, but "evolutionary," that is, a superior psychic state.

13. Lynda Hart, "Motherhood according to Karen Finley," *Drama Review* 36, no. 1 (1991): 127, 129.

14. Karen Finley, *Constant State of Desire*, in Champagne, *Out from Under.*

15. Finley, *Constant State of Desire*, 60.

16. Finley, *Constant State of Desire*, 59.

17. Champagne, in her introduction to Finley's work in *Out from Under*, 58.

18. C. Carr, *On Edge: Performance at the End of the Twentieth Century* (Hanover: Wesleyan University Press, 1993), 127.

19. Carr, *On Edge*, 130.

20. Finley, *Constant State of Desire*, 59–60.

21. See, again, Schwartz, *Culture of the Copy*, for an interesting, if somewhat lengthy, discourse on the double. The book discusses at various points the intersection of doubling, theater, and MPD.

22. Finley, *Constant State of Desire*, 67–68.

23. Carr, *On Edge*, 128.

24. Valerie Sinason, *Treating Victims of Satanist Abuse* (New York: Routledge, 1994), 72.

25. Carr, *On Edge*, 128.

26. Carr, *On Edge*, 131.

27. Christopher Busa, "Talking with Karen Finley," in the Provincetown Arts section of *Provincetown Gallery*, 1996. See also a reprint of the article at www.capecodaccess.com/Gallery/Arts/talkingKaren.html. August 15, 2000.

28. For a more thorough discussion of the relationships between terror and theater see my *Stages of Terror.*

29. James Glass, *Shattered Selves: Multiple Personality in a Postmodern World* (Ithaca: Cornell University Press, 1993), 56.

30. Some individuals have alters that function as demigods, aloof, omnipotent, detached from their surroundings. Others take on the identities of ducks, dogs, and other animals.

31. Glass, *Shattered Selves*, 104.

32. See Ian Hacking's *Rewriting the Soul: Multiple Personality and the Sciences of Memory* (Princeton: Princeton University Press, 1995), esp. chap. 12.

33. See Hacking, *Rewriting the Soul*, 32.

34. It is important to note here that not all cases of recovered memories involve DID, and not all DID patients have "repressed" their memories, although most DID patients do not recall the original trauma and must rediscover it. This provides an intriguing link between DID and the somewhat more widespread phenomena of "recovered memory."

35. This very issue lies at the center of *Primal Fear*, a recent Hollywood movie about DID.

36. Indeed, some recent reports have suggested that recovering memories and "reintegration therapy" may, in the long run, be more harmful than no therapy at all.

37. Antonin Artaud, "The Theater of Cruelty (First Manifesto)," in *Theater and Its Double*, 92.

38. Ellen Bass and Laura Davis, *The Courage to Heal*, 2d ed. (New York: Harper and Row, 1992), 74.

39. Bass and Davis, *The Courage to Heal*, 74–75.

40. Along with Bass and Davis's proclamation that "if you think it might have happened, it probably did," goes the presumption in early DID therapies that the patients' memories are never to be doubted. There is, for example, in the work of Bass and Davis a blithe acceptance of the empirical veracity of patient memory, a veracity now deeply questioned by therapists and memory experts of all stripes.

41. Constantin Stanislawski, *An Actor Prepares* (New York: Theater Arts Books, 1936), 156, 163.

42. Harold Bloom, *The American Religion: The Emergence of the Post-Christian Nation* (New York: Simon and Schuster, 1992).

43. See Hart, "Motherhood," 125.

44. Donna Haraway, "A Cyborg Manifesto: Science, Technology, and Socialist-Feminism in the Late Twentieth Century," chap. 8 in her *Simians, Cyborgs, and Women* (New York: Routledge, 1991).

45. A point that leftist and feminist defenders of DID therapies ought to note.

46. The following account is contained in Loftus's *Myth of Repressed Memories* and is itself a recounting of Richard Ofshe's *Remembering Satan* (New York: Knopf, 1994).

47. Lynch's roughly contemporaneous series was set, in fact, in the same Pacific Northwest area as the Ingram case and followed the same "make it up as you go" ethos as the Ingram stories.

48. See Loftus, *Myth of Repressed Memories*, 258.

49. It is interesting, in light of what we've seen regarding the figure of the murdered infant in American drama, how often this image appears in the "recovered memories" of SRA (Satanic Ritual Abuse).

50. See Loftus, *Myth of Repressed Memories*, 239.

51. Loftus, *Myth of Repressed Memories*, 257.

52. Loftus, *Myth of Repressed Memories*, 234; emphasis added.

53. See Glass, *Shattered Selves*, 115; emphasis added.

54. Many of the "symptom lists" of DID, in fact, note that shifting identities may appear to the "casual observer" to be nothing more than shifts in mood.

55. As Laurie Anderson would have it—"O Superman. O Judge. O Mom and Dad . . ."

56. Jean Laplanche, *Seduction, Translation, Drives*, trans. Martin Stanton (London: Institute of Contemporary Arts, 1992), 167.

57. Cathy Caruth, *Trauma: Explorations in Memory* (Baltimore: Johns Hopkins University Press, 1995), 152.

58. Caruth, *Trauma*, 153.

59. Caruth, *Trauma*, 153.

60. Caruth, *Trauma*, 155.

61. Caruth, *Trauma*, 153.

Chapter Seven

1. Tony Kushner, *Angels in America,* part 1, *The Millennium Approaches* (New York: Theater Communications Group, 1992), 115. Hereafter I will cite this play as *Angels I.*

2. Shoshana Felman and Dori Laub, *Testimony: Crises of Witnessing in Literature, Psychoanalysis, and History* (New York: Routledge, 1992), 4–5.

3. Kushner, *Angels I,* 87.

4. Antonin Artaud, "Theater and the Plague," in *Theater and Its Double,* 30.

5. This is quoted on several websites (see, for example, http://www .geocities.com/Athens/Forum/2081/temple2.htm. For a recording of a portion of the ceremony, see http://www.lds-mormon.com/veilworker/creation.shtml and is taken from Jerald and Sandra Tanner's *Mormonism: Shadow or Reality,* 5th ed. (Salt Lake City: Utah Lighthouse Ministry, 1987).

6. Artaud, "Theater and the Plague," 27.

7. This change was actually initiated in 1978.

8. "Race Problems-as They Affect the Church," an address by Mark E. Petersen at the Convention of Teachers of Religion on the College Level, Brigham Young University, Provo, Utah, August 27, 1954. Quoted by Bill McKeever in "The Black Seed of Cain," http://www.mrm.org/articles/seed-of-cain.html. See also http://www.lds-mormon.com/racism.shtml

9. See http://www.inlink.com/~rife/ldsendow31. See, for example, http://nowscape.com/mormon/mormcr3.htm and note also http://nows-cape.com/mormon/mormcrlb.htm. Taken from Jerald and Sandra Tanner's *Mormonism.*

10. Artaud, "Theater and the Plague," 85.

11. See my *Stages of Terror,* 48–50.

12. "In the Church we are not neutral. We are one-sided. There is a war going on and we are engaged in it. It is the war between good and evil, and we are belligerents defending the good. We are therefore obliged to give preference to and protect all that is represented in the gospel of Jesus Christ, and we have made covenants to do it. . . . There is much in the scriptures and in our Church literature to convince us that we are at war with the adversary. We are not obliged as a church, nor are we as members obliged, to accommodate the enemy in this battle." Boyd K. Packer, a talk given at the Fifth Annual Church Educational System Religious Educators' Symposium, August 22, 1981, Brigham Young University, Provo, Utah. For an official transcript see Brigham Young University Studies, summer 1981.

13. Tony Kushner, *Angels in America,* part 2, *Perestroika* (New York: Theater Communications Group, 1992), 38. I will henceforth cite this text as *Angels II.*

14. Kushner, *Angels II,* 41.

15. Kushner, *Angels II,* 45.

16. Kushner, *Angels II,* 40

17. Kushner, *Angels II,* 49.

18. Kushner, *Angels II*, 39–46.

19. Thomas G. Alexander, "The Reconstruction of Mormon Doctrine: From Joseph Smith to Progressive Theology," in *Sunstone*, July–August 1980; emphasis added.

20. The "contingency debate" among literary and political theorists (how contingent is contingent truth?) is perhaps the most important debate in critical theory into the first decade of the twenty-first century. Is contingency absolute, and if absolute, doesn't that absoluteness imply noncontingency, or the presence within the contingent (within "change," in Kushner's text) of the unmovable, the static, the essential? See *Contingency, Hegemony, Universality: Contemporary Dialogues on the Left*, by Judith Butler, Ernesto Laclau, and Slavoj Žižek (New York: Verso, 2000). This book represents a series of debates among the three contributors on contemporary political theory. The issue here is best summed up in the discussions between Slavoj Žižek (whose engagement with American culture names him as an American cultural critic more than a Slovenian) and Judith Butler. In this debate, Butler asks, finally, whether it is not the case that Žižek's attempt to ratify the Oedipal "law of castration" as law, and moreover as law that excludes the feminine as "a stain" outside the circumstance of the symbolic, is not an evacuation of the very notion of contingency that Žižek holds to be central to all forms of ideology. Doesn't maintaining the "law of castration" (or any law, for that matter) violate the entire edifice of poststructural/contingency theory? Isn't the issue, at its most personal level, that Žižek represents the very "law" of mastery that Butler both abhors and embodies? Žižek, on the other hand, moves surreptitiously, I think, in the direction of the tragic, though he does not admit it—perhaps cannot admit it. He asks, rather too indirectly, if the all-important notion of contingency is not itself contingent. (Is the statement "All truth is contingent" itself contingent?) That is to say, Žižek asks if the contingency of ideological truth requires the admission of a noncontingency that would supply its meaning—the unitary "law of castration"?

21. Kushner, *Angels II*, 14.

22. Artaud, "Theater and the Plague," 31.

23. Finkielkraut, *Defeat of the Mind*, 125.

24. Caruth, *Trauma*, 5.

25. Caruth, *Trauma*, 7.

26. Suzan-Lori Parks, *The America Play* (New York: Theater Communications Group, 1995), 160. Subsequent references are given in the text.

Epilogue

1. Again, for a lengthy and fascinating description of this moment, and the entire interplay between the theater, and the assassination, between the Booth family as actors and the notoriety of John Wilkes, see *Assassin on Stage* by Furtwangler, 100–107.

2. James W. Clarke, *American Assassins* (Princeton: Princeton University Press, 1982), 175.

BIBLIOGRAPHY

Ackerman, Alan L. *The Portable Theater: American Literature and the Nineteenth-Century Stage*. Baltimore: Johns Hopkins University Press, 1999.
———. "The Right to Privacy: William Dean Howells and the Rise of Dramatic Realism." *American Literary Realism* 30, no. 1 (1997): 1–19.
Albee, Edward. *Who's Afraid of Virginia Woolf?* New York: Atheneum Press, 1981.
Alexander, Thomas G. "The Reconstruction of Mormon Doctrine: From Joseph Smith to Progressive Theology." *Sunstone*, July–August 1980, 24–33.
Artaud, Antonin. *The Theatre and Its Double*. Trans. Mary Caroline Richards. New York: Grove Press, 1958.
———. "Theatre and the Plague." In *Theatre and Its Double*. Trans. Mary Caroline Richards. New York: Grove Press, 1958.
———. "The Theatre of Cruelty (First Manifesto)." In *Theatre and Its Double*. Trans. Mary Caroline Richards. New York: Grove Press, 1958.
Bank, Rosemarie K. *Theatre Culture in America, 1825–1860*. Cambridge: Cambridge University Press, 1997.
Bass, Ellen, and Laura Davis. *The Courage to Heal*. 2d ed. New York: Harper and Row, 1992.
Bataille, George. "The Eye." In *Visions of Excess: Selected Writings, 1927–1939*. Minneapolis: University of Minnesota Press, 1985.
Bell, Michael Davitt. *The Problem of American Realism*. Chicago: University of Chicago Press, 1993.
Berthoff, Warner. *The Ferment of Realism: American Literature, 1884–1919*. New York: Free Press, 1965.
Bhabha, Homi K. "Of Mimicry and Man: The Ambivalence of Colonial Discourse." In *The Location of Culture*. New York: Routledge, 1994.
———, ed. *Nation and Narration*. New York: Routledge, 1990.
Blau, Herbert. "Ideology and Performance." *Theatre Journal* 35 (December 1983): 441–60.
———. *Take Up the Bodies: Theater at the Vanishing Point*. Urbana: University of Illinois Press, 1982.
———. *To All Appearances: Ideology and Performance*. New York: Routledge, 1992.

Bloom, Harold. *The American Religion: The Emergence of the Post-Christian Nation.* New York: Simon and Schuster, 1992.

Boucicault, Dion. *The Octoroon.* In *Representative American Plays,* ed. Arthur Hobson Quinn. New York: Appleton-Century-Crofts, 1957.

Brooke, John L. *The Refiner's Fire: The Making of Mormon Cosmology, 1644–1844.* Cambridge: Cambridge University Press, 1996.

Burroughs, Stephen. *The Memoirs of Stephen Burroughs.* Boston: Northeastern University Press, 1988.

Busa, Christopher. "Talking with Karen Finley." *Provincetown Arts, Provincetown Gallery,* 1996. See also a reprint of the article at www.capecodaccess.com/Gallery/Arts/talkingKaren.html.

Butler, Judith. *Bodies That Matter.* New York: Routledge, 1993.

———. "Performative Acts and Gender Constitution." In *Performing Feminisms: Feminist Critical Theory and Theatre.* Baltimore: Johns Hopkins University Press, 1990.

Butler, Judith, Seyla Benhabib, Drucilla Cornell, and Nancy Fraser. In *Feminist Contentions: A Philosophical Exchange,* ed. Linda Nicholson. New York: Routledge, 1995.

Butler, Judith, Ernesto Laclau, and Slavoj Žižek. *Contingency, Hegemony, Universality: Contemporary Dialogues on the Left.* New York: Verso, 2000.

Cameron, Sharon. *The Corporeal Self: Allegories of the Body in Melville and Hawthorne.* Baltimore: Johns Hopkins University Press, 1981.

Carr, C. *On Edge: Performance at the End of the Twentieth Century.* Hanover, N.H.: Wesleyan University Press, 1993.

Carson, Ada Lou, and Herbert L. Carson. *Royall Tyler.* Boston: Twayne, 1979.

Caruth, Cathy. *Trauma: Explorations in Memory.* Baltimore: Johns Hopkins University Press, 1995.

Champagne, Leonora, ed. *Out from Under: Texts by Women Performance Artists.* New York: Theatre Communications Group, 1990.

Clarke, James W. *American Assassins.* Princeton: Princeton University Press, 1982.

Cockrell, Dale. *Demons of Disorder: Early Blackface Minstrels and Their World.* Cambridge: Cambridge University Press, 1997.

Cole, Simon. "Smudged! The Blurry Science of Fingerprints." *Lingua Franca,* November 2000, 54–62.

Conklin, Paul A. *Cane Ridge: America's Pentecost.* Madison: University of Wisconsin Press, 1990.

Copjec, Joan. *Read My Desire: Lacan against the Historicists.* Cambridge: MIT Press, 1995.

Crary, Jonathan. *Techniques of the Observer.* Cambridge: MIT Press, 1992.

Daigrepont, Lloyd M. "'Rip Van Winkle' and the Gnostic Vision of History." *Clio* 15, no. 1 (1985): 47–59.

Davis, Walter A. *Get the Guests: Psychoanalysis, Modern American Drama, and the Audience.* Madison: University of Wisconsin Press, 1994.

Deleuze, Gilles. *Difference and Repetition.* Trans. Paul Patton. New York: Columbia University Press, 1968.

Derrida, Jacques. *Dissemination.* Trans. Barbara Johnson. Chicago: University of Chicago Press, 1981.

——. *Monolingualism of the Other; or, The Prosthesis of Origin.* Stanford: Stanford University Press, 1998.

——. *Spectres of Marx: The State of the Debt, the Work of Mourning, and the New International.* Trans. Peggy Kamuf. New York: Routledge, 1994.

——. *Writing and Difference.* Trans. Alan Bass. Chicago: University of Chicago Press, 1978.

Diamond, Elin. *Unmaking Mimesis: Essays on Feminism and Theatre.* New York: Routledge, 1997.

Dolan, Frederick. *Allegories of America: Narratives, Metaphysics, Politics.* Ithaca: Cornell University Press, 1994.

Dolan, Jill. *Presence and Desire: Essays on Gender, Sexuality, Performance.* Ann Arbor: University of Michigan Press, 1993.

Emerson, Everett. *Puritanism in America: 1620–1750.* Boston: G. K. Hall, 1977.

Erdman, Harley. "Caught in the 'Eye of the Eternal': Justice, Race, and the Camera, from *The Octoroon* to Rodney King." *Theatre Journal* 54 (October 1993) 333–48.

Evelev, John. "The Contrast: The Problem of Theatricality and Political Crisis in Postrevolutionary America." *Early American Literature* 31, no. 1 (1996): 74–97.

Felman, Shoshana, and Dori Laub. *Testimony: Crises of Witnessing in Literature, Psychoanalysis, and History.* New York: Routledge, 1992.

Fink, Bruce. *Lacanian Psychoanalysis: Theory and Technique.* Cambridge: Harvard University Press, 1997.

Finkielkraut, Alain. *The Defeat of the Mind.* Ed. and trans. Judith Friedlander. New York: Columbia University Press, 1995.

Finley, Karen. *Constant State of Desire.* In *Out from Under: Texts by Women Performance Artists*, ed. Lenora Champagne. New York: Theatre Communications Group, 1990.

Forte, Jeanie. "Women's Performance Art: Feminism and Postmodernism." In *Performing Feminisms.* Baltimore: Johns Hopkins University Press, 1990.

Foucault, Michel. *The Archaeology of Knowledge and the Discourse on Language.* Trans. A. M. Sheridan Smith. New York: Pantheon, 1972.

Furtwangler, Albert. *Assassin on Stage.* Urbana: University of Illinois Press, 1991.

Gainor, J. Ellen. "The Provincetown Player's Experiments with Realism." In *Realism and the American Dramatic Tradition*, ed. William W. Demastes. Tuscaloosa: University of Alabama Press, 1996.

Galassi, Frank S. "Slavery and Melodrama: Boucicault's *The Octoroon.*" *Markham Review* 6 (1977): 77–80.

Gibbs, Nancy, and Timothy Roth. "The Columbine Tapes." *Time*, December 20, 1999, 42–47.

Glass, James. *Shattered Selves: Multiple Personality in a Postmodern World.* Ithaca: Cornell University Press, 1993.

Goldstein, Malcolm. *The Political Stage: American Drama and Theater of the Great Depression.* New York: Oxford University Press, 1974.

Goux, Jean-Joseph. *Symbolic Economies.* Ithaca: Cornell University Press, 1990.

Grimsted, David. *Melodrama Unveiled.* Berkeley and Los Angeles: University of California Press, 1968.

Guzzoni, Ute. "Do We Still Want to Be Subjects?" In *Deconstructive Subjectivities,* ed. Simon Critchley and Peter Dews. New York: State University of New York Press, 1996.

Hacking, Ian. *Rewriting the Soul: Multiple Personality and the Sciences of Memory.* Princeton: Princeton University Press, 1995.

Halttunen, Karen. *Confidence Men and Painted Women: A Study of Middle-Class Culture in America, 1830–1970.* New Haven: Yale University Press, 1982.

Haraway, Donna. *Simians, Cyborgs, and Women.* New York: Routledge, 1991.

Hart, Lynda. "Motherhood according to Finley." *Drama Review* 36, no. 1 (1991): 124–34.

Hawthorne, Nathaniel. *The Complete Novels and Selected Tales of Nathaniel Hawthorne.* New York: Modern Library, 1937, 1965.

Hay, Samuel A. *African American Theatre: An Historical and Critical Analysis.* New York: Cambridge University Press, 1994.

Herne, James. *Margaret Fleming.* In *Representative American Plays,* ed. Arthur Hobson Quinn. New York: Appleton-Century-Crofts, 1957.

Huerta, Jorge A. *Chicano Drama: Performance, Society, and Myth.* New York: Cambridge University Press, 2000.

———. *Chicano Theater: Themes and Forms.* Ypsilanti, Mich.: Bilingual Press, 1982.

Irving, Washington. *The Complete Tales of Washington Irving.* Ed. Charles Neider. New York: Da Capo Press, 1998.

Jefferson, Joseph. *The Autobiography of Joseph Jefferson.* Ed. Bernard Bailyn. Cambridge: Harvard University Press, 1964.

———. *Rip Van Winkle* "as played by Joseph Jefferson." In *Representative American Plays,* ed. Arthur Hobson Quinn. New York: Appleton-Century-Crofts, 1957.

Kritzer, Amelia Howe, ed. *Plays by Early American Women, 1775–1850.* Ann Arbor: University of Michigan Press, 1995.

Kubiak, Anthony. "America/Amnesis," *Performance Research* 5, no. 1 (2000): 30–36.

———. "Modern Theatre and Melville's Moby-Dick: Writing and Sounding the Whale." *Modern Drama* 34, no. 1 (1991): 107–17.

———. "Scene One/Warning Signs: Puritanism and the Early American Theatres of Cruelty." *Journal of Dramatic Theory and Criticism* 12, no. 2 (1998): 15–34.

———. "Splitting the Difference: Performance and Its Double in American Culture." *Drama Review* 42, no. 4 (T160) (1998): 91–114.

———. *Stages of Terror: Terrorism, Ideology, and Coercion as Theatre History.* Bloomington: Indiana University Press, 1991.

Kushner, Tony. *Angels in America.* Part 1, *The Millennium Approaches;* part 2, *Perestroika.* New York: Theatre Communications Group, 1992.

Lacan, Jacques. *Ecrits: A Selection.* Trans. Alan Sheridan. New York: Norton, 1977.

———. *The Four Fundamental Concepts of Psychoanalysis*. Ed. Jacques-Alain Miller. Trans. Alan Sheridan. London: Penguin, 1986.

Laclau, Ernesto. *Emancipation(s)*. New York: Verso, 1996.

———. Introduction to *The Sublime Object of Ideology*, by Slavoj Žižek. New York: Verso, 1989.

Laplanche, Jean. *Seduction, Translation, Drives*. Trans. Martin Stanton. London: Institute of Contemporary Arts, 1992.

Leclaire, Serge. *A Child Is Being Murdered*. Trans. Marie-Claude Hays. Stanford: Stanford University Press, 1998.

Lindberg, Gary. *The Confidence Man in American Literature*. New York: Oxford University Press, 1982.

Loftus, Elizabeth. *The Myth of Repressed Memory: False Memories and Allegations of Sexual Abuse*. New York: St. Martin's Press, 1994.

Lott, Eric. *Love and Theft: Blackface Minstrelsy and the American Working Class*. New York: Oxford University Press, 1993.

Mason, Jeffrey. *Melodrama and the Myth of America*. Bloomington: Indiana University Press, 1993.

McConachie, Bruce. *Melodramatic Formations: American Theatre and Society, 1820–1870*. Iowa City: University of Iowa Press, 1992.

———. "Using the Concept of Cultural Hegemony to Write Theatre History." In *Interpreting the Theatrical Past*, ed. Thomas Postlewait and Bruce McConachie. Iowa: University of Iowa Press, 1989.

Melville, Herman. *Moby Dick; or, The Whale*. Vol. 6 of *The Writings of Herman Melville*, ed. Harrison Hayford, Hershel Parker, and G. Thomas Tanselle. Northwestern-Newberry Edition. Evanston: Northwestern University Press and the Newberry Library, 1988.

———. *Moby-Dick*. Norton Critical Edition. Ed. Harrison Hayford and Hershel Parker. New York: Norton, 1967.

Merleau-Ponty, Maurice. *The Visible and the Invisible*. Ed. Claude Lefort. Trans. Alphonso Lingis. Evanston: Northwestern University Press, 1968.

Meserve, Walter J. *American Drama to 1900: A Guide to Information Sources*. Detroit: Gale, 1980.

———. *Discussions of American Drama*. Boston: D. C. Heath, 1966.

———. *An Emerging Entertainment: The Drama of the American People to 1828*. Bloomington: Indiana University Press, 1977.

Michaels, Walter Benn. *The Gold Standard and the Logic of Naturalism*. Berkeley and Los Angeles: University of California Press, 1987.

Morgan, Edmund S. Review of *Sermons*, ed. Michael Warner. *New York Review of Books*, September 23, 1999, 40–41.

Mouffe, Chantal, and Ernesto Laclau. *Hegemony and Socialist Strategy: Towards a Radical Democratic Politics*. New York: Verso, 1985.

Nasio, Juan-David. *Five Lessons on the Psychoanalytic Theory of Jacques Lacan*. Trans. David Pettigrew and Francois Raffoul. Albany: State University of New York Press, 1998.

———. *Hysteria: The Splendid Child of Psychoanalysis*. Trans. and ed. Susan Fairfield. Northvale: Jason Aronson, 1997.

Nietzsche, Friedrich. *On the Advantage and Disadvantage of History for Life.* Trans. Peter Preuss. Indianapolis: Hackett, 1980.

Ofshe, Richard. *Remembering Satan.* New York: Knopf, 1994.

Olson, Charles. *Call Me Ishmael.* San Francisco: City Lights Books, 1947.

O'Neill, Eugene. *Desire under the Elms.* In *Complete Plays, 1920–1931.* New York: Library of America, 1988.

Parks, Suzan-Lori. *The America Play.* New York: Theatre Communications Group, 1995.

Petersen, Mark E. "Race Problems as They Affect the Church." Address at the Convention of Teachers of Religion on the College Level, Brigham Young University, Provo, Utah, August 27, 1954. Petersen is quoted in *The Changing World of Mormonism* by Jerald and Sandra Tanner (Chicago: Moody Press, 1981), 307. The full original text of this book can be found at http://www.utlm.org/onlinebooks/changecontents.htm

Phelan, Peggy. *Unmarked: The Politics of Performance.* New York: Routledge, 1993.

Putnam, Hillary. *Realism with a Human Face.* Cambridge: Harvard University Press, 1990.

Quinn, Arthur Hobson. *Representative American Plays.* New York: Appleton-Century-Crofts, 1957.

Richardson, Gary A. *American Drama from the Colonial Period through World War I: A Critical History.* New York: Twayne, 1993.

———. "Boucicault's *The Octoroon* and American Law." *Theatre Journal* 34 (May 1982): 155–64.

Roach, Joseph. "Slave Spectacles and Tragic Octoroons: A Cultural Genealogy of Antebellum Performance." *Theatre Survey* 33 (November 1992): 167–87.

Robinson, James A. "Buried Children: Fathers and Sons in O'Neill and Shepard." In *Eugene O'Neill and the Emergence of American Drama,* ed. Marc Maufort. Atlanta: Rodopi, 1989.

Robinson, Marc. *The Other American Drama.* Baltimore: Johns Hopkins University Press, 1997.

Roth, Beatrice. *The Father.* In *Out from Under: Texts by Women Performance Artists,* ed. Lenora Champagne. New York: Theatre Communications Group, 1990.

Schroeder, Patricia R. *The Presence of the Past in Modern American Drama.* Rutherford, N.J.: Fairleigh Dickinson University Press, 1989.

Schwartz, Hillel. *The Culture of the Copy: Striking Likenesses, Unreasonable Facsimiles.* New York: Zone Books, 1996.

Shepard, Sam. *Buried Child.* In *Seven Plays.* New York: Bantam Books, 1984.

Shepard, Thomas. *God's Plot.* Ed. Michael McGiffert. Amherst: University of Massachusetts Press, 1972, 1994.

Showalter, Elaine. *Hystories.* New York: Columbia University Press, 1997.

Siebert, Donald T., Jr. "Royall Tyler's 'Bold Example': *The Contrast* and the English Comedy of Manners." *Early American Literature* 13 (1978): 3–11.

Sinason, Valerie. *Treating Victims of Satanist Abuse.* New York: Routledge, 1994.

Smith, Barbara Herrnstein. "Narrative Versions, Narrative Theories." *Critical Inquiry* 7, no. 1 (1980): 219.

Smith, Susan Harris. *American Drama: The Bastard Art.* Cambridge: Cambridge University Press, 1997.

Sollers, Werner. "The Bluish Tinge in the Half-Moons, or Fingernails as a Racial Sign: The Study of a Motif." In *Thematics: New Approaches,* ed. Claude Bremond, Joshua Landy, and Thomas Pavel. Albany: State University of New York Press, 1995.

Stanislawski, Constantin. *An Actor Prepares.* New York: Theatre Arts Books, 1936.

Stavrakakis, Yannis. *Lacan and the Political.* New York: Routledge, 1999.

Stuhr, John J., ed. *Classical American Philosophy: Essential Readings and Interpretive Essays.* New York: Oxford University Press, 1987.

Tanner, Jerald, and Sandra Tanner. *Mormonism: Shadow or Reality.* 5th ed. Salt Lake City: Utah Lighthouse Ministry, 1987.

Taylor, Thomas J. *American Theater History: An Annotated Bibliography.* Pasadena: Salem Press, 1992.

Taylor, Tom. *Our American Cousin.* N.p., 1869.

Thomas, Brook. *American Literary Realism and the Failed Promise of Contract.* Berkeley and Los Angeles: University of California Press, 1997.

Thompson, George A., Jr. *A Documentary History of the African Theatre.* Evanston, Ill.: Northwestern University Press, 1998.

Tocqueville, Alexis de. *Democracy in America.* Trans. George Lawrence. Ed. J. P. Mayer. New York: Harper and Row, 1966.

Toll, Robert C. *Blacking Up: The Minstrel Show in Nineteenth-Century America.* New York: Oxford University Press, 1974.

Wadlington, Warwick. *The Confidence Game in American Literature.* Princeton: Princeton University Press, 1975.

Wells, Robert V. "While Rip Napped: Social Change in Late Eighteenth-Century New York." *New York History,* January 1990, 5–23.

Wigglesworth, Michael. *The Diary of Michael Wigglesworth.* Ed. Edmund S. Morgan. New York: Harper and Row, 1946.

Wilden, Anthony. *System and Structure: Essays in Communication and Exchange.* 2d ed. New York: Tavistock/Methuen, 1972.

Wilmeth, Don B. *The Cambridge History of American Theatre.* Vol. 1, *Beginnings to 1870;* vol. 2, *1870–1945.* Cambridge: Cambridge University Press, 1998.

Wilson, Garff B. *Three Hundred Years of American Drama and Theatre: From "Ye B(are) and Ye Cubb" to "Hair."* Englewood Cliffs, N.J.: Prentice-Hall, 1973.

Winthrop, John. "A Modell of Christian Charity." In *An American Primer,* ed. Daniel Boorstin. New York: Penguin, 1966.

Worthen, W. B. "Drama, Performativity, and Performance." *PMLA* 113, no. 5 (1998): 1093–1107.

Young, William C. *Documents of American Theater History.* Vol. 1, *Famous American Playhouses, 1716–1899;* vol. 2, *Famous American Playhouses, 1900–1971.* Chicago: American Library Association, 1973.

Zinn, Howard. *A People's History of the United States.* New York: HarperCollins, 1980, 1990.

Žižek, Slavoj. "The Cartesian Subject versus the Cartesian Theatre." In *Cogito and the Unconscious*, ed. Slavoj Žižek. Durham: Duke University Press, 1998.

————. *Looking Awry: An Introduction to Jacques Lacan through Popular Culture.* Cambridge: MIT Press, 1997.

————. *The Metastases of Enjoyment: Six Essays on Women and Causality.* New York: Verso, 1994.

————. *The Sublime Object of Ideology.* New York: Verso, 1989.

————. *The Ticklish Subject: The Absent Centre of Political Ontology.* New York: Verso, 1999.

INDEX